L'Oréal Took My Home

Advance praise for *L'Oréal Took My Home*:

'A shame-filled story of cover-up, deceit and Nazi collaboration. Utterly convincing. And a compelling read. L'Oréal needs to turn over its profits from their wrinkle-disappearing products to compensate for and rid themselves of the terrible blemish perpetrated on the Rosenfelder family rather than using it to create more tricks of artifice and cunning to sell us unattainable youthful looks'
– Susie Orbach

'It is right that this book should be published. It is a painful story, passionately told and fully documented, of the forcible appropriation of the home of a Jewish family by the Nazis in 1938, which finally came into the possession of the cosmetics giants, L'Oréal. Though the company denies any knowledge of the provenance of the property, it seems that they were complicit in its acquisition from the start. Despite the present climate of opinion in Europe, in favour of compensation for victims such as Monica Waitzfelder's family, the company has made no admission of moral responsibility. The case is now to come before the European Court of Human Rights'
- **Mary Warnock** (Baroness Warnock, member of the Government Spoilation Advisory Panel)

'Monica Waitzfelder tells a powerful story, and asks the perfectly obvious question-why won't L'Oréal recognise what they did before and during the war, and compensate her mother for their house in Karlsruhe? Court after court has decided that it is not a 'French' case, yet other courts in other jurisdictions have not had such problems. Read the book to see how the system just does not want to listen- but be assured that the Waitzfelder family will win in the end, because their case is just' - **Rabbi Julia Neuberger**

'France's richest resident, cosmetics heiress Liliane Bettencourt, is in desperate need of some concealer. The 82-year-old controlling shareholder in L'Oréal, worth some $17.2 billion, is fending off allegations of ugly behaviour by her father, L'Oréal founder and alleged Nazi sympathizer Eugene Schueller . . . *L'Oréal Took My Home* details [the family's] fight with L'Oréal, replete with detailed documentation' - *Forbes* **magazine**

'Puts Waitzfelder at the centre of a painful debate in France about the country's role in the Nazis' effort to destroy Jews and strip them of their possessions. Indeed, the case is forcing France, which once prided itself on being a nation of resisters, to face difficult questions about its involvement with Nazi activities'
- *Christian Science Monitor*

Monica Waitzfelder

L'Oréal Took My Home

The Secrets of a Theft

Translated from the French by Peter Bush

With a Preface by Serge Klarsfeld

ARCADIA BOOKS

Arcadia Books Ltd
15–16 Nassau Street
London W1W 7AB

www.arcadiabooks.co.uk

First published in the United Kingdom 2006
Copyright © Hachette Littératures, 2004.
First published by Hachette as *L'Oréal a pris ma maison* in 2004
Translation © Peter Bush 2006

A catalogue record for this book is available from the British Library.

ISBN 1-905147-11-2
ISBN 1-905147-53-8 Export paperback edition published simultaneously

Typeset in Bembo by Basement Press
Printed in Finland by WS Bookwell

Arcadia Books supports English PEN, the fellowship of writers who work together to promote literature and its understanding. English PEN upholds writers' freedoms in Britain and around the world, challenging political and cultural limits on free expression. To find out more, visit www.englishpen.org or contact English PEN, 6–8 Amwell Street, London EC1R 1UQ

Arcadia Books distributors are as follows:

in the UK and elsewhere in Europe:
Turnaround Publishers Services
Unit 3, Olympia Trading Estate
Coburg Road
London N22 6TZ

in the USA and Canada:
Independent Publishers Group
814 N. Franklin St.
Chicago, IL 60610

in Australia:
Tower Books
PO Box 213
Brookvale, NSW 2100

in New Zealand:
Addenda
Box 78224
Grey Lynn
Auckland

in South Africa:
Quartet Sales and Marketing
PO Box 1218
Northcliffe
Johannesburg 2115

Arcadia Books is the *Sunday Times* Small Publisher of the Year

I dedicate this book to the Queirel family,
to all those in the Resistance,
to all those still brave enough to fight
against injustice.

Contents

Preface

When it comes to robberies and reparations, compensation, indemnification or restitution, the possible outcomes are many and varied. Although they lost not a single loved one in the Shoah, some victims may unearth paintings seized by the Nazis, get them unhooked from where they hang in museums and regain canvasses to the value of €250 million, while other may not even recover a quarter of the value of a much more modest belonging.

Many factors are at play in these situations, particularly persistence and chance. Persistence allows solid, well documented cases to be established, the climax of long researches begun in family archives and pursued in the public archives of one or several countries.

Chance enters the scene when, at the end of a long process, a judgement grants you the right to recover all or part of what belonged to you, or else when the legal entity or individual that has been benefiting for several decades from the initial theft decides that someone is within their rights to reclaim the property they are profiting from and agrees to return it or pay the proper price for it.

Edith Rosenfelder and her daughter have been persistent beyond the call of reason; but luck has not come their way: L'Oréal, their adversary, has not had the elegance to make an offer in order to put an end to litigation and, in the last resort, the legal system has not forced L'Oréal to return the Rosenfelder's building that was seized in 1938 in Karlsruhe by Hitler's Germany.

Edith Rosenfelder is now seventy-eight years old. She is the daughter of German Jews: Fritz and Kaethe. Her mother was deported from France to Auschwitz on September 7 1942; her father died of sorrow and deprivation in 1945. She left for Brazil at the age of seventeen and married there; her daughter Monica Waitzfelder has dedicated herself to this David-against-Goliath struggle represented by the attempt to recover the land where their fine family home once stood in Karlsruhe.

Fritz R. was the first to seek refuge in Paris in 1936 and signed a power of attorney on May 24 at the German Consulate authorizing a person he didn't even know in Germany to look after all his property and business. The document was signed under constraint, Fritz's wife and daughter being still in Germany and under threat from the Nazis. The next day, May 25, Fritz received as if miraculously a residence card from the Prefecture of Police. On January 20 1938, thanks to the powers of attorney signed by Fritz, the property of Fritz Rosenfelder and his brother Karl was transferred to the BGV insurance company. After this sale, Kaethe and his daughter could finally leave Germany and join Fritz in Paris. As soon as war began they were imprisoned as Germans and, after the fall of France, as foreign Jews. Kaethe perished, Fritz died; Edith survived. As for the building in Karlsruhe, it was resold in 1954 to a German subsidiary of L'Oréal, in spite of the proven continued existence of its owners who had been dispossessed by the greed and violence of the Nazis. In 1961 L'Oréal became the direct owner of the land.

In 2004 at the Supreme Court dealing with this case, the Deputy Director of Public Prosecutions who presided advised that the fact the robbery took place in France at the German Consulate in 1937 meant that neither the considerable time that had gone by, nor the fact the consequences were felt in Germany, should prevent the French legal system from ascertaining whether that criminal gain from stolen property was well-founded and who were the beneficiaries. In the end the Supreme Court unfortunately did not find this was so and refused to pursue enquiries relating to the extortion of the signature for the order of sale.

L'Oréal could have reached an amicable settlement as suggested by Monica Waitzfelder, who valiantly picked up the baton from her mother, Edith. She carried out multiple searches in French and German archives and threw light on each phase in the persecution of her family and the way it was dispossessed of its wealth, discovering on the many detours in her search for justice black marks not only over those opposing their demands but also over Jews and non-Jews who placed obstacles in her way rather than help her.

L'Oréal's past should have led this giant company to develop greater understanding of Edith and Monica: Eugène Schueller, the creator of L'Oréal, was also one of the founders of La Cagoule, the extreme right wing movement which collaborated with the Nazis and, which, among other things, blew up six synagogues in Paris in October 1941. Jacques Corrèze who was responsible for L'Oréal's business activity in the United States was forced to resign in 1991 when I revealed that, as head of the collaborationist organisation, MSR, he had expelled Jews from their dwellings in 1941. As for André Bettencourt, the husband of L'Oréal's owner, Eugène Schueller's daughter, he began his brilliant political career in the foulest of ways by publishing dozens of articles between 1940 and 1942 in *La Terre française,* a prominent agricultural affairs newspaper created by the Germans. Several of these articles have an undeniably anti-Semitic character.

L'Oréal has refused to take on board the nature of its own history as well as the nature of the history of the Rosenfelder family. In spite of everything, that might have led to a moving reconciliation, to a gesture of fraternity and an end to confrontations based as much on ideology as cupidity! What might have been never was. Monica will perhaps still be forced to fight for a long time on several fronts in order to defend their House in Karlsruhe, which has become more than a virtual house and a financial issue: a genuine matter of principle.

Serge Klarsfeld

1

It All Began...

First of all, I thought it must be a joke.

'Hello, I would like to speak to Monica Waitzfelder.'

'Speaking.'

'I am calling from the Prime Minister's Office.'

I wanted to laugh. And he wanted to continue:

'You never sent back our questionnaire.'

'Oh, it's only about a questionnaire!'

In cheeky, humorous vein. And then I chanced my arm:

'That you, Manu?'

'It's the second time I've rung you from the Prime Minister's Office. We are setting up a commission to look into the stealing of Jewish property. I believe your grandparents were deported?'

Then I changed my tone of voice: 'I'm sorry. I thought a friend was having me on... My grandparents did indeed live in France and were deported. And what's this questionnaire you mentioned all about?'

'A questionnaire about the stealing of Jewish property. Did you receive one?'

'Yes, but it asked impossible things of me...'

'Such as?'

'Whether I possessed a whole stack of documentation. How on earth could I? Everybody who was deported died. And all their papers bit the dust with them. Excuse my language, but that questionnaire really riled me.'

Completely unfazed by my outburst, he went on: 'You don't have anything then?'

'If my mother got out, it's only because the person who came to rescue her ordered her not to put her shoes on, to save time; so, you can imagine, documents... All I've known since I was a child is that my grandparents were the owners of a large Victorian-style house in Karlsruhe. My mother showed me a photo. It's all she has.'

'Well, that's a good start. Perhaps your mother remembers other things?'

'It's very difficult to talk to her about all that. She's pulled down the curtain on that period of her life. When I was small, I could see it upset her, but she never said very much. She would just mention the house.'

'Try to speak to her. See what you can learn from her and try to obtain documentation on the house. Perhaps you should start there.'

'I've tried time and again to get documents... I've never managed to put my hands on any.'

'What do you mean? You've never managed to?'

'They refuse to give them to me, my mother has been asking for them for years and I've tried several times.'

Now, I thought my interlocutor sounded slightly doubtful: 'But this house did belong to you?'

'My mother said it did.'

'Well, they must supply you with all the documents. You know, things are changing now.'

'Perhaps...'

My interlocutor left me his details. I apologized again for the way I'd greeted him and asked a few questions about the measures the Prime Minister's Office was taking. I should call him back and provide him with more information, and in the long run even meet him.

This all took place mid–December 1999.

The house... From my early childhood, my mother had told me: 'L'Oréal took my home'. As a little girl I didn't really understand what that meant. The only thing L'Oréal meant to me was shampoo, and I didn't like it very much because it made my eyes smart.

Later on, I saw a photo of the house taken by my great-uncle at the end of the 1920s, a photo he subsequently gave to my mother. The only record we possessed of that period.

I should add that in Brazil, where I was born, history has more to do with carnival and football than the Second World War. Not that the latter was never mentioned: in the Jewish community – comprising mainly various escapees from the Shoah – which we saw on a daily basis and which became almost a substitute for the family, some people would tell their stories. But my mother never told hers. I heard it said that she had suffered too much and should be left in peace. From time to time she had 'fits' which my brother and I never understood: she would sometimes cry, or be shaken by an unspeakable fear, and she'd be left prostrate... We'd then go and seek refuge with our neighbours.

As a child, I realized my mother was one of those who had suffered most among this group of immigrants. And then there was the story of the stolen house, which kept returning like a leitmotif.

2

The Redheaded Witch

I was born in Rio de Janeiro. Apparently I was a very placid child, but one to be watched carefully because I was interested in everything going on around me and often almost fell out of my cradle or pushchair.

My first word was *Wasser*. I like water: the sea, the swimming pool, rivers…

At home, we spoke German because my parents expressed themselves poorly in Portuguese. My mother also spoke French, but my father didn't. Nonetheless, they enrolled me in an English school. There were children of every nationality: Japanese, French, Irish and Yugoslav…and every religion. We had lots of fun discovering one another's culture. We also learned music, painting and dance, but by my third year in primary school, I was still unable to read or write, so my parents decided to send my brother and me to a Brazilian school. In less than six months we could read and write and had adjusted to our new school.

From the age of four and three respectively, my brother and I took recorder and piano lessons. We had terrific teachers. They were Jewish concert artists who had had to flee Nazi Germany and now taught beginners in order to make ends meet. But we had no idea of any of that at the time. After our lessons, our two teachers would tell us to sit down and played us a beautiful concerto.

I also had dance lessons from the age of three. I loved dancing. I was a very shy child, and the movements allowed me to express myself without having to talk too much. I also read a lot, particularly French writers translated into Portuguese: the Countess of Ségur, Dumas, Valéry, Saint-Exupéry, and later on Stendhal, Zola, Maupassant, Gide, Sartre, Camus... I loved to read and would devour everything that fell into my hands. I also loved to study. As the atmosphere at home was very fraught, I think I sought refuge in my studies.

My father had a job that forced him to travel a lot: he would sometimes be away for three weeks, spend a week at home and then be off again.

The Jews in Rio helped each other a lot. There was a large number, especially Germans and Austrians. Some had fled persecution; others had escaped the camps. All were slightly lost in this country that was so different to their European culture. My mother was one of the few who had come from France. She had a French friend, also called Edith, but who was called Editinha. Unlike my mother's parents Editinha's weren't deported; her father committed suicide before they could take him away. The other day, in conversation, she told me she was quite astonished by the amount I'd found out, for my mother, although a close friend, had never told her anything, not even that her own mother had died in Auschwitz.

I have a confession to make: up to the age of ten I was afraid I was a witch. I should add that I am a redhead and that there can't be more than ten redheads in Rio. People used to stop us in the street and talk to my mother about the colour of my hair and that would really upset me: I had read in books how in the Middle Ages redheads were thought to be witches and were consequently burned. I think it was around this time that I had an inkling of knowledge about Nazism. However, I didn't read books or go to films dealing with the subject, perhaps as a self-defence mechanism.

Later on, I studied medicine and worked as an intern in a hospital. I discovered another universe and tried to understand and help people who were in pain. Nonetheless, I was always attracted by music and dance, options my family didn't consider to be real jobs. I finally abandoned medicine and decided on the arts, despite the lively arguments such a choice provoked among my nearest and dearest.

I then began to study to be an actress, while continuing with dance. I also took singing lessons. I got my professional card as an actress. I belonged to some prestigious companies of the time that fused dance and theatre, and all was well with my life. But I felt something was still missing.

I woke up one fine morning in Rio, in the pretty maisonette I was sharing in Botofago, my head abuzz with a single idea: I must go to Paris. Initially, it seemed strange that I should have been visited by such a wish: I didn't know anyone there, didn't speak French and didn't even remember seeing a film recently about this city or anything else that might have suggested it. In the end I could only laugh at the fact that such a preposterous idea had passed through my mind.

It had no basis in reason; I was at last leading a calm, settled life after a difficult separation (even though I was the one who had initiated the break), I'd got over my father's death in 1979 and was getting to grips with a new job I really liked. I had written a master's dissertation in philosophy with great panache, my artistic career was more secure, I'd joined a company that was much in vogue, and I also enjoyed a good circle of friends. Moreover, while Brazil might still be governed by a military dictatorship, we felt the end of the regime was nigh.

But nothing I did could chase this strange idea from my head. The weather or my daily routines certainly couldn't; on the contrary, it became such an obsession that my head was full of nothing else every morning when I woke up. I found it all extremely unsettling.

I then told myself the only way I could calm down would be to collect information about Paris. But even if the dictatorship were on its way out, it was still a constraining factor and made it very difficult to get proper information about anything happening abroad.

Nevertheless, I finally yielded to the persistence and power of desire: I *would* go to Paris. I'd never behaved this way before, but now desire had been transformed into necessity.

My mother and I had never agreed on anything at all. She continually criticized the choices I made, to the point that I was now inured to her attitude. Despite our stormy relationship, we spoke on the telephone every day, and I told her what I was planning by telephone.

'I think that's an excellent idea', she responded.

To my amazement, for the first time in a long, long time, I heard her voice express approval of one of my initiatives. She didn't even ask me how I reckoned I'd survive materially over there or what money I'd use to buy my ticket, nor did she use the language barrier as a counterargument. Not a single reproach.

Despite her encouragement, I used to temper my ardour by telling myself I'd give up my plans at the first obstacle to appear on my path. It was in such a state of mind that I went to the embassy to ask for a European passport: if I were refused, I would stay in Brazil. I obtained one within a week.

I had mentioned this sudden desire to go to Paris to my contemporary dance teacher. This woman was a real character, a great artist and was very sensitive to issues of human nature. She carefully considered each and every one of her words; no remark was ever superfluous. She was as supportive as my mother: 'I think it will do you good.'

And added: 'I've always thought of you as a producer...'

She said nothing else. Producing... That was something which had certainly never crossed my mind.

It was only from the moment things began to take shape that I began to question the reasons impelling me to leave: what would I do once I got there? My music theory teacher also encouraged me in vain – 'you think like a European, go for it' – I still didn't understand the meaning of the steps I was taking.

One day, as I was leaving a music class, my teacher asked me for help: 'A great Italian guitarist is in Rio to give a series of concerts. Can you help him get to know Rio?'

I drove over to pick the guitarist up, and after we'd made our introductions he asked if it would be all right for a friend of his to join us who happened to be in Rio.

'Of course,' I replied.

His friend was called Philippe and lived in…Paris. It wasn't difficult to show off Rio; it's a wonderful city, the weather is always good and, for someone familiar with it, is packed with interesting places to show people. On that pleasant day we spent together, I told Philippe of my plans, however ridiculous they may have seemed, to go and live in Paris. He offered to put me up until I decided to return. And he added that he would even come to meet me at the airport. All I had to do was ring him and let him know when I'd be arriving.

Right then, I still didn't know what exactly was motivating my desire to leave. It was only in the course of my stay in France that I realized I'd come to discover my roots. And gradually, history took over.

I signed up at the music conservatory as soon as I arrived in France. I soon began to attend courses in opera production. And some theatre studies in order to learn particular stage techniques. I worked with great producers, like Strehler, who taught me a lot. I started working for the Opéra National de Paris in 1991, as assistant producer on Roman Polanski's *The Tales of Hoffmann*. Since then I have worked with a number of producers on many, many productions. For the Opéra, but also the Théâtre du Châtelet, the Capitole in Toulouse, as well as abroad; in particular, I produced Bartok's *Bluebeard's Castle* at the National Opera in Rio

3

A Deafening Silence

I arrived in Paris in August 1984. From the following year, as I was in Europe, I started investigating the house my mother talked about so much. I made contact with various people I thought might be of help but drew only blanks. For Jews who had survived the Shoah there existed a process for returning property called *Wiedergutmachung*. Now, whenever my mother had recourse to it, she could never get hold of any documentation, and her lawyers told her that her case was already closed. I didn't understand why my mother had never received any compensation as other people had. I then asked myself this question: had my grandparents in fact owned this house or were they simply tenants? By now it was impossible to speak to my mother about anything related to the Shoah; time had turned silence into a habit. It was my father who had told me the little that I knew.

After these first futile steps, I didn't labour the point. I had to integrate myself into French life, learn the language and earn a living. I had come knowing hardly anyone and it seemed more difficult to set up contacts than in Brazil. Nonetheless, I started to hassle the bureaucracies whenever I had an opportunity. But the new friends I confided in began to make fun of me; some even said I was inventing everything. So I became reticent on the subject.

I have a paternal uncle by marriage, and he lives in Basle, Switzerland. I took advantage of a visit of his to Karlsruhe in 1993 to ask him to go to the land registry and order a copy of the deeds the German authorities keep of the current and previous owners of properties. When he informed them of the address, he was told it didn't exist. My uncle was fobbed off by this laconic response. He enjoyed no more luck than we did.

My head buzzed with the words my mother had so often repeated about the home L'Oréal had stolen from her.

'Didn't you even ask for the address of L'Oréal?'

'If they told me they've never heard of that address, it's because it doesn't exist.'

I found this strange, to put it mildly: an address can be altered, the name of a street can be changed, but to do that and not inform the city land registry! I mentioned it to Angela who helped me write letters in German (although German is my mother tongue, I've never learned to write it). Angela was – and still is – my translator and, as she translated a series of documents for me, I watched her wax more and more indignant. She was also always extremely supportive. We then decided to write to the mayor of Karlsruhe to ask him for the new name of the street, explaining that my family had lived there and I wanted to pay the town a visit. His reply was long in coming but, in a helpful letter, he indicated that the street still existed, that unfortunately the house had been bombed in the war and that it had been replaced by an office block; nonetheless, he encouraged me to visit the town of my grandparents.

Now, if this street and number still existed, why were they refusing to supply us with the documentation we requested? I realized we had to proceed carefully and play the bureaucracy at its own game. I asked Angela to find out the names of the firms working in the building. No L'Oréal. We went on with our research. I called the registry once again to ask for a copy of the deeds.

'We only send these documents to the owners or previous owners.'

'But my grandparents owned the property, at least before the war.'

'Their surname?'

'Rosenfelder.'

'No Rosenfelder is mentioned at this address.'

'Go back to the beginning of the century…'

'I've already told you that I went back to the eighteenth century, and particularly from the beginning of this century to the 1940s.'

'But my mother…'

'She made this story up or perhaps they were just tenants. You know, lots of people went slightly mad after what they lived through in the war.'

'Thanks anyway…'

A few days before Christmas 1999, I got another call from my interlocutor at the Prime Minister's Office. He explained how he was going to be the spokesman for a committee that was being set up, that he was a judge and was responsible for my case and that, even though the committee hadn't yet received its rubric, we could fix a meeting early in 2000. I was then rehearsing *Don Giovanni* at the Opéra, and my hours weren't exactly the same as the bureaucracy's.

'I can see you, even if it's late.'

In the event we met one evening after a late rehearsal. I gave him the various bits of information I had managed to extract from my mother by dint of patience and tender care. Of course, she hadn't told me the whole story. I still had work to do because she was resistant. But I couldn't put any more pressure on her; I already felt I was torturing her simply by evoking that period of her life.

I thus learned that after fleeing Karlsruhe in 1938, my grandparents had taken up residence in the eighth *arrondissement*, 6 rue des Saussaies, on the third floor. A large apartment filled with furniture they'd brought with them from Germany. Paintings by the great masters hung on some of the walls. They rented, since Jews didn't have the right to own property by then. My mother had also revealed that my grandfather was an important lawyer. He played the piano and violin brilliantly and had even initially contemplated a career as a conductor, but the wounds he received in the First World War had prevented him from following that route.

I showed the photo of the house to the report-writer.

'Have you written to Karlsruhe to get confirmation that your family lived there?'

'Yes, I even made it plain that the French government was requesting this information. I hope to get a reply soon; I only just sent my letter.'

Several months passed by, I wrote repeatedly, all my letters remained unanswered. I couldn't understand this fresh silence at all. But the ballgame had changed. I had more sway now that I could insist the French government was behind me. I finally picked up my phone to speak directly to the mayor who 'naturally' was unable to take the call. It was his secretary who endured my anger: 'All I want is evidence that my family lived at a specific address in Karlsruhe. I've been requesting a copy of the deeds for years, and now the French government is requesting a copy. I've sent several letters over recent months, and you haven't even deigned to reply. I will take legal action, if needs be!'

'We certainly received your letters. I don't understand what has happened. Here's Mrs V.'

Mrs V. was very embarrassed. Yes, there'd been a mistake: in what way could she be of help? Then she repeated how, in order to get the documentation on the house, one had to contact the land registry.

I felt the Kafkaesque nightmare was resurging: the land registry had been refusing us any documentation at all for years by employing ever more fantastic excuses. I told Mrs V. of the steps I'd taken over the years, that I was desperate and couldn't think what to do next. I told her of the French government's request. I argued that, even if my family had rented this house, they could still send me something that proved they had lived there, anything, an invoice, any scrap of paper... And on that note, I left her my details.

A few hours later, I received a fax that was very difficult to read. I took a magnifying glass and saw the name 'Rosenfelder'. The document, dated 1938, was a Nazi request for a building permission[1] relating to Wendstrasse 19 – the address my mother always mentioned – and carried this information: '*previous owners Isaak and Sophie Rosenfelder née Schnurmann*'. I would later learn that Isaak and Sophie were my great-grandparents, father and mother respectively of Fritz Rosenfelder, my maternal grandfather.

I immediately called Angela: 'I'll send you the fax. Tell me what you can decipher. I'd like to know if you read there what I read.'

The telephone soon rang: 'How did you get your hands on this?'

I told her quickly, burning to know what she thought.

'Well, yes, it's proof this house belongs to you. It's incredible how they've lied to you for so many years! How could they?'

I called back the land registry, feeling full of energy, and asked the perennial questions of my interlocutor, who was really rude: 'I told you your mother is out of her mind!'

'I'll send you a fax right away.'

I sent him the document and kept my temper.

'You've received it? Perfect. Please send the extracts from the land registry mentioning my family's ownership. You have my address.'

And I hung up.

---

1 The permission was to build a parking lot in the place where the house stood. The document was incomplete and too illegible to see who had made the request. I found that out later, through some cross-referencing.

I received a copy of the extracts a few days later in the post. An apologetic note accompanied the unsigned letter using 'the holidays' as an excuse for the tardiness of the reply.

I quickly read the contents of the extracts. What my eyes could see — even if after several readings I still didn't understand the whole document — was edifying: the name Rosenfelder stood out very clearly[2]. I did not understand why it had been so difficult to get hold of this document. I was soon to find out.

2 See Appendix 1.

4

My Mother

Edith Rosenfelder Waitzfelder is the only daughter of Kaethe and Fritz Rosenfelder. They lived in Karlsruhe, in a magnificent 2,000-square-metre property, Wendstrasse 19. Fritz came from a wealthy family: his mother, Sophie Schnurmann, was the daughter of an industrialist who had prospered in the manufacture and marketing of paper and textiles. Sophie's sister, Cornelia, managed several of the family enterprises. As Cornelia never married, Sophie's children inherited the family patrimony. Max, the eldest, died in the First World War. Karl and Fritz were left. Karl, who was a playwright, left no children. Fritz had one daughter: Edith, my mother, born in July 1928, in the house at Wendstrasse 19.

The position of Jews in Germany started to deteriorate between 1932 and 1934; by the end of 1936, Fritz decided to take his family to Paris in order to escape the Nazi persecutions. Germany was going through a bad period and Paris would provide shelter while they waited for happier times. He knew the city because he had studied there, as well as in London and Geneva. He spoke French and worked as lawyer for the French consulate in Karlsruhe. He went to Paris alone to look for accommodation with the idea of bringing his family over when he had found something. While waiting, he stayed at a hotel, and the family was only reunited in France in September 1938 when it moved to the rue des Saussaies.

But by 1939 Fritz was already being interned in different French prison camps. These included Tence in Haute-Loire, Gurs in the Pyrenees and Les Milles near Marseille. Edith, my mother, Kaethe, my grandmother, and Emma, Kaethe's mother, stayed on at the rue des Saussaies. Edith went to school and played on the Champ-de-Mars.

Fritz had managed to get visas so they could emigrate to the United States, but Emma, who didn't understand what was happening and couldn't imagine the extent of the threat hanging over the family, refused to set off for a country which, according to her, 'had no culture'.

When, in 1941, the situation became untenable in Paris, Kaethe decided to flee with her daughter and mother to an unoccupied area in Allauch, a small village close to Marseille. That was where my mother continued her education. At the very same time Fritz was released from the camp at Les Milles.

In 1942, after a roundup, he was interned again in the camp at Les Milles but this time was on the list of those to be deported to Auschwitz. He managed to escape, but while he was on the run in August 1942, it was his wife Kaethe's turn to be rounded up and sent to Auschwitz where she was gassed to death, then burned in a crematory oven. Miraculously my mother had gone to the beach that day with her teacher and owed her salvation to an intervention by Rosette, a young village girl who arrived before the gendarmes and saved her from being rounded up.

When he learned his wife had been captured and could never return, Fritz worked quickly to recover his daughter, and they reached Switzerland after a perilous crossing of Lake Geneva. There they were first kept in prison before being sent to a refugee camp.

But Fritz was already quite ill; his many long stays in internment camps – cold, locked up and starved of food – had taken their toll of his health. He died on December 31, 1945 in a Geneva hospital.

A large number of the family, cousins, uncles and aunts, who had also sought refuge in France and were then interned, had similarly died of cold or dysentery in the camp at Gurs.

My mother, aged seventeen, found herself alone at the end of the war. She stayed in a refugee camp in Montreux and was fed by a Jewish institution until a responsible relative was found to look after her, as she was still a minor. By the end of 1946, Ernest, an uncle who had emigrated to Sao Paolo, had agreed to take her in. So Edith left for Brazil, not knowing anything about this country's language or culture.

Three months after her twenty-third birthday, she married my father, who lived in Rio de Janeiro. They had two offspring, my brother and I; after our father's death, we have been the ones who see to her needs, for she lives in particularly precarious circumstances.

My mother was prey to great changes of mood. She had moments of pure joy: she told us stories like nobody else, made puppets for us or got out her paint box to sketch our portraits. Then suddenly, quite unexpectedly, she would have periods of melancholy and great sadness that turned her into a quite different woman. She would cry for no reason, and my brother and I took great care not to upset her. We would never talk about such moments at school: children don't like to be different from other children.

Moreover for years I wouldn't let myself cry. I have reneged on that pledge frequently since I started on this process of property reclamation!

The story my mother most liked to tell was the one called 'The Princess and the Pea'. It was her favourite story. My friends often described my mother as a princess. She always kept a noble mien, despite the premature wrinkles. Her face is so lined that when she starts to laugh, one wonders if in fact she isn't really going to cry. L'Oréal beauty creams, very good products all else notwithstanding, have been unable to spare her face the signs of her suffering. On the contrary...

I remember a strange incident – my father told me about it – that happened when they were on their honeymoon in Argentina.

My father was a very good dancer and often took my mother out dancing. That evening they had gone to a small village. I don't know what the place can have been like, I don't think there can have been any discotheques at the time, but she suddenly stopped dancing, picked her things up and said she couldn't stay there any longer. She thought she'd spotted Mengele[3] in the crowd, and that had reminded her of her mother's death. My father tried to reassure her by saying that Mengele had died with Hitler.

'Don't keep on,' she replied. 'People say he's dead, but I know it's him.'

My father died in 1979 and would never know that, in the 1980s, historians testified to this Nazi criminal's presence in Argentina at that time. There is a strong possibility that he was the man my mother saw.

My mother only returned to Europe twice after leaving Switzerland in 1946. Once with my father, and a second time to visit me. She has nevertheless not forgotten her German roots; whenever friends went to Germany and asked her what she wanted, she used to reply: 'Take a photo of my house, Wendstrasse 19, for me.' One day she was at last sent a present of a very beautiful photo annotated by friends: that's when she discovered L'Oréal had established its German head office there.

My mother really adored France. She had taught French language and literature at the Alliance Française in Rio. When we were small, although we didn't speak a word of French, we would sing nursery rhymes like '*Frère Jacques*', '*Alouette, gentille alouette*' and many others. We even knew '*La Marseillaise*' by heart. My mother listened to Piaf, Montand, Aznavour, Trénet and Barbara. She would talk to us

---

3 Dr Josef Mengele, the Nazi doctor in Auschwitz, carried out horrific medical experiments on those held there. He was nicknamed 'the Angel of Death'. He fled to Argentina and it is believed he died in Brazil in 1979.

about the *maquis* and the French Resistance fighters who had obtained fake passports for her and her father; they were her heroes.

If they were certainly that, there were many others who borrowed this glorious name at the end of the war: the famous 'last-minute resisters'.

When L'Oréal established itself in Karlsruhe, its reputation was still unblemished. On the contrary, as its arrival in the region coincided with the Allies, the liberators of Europe and conquerors of Nazism, the company enjoyed a more than positive image. L'Oréal belonged to that band of heroes who were about to rebuild the country. One of the Allies's tasks was to ensure that property stolen from the Jews was returned. I was soon to be disenchanted on that front.

5

A Bad-Smelling Perfume

Angela needed the help of another translator and a good four months to complete a first translation of the deeds. As she proceeded with her task, she was shocked by what she uncovered. If some passages still remained opaque, one thing was certain: the house had definitely belonged to the Rosenfelders until 1938, the date when it was 'sold'. The text concerning the 'sale' is not very clear. At the end of the war, the American military government placed an embargo on it – as with all Jewish property purloined by the Nazis – and it was subject to a restitution order. The deeds then signal a new sale to the company, Haarfarben und Parfümerien GmbH.

When I read this name, my mother's phrase immediately echoed in my head: even if L'Oréal wasn't mentioned, it was obviously something related to hair-care products. Perhaps my mother was right. She reacted vociferously when she caught sight of the document: 'You see, I'm not mad! I've been saying that house is mine for sixty years.'

If only for that, the fact that I had recovered this document was a source of satisfaction.

I typed Haarfarben und Parfümerien GmbH into my computer and was able to track the company down very quickly. A few clicks on the Internet were enough to make the link with L'Oréal. I sent my thanks and some sweets to Karlsruhe, in order to thank Mrs V. She called a few days afterwards to thank me, to say that it wasn't necessary, that she was sorry…

'Sorry for what? You did the most one could do for anyone! My mother has been waiting for this document for sixty years. Tell me, Mrs V., how is it possible we've been lied to for so many years when people quite clearly knew this house was ours?'

Mme V. started to whisper: 'You know that before the war things here were done rather…. Equally, after the war, they were done rather deviously[4]. L'Oréal is very important here. I'm sorry. I must hang up. Thank you.'

'I am the one who should be thanking you.'

I felt this story was too much for me. I didn't know what to think or do. Besides, I had operas to study. I hadn't the time to keep everything on the boil.

A few months after the call from the Prime Minister's Office, I went to the CDJC[5] to search for documents related to my grandparents' deportation. En route, I remembered an incident that had occurred six years earlier. I had called the Sons and Daughters of Jewish French Deportees to get any possible information. All I knew then was their name and final destination, Auschwitz. My mother had never said anything to me, so everything else was a great blur for me.

'What was your grandparents' name?'

'Kaethe Rosenfelder, née Hirsch, and Fritz Rosenfelder.'

'Kaethe, train number 29, destination Auschwitz, died in a gas chamber.'

These words cut through my body like a sharp knife, and I hung up at once, distraught. I'd made that call to Serge Klarsfeld's association years ago and now felt strong enough to search out the documents and face their content.

4 Mrs V. used the German word '*krumm*'.
5 Centre de documentation juive contemporaine – the Centre for Contemporary Jewish Documentation.

The CDJC employees could only give me the deportation book for my grandmother, Kaethe. They had nothing on her husband, Fritz. They gave me addresses where I could continue my research.

I read and read when I got home. On the first page, the acronyms RF (République française) and SS are printed side by side. The book is written half in French, half in German. Even though you know what's coming, its content is horrific. It speaks of people as if they were ordinary freight divided up in sections, by age, sex and exit camps. The cargo left on time, so many died on the journey, so many reached their destination, so many passed through the gas chambers. Orders were carried out to the letter, all women died. Only a few men (a number is mentioned) escape immediate death; they will be allocated to forced-labour gangs.

Then come the signatures. It is SS *Sturmbannführer* Hagen who carried out the orders, executing decisions taken at a round table by Eichmann and Laval.

I knew who Eichmann was[6]. When his death was announced my father had declared that it was a day to remember before explaining who this character was. At the time, I didn't try to find out anything else. I went to see one of my neighbours.

'Have you heard of this man Laval?'

She looked at me in astonishment as if I'd asked something quite foolish. Then she remembered I hadn't been brought up in France.

'He was the prime minister in the Vichy government. Why?'

'Because he and Eichmann signed the deportation order for my grandmother. It's strange. I thought only Germans were responsible for the deportation of Jews and that the French government only followed orders. However, it is quite clear they took the decision jointly.'

6 Adolf Eichmann (1906–1962), German civil servant, member of the SS, directed the Jewish office at the German High Command. He was in charge of the extermination of all Jews in Europe (the 'Final Solution'). In 1945 he sought refuge in Argentina, but was tracked down by the Israeli police in 1960. He was hanged after a long trial in Jerusalem.

'Where did your grandparents live?'

'In Paris, 6 rue des Saussaies.'

She sat down when she heard those words.

'What's the matter?'

'The headquarters of the Gestapo was on the rue des Saussaies.'

Then a childhood memory suddenly flashed back: 'Hide, the Gestapo's opposite, hide.' Another sentence I'd heard from my mother's lips. Some things were beginning to make sense.

A few days later, I was buying a newspaper when my eyes were drawn to the cover of *L'Express* featuring Liliane Bettencourt, the L'Oréal heiress. The article rather sang her praises. Reference was certainly made to a few shadowy areas darkening the family past, but the point wasn't laboured. I couldn't stop myself from thinking she couldn't be the great lady they described, that her family had taken our house, that we had deliberately – and for many years – been refused access to the deeds mentioning our title deed and that after all that our property had never been returned to us. I'll write to *L'Express*, I told myself, and reveal some other sides to the lady in question. How naive I was!

I called my uncle to tell him what I was planning. He advised me against writing such a letter: I would be challenging powerful people and exposing myself to eventual retaliation. Besides, I didn't know the exact nature of their relationship with the magazine. According to him, even if I were in the right, it would be better to get a lawyer to write the letter. Easy enough to say when you don't mix in this world, when you don't always have the means and you have no time!

Several people commented on the article and asked me questions. I replied timidly that I'd thought of writing to *L'Express*, that I'd been advised to see a lawyer and had finally dropped the whole business.

In fact, I didn't really know which way to turn because some of my friends insisted it was important to do something.

Two months later, I telephoned *Maître* Charles Korman.

6

The Price of a Great Fortune

Born in 1922, Liliane Bettencourt is the daughter and sole heiress of Eugène Schueller, the founder of L'Oréal[7]. She married André Bettencourt in June 1950. The latter met Eugène Schueller at the end of the 1930s. André pursued a political career after the war. Well to the right, he was nonetheless a close, loyal friend of François Mitterand; the two men had met each other and got on well since their youth.

Liliane Bettencourt, with a fortune worth € 14.9 billion[8], is the richest woman in France and occupies thirteenth position in the world ranking of millionaires. According to the Fininfo company, her estimated fortune, including her holdings of stocks and shares, was in the region of $18.4 billion.

And the Bettencourts grow a further € 590,000 richer by the hour, even when they are asleep[9]:

Mme Liliane Bettencourt lives in a large house in Neuilly-sur-Seine, with an array of servants [...] But there is

7 Most of the information in this chapter comes from the following books: Emmanuel Faux, Thomas Legrand, Gilles Perez, *La main droite de Dieu: enquête sur François Mitterand et l'extrême droite*, Paris, Le Seuil, 1994, pp. 150-153; and Michel Bar-Zohar, *Une histoire sans fard: L'Oréal des années sombres au boycott arabe*, translated by Serge Moran, Paris, Fayard, 1997, pp. 50-54.

8 *Le Monde*, February 2002.

9 Bruno Abescat, *La Saga des Bettencourt: L'Oréal, une fortune française*, Paris, Plon, 2002, pp. 28, 29.

no doubt that the most beautiful of her properties is in Arcouest, in Britanny [...] With its swimming pool full of warm sea water and exquisite view of the island of Bréhat – that changes at every moment of the day as the tides cover and uncover the rocks – magnificently equipped and sheltered by a clump of eucalyptus trees, the villa enjoys more than a touch of paradise[10].

The Bettencourts mingle with Parisian high society (or perhaps it would be more accurate to say that Parisian high society mingles with the Bettencourts). They enjoy privileged relationships in the political world, on the right and left, starting with successive presidents of the Republic and their wives. Members of the government, of legislative assemblies, the Constitutional Council and the Central Bank pay them court. Beyond political and financial spheres, they have created links in the worlds of media, culture and science; the Bettencourts have established a foundation[11] that sponsors different projects arising from within these same domains. In other words, you can find the Bettencourt touch wherever you probe the decision-making areas in French society.

Eugène Schueller, a chemist, founded L'Oréal in 1907 under the name of the French Company for Harmless Hair Dyes (Société française de teintures innoffensives pour cheveux). The firm quickly prospered, and Schueller found he had a substantial fortune on his hands.

---

10 Ibid., p. 27

11 Apart from the founders, Mr and Mrs Bettencourt, their daughter Françoise and son-in-law Jean-Pierre Meyers, the members of the board of this foundation include three well qualified people, ex-directors of L'Oréal – François Dalle, Pascal Castres Saint-Martin and Guy Landon – two representatives belonging to leading state bodies – Michel Albert, inspector of finances and member of the National Institute of France, and Jean-Luc Silicani, state counsellor – and finally three upstanding members – Jean-Pierre Duport, Prefect for the Île-de-France, Prefect of Paris, Professor of Medicine Alain Pompidou and businessman Marc Ladreit de Lacharrière, also a former collaborator with L'Oréal and now occupying the position of treasurer.

In 1935 he viewed with distaste the probable rise to power of the Popular Front and joined the most extreme nationalist grouping, which loudly proclaimed that it preferred Hitler to the Popular Front. Schueller didn't hesitate to put his wallet where his mouth was and supplied generous support. Thus, from the very start, the CSAR (Secret Committee for Revolutionary Action) sought his help, and it was then that he met its founder, Eugène Deloncle. The group, which met several times at L'Oréal headquarters, 14 rue Royale in Paris, soon became very famous under the name of La Cagoule – 'The Hood'. Schueller was not happy merely investing large sums of money in this clandestine organization that championed violent action: he was one of its most outlandish ideologues.

There was another key man in La Cagoule: Jacques Corrèze, Deloncle's assistant. His codename was *la Bûche* –'The Log'. He was involved in most of the bloody actions or murders committed by La Cagoule before the war. In fact, no sooner was it created than the organization embarked on a series of political murders. A villa in Rueil harboured a strong-room and torture chamber. Poison was stolen from research institutes in order to suppress traitors to the cause. Four aeroplanes on their way to Spain exploded in flight. In Paris, two bombs destroyed the buildings of the General Confederation of French Industry and the Inter-professional Employers Union, in an attempt to lay blame for the attacks on the Communists.

Moreover, to support the *coup d'état* it was preparing against the Republic, the organization assembled an impressive stockpile of arms. Thousands of hand grenades, hundreds of rifles and machine guns and munitions were seized in their Paris warehouse.

In 1937 the organization walked straight into a trap set by the police, who spread the rumour that the Communists were preparing an insurrection in Paris. The 'red' threat mobilized almost all the members of La Cagoule, and the police, under the orders of Marx Dormoy, Minister of the Interior, arrested fifty-seven of them. Schueller escaped, but Deloncle wasn't so lucky. But he wouldn't stay long behind bars: the war and the Occupation soon put an end to judicial investigations.

The defeat in 1940 and advent of the Pétain government were a godsend for La Cagoule; it could finally become enmeshed in the structures of power. Thus, in Vichy, from among the leading members of La Cagoule, François Méténier was put in charge of the armed groups protecting the head of the National Revolution; Gabriel Jeantet was Marshal Pétain's right-hand man; and Colonel Goussard his loyal follower. He would in the end join the Resistance.

In Paris, Deloncle openly collaborated with the Gestapo and the SS via a legal avatar of La Cagoule, the Movement for Social Revolution (Mouvement social révolutionnaire, or MSR) founded with Schueller in September 1940. The names of the two men appeared side by side on posters, tracts and invitations. The first manifesto of the movement – entitled 'Revolution! MSR. Resurrection!' – included the signatures of, among others, Deloncle, Schueller and Corrèze. The latter was a member of its political bureau as was that veteran *cagoulard*, Jean Filliol. The MSR officially published its chain of command. Schueller was part of the executive committee as chair of all the technical committees. The secretariat for these committees was established at L'Oréal headquarters, 14 rue Royale[12].

The MSR was an umbrella for two organizations that trumpeted anti-Semitic battle cries: the Anti-Jewish Movement and the French Community, to which Corrèze belonged. This gentleman requested and engineered the setting up of a General Commissariat for Jewish Questions (Commissariat général aux questions juives, or CGJQ) that then became the Institute for the Study of Jewish Questions (l'Institut d'étude des questions juives, or IEQJ) directed by a man by the name of Sézille. On April 5 1941, Sézille wrote to Deloncle: 'The MSR must and will be the

---

12 See Appendices 17 and 18.

executive arm and the French Community, through its sphere of study and documentation, will provide the means.' And, when the IEQJ created its anti-Jewish brigades in July 1941, the MSR was responsible for remunerating the district leaders[13].

But the time had come for the MSR to expand its base and enhance its status from a group to that of a party. Under the approving gaze of the German Embassy, it published a violently anti-Semitic, anti-democratic and racist platform before merging with another pro-Nazi organization led by Marcel Déat in order to set up the National Popular Assembly (Rassemblement national populaire, or RNP) the Parisian secretary of which was none other than Corrèze.

The RNP programme was as follows: 'Our goal is to pursue, in a planned, methodical way, the exclusion of the Jews and to defend the interests of the French damaged by the Jews.' In the course of the first RNP Congress in June 1941, one speaker after another took to the podium to encourage the French to 'cleanse the country of Jews and its latest bastard offspring, Gaullism'. Schueller, head of the RNP technical committees, described the three axes of the economic revolution to be carried through: wages, management and capital. For the revolution to succeed he harangued his audience, 'we must quickly execute fifty or a hundred important people'.

Intoxication with power didn't mean La Cagoule forgot its former enemies: in July 1941, the former Minister of the Interior, Marx Dormoy, paid with his life for having defused the plot they were hatching before the war. A bomb was placed under his pillow. When La Cagoule went on trial, the official report of which I managed to track down, a witness declared that Deloncle and the leadership of La Cagoule ordered this attack.

Marx Dormoy was not the only man to suffer the murderous vengeance of La Cagoule. As if the blood already spilt wasn't

13 Anti-Jewish services were concentrated at 11 rue des Saussaies.

enough to appease it, Deloncle – who still needed so sorely to prove to the Occupier that he was a genuine collaborator – had seven synagogues blown up on the night of 2 October.

In the aftermath of the war, L'Oréal was there to allow former collaborators and a number of *cagoulards* to discreetly restore their virginity. Thus, Jacques Corrèze (*cagoulard* number 552) secretary general of the MSR and involved in the LVF[14] resurfaced in the Spanish branch of L'Oréal, then became President of Cosmair, the branch of L'Oréal in the United States. Jean Filliol (*cagoulard* number 43), the main thug in La Cagoule, was taken on under the pseudonym of André Lamy. Gabriel Jeantet (*cagoulard* number 467) and Jean Leguay were also recruited. For the record, the latter – Bousquet's assistant at the General Secretariat for the Police in the Occupation and representative for the Secretariat in the Northern region – is considered to be one of those with most responsibility for the Vél d'Hiv[15] roundup.

At the time of the Liberation, Schueller employed François Mitterand, making him Executive Director of Editions du Rond-Point (a L'Oréal financed activity). He encouraged him to get involved in politics, and it was L'Oréal that financed his first campaign. Very soon after he was elected a deputy in November 1946, Schueller's young protégé received his first ministerial portfolio[16].

---

14 Légion des volontaires français – the Legion of French Volunteers.

15 On 16 and 17 July 1942 more than 8,000 Jews including 4,000 children were gathered in the Vélodrome d'Hiver in Paris in atrocious conditions. Organized by the French police, this roundup was one of the most important acts of anti-Semitic persecution committed by the French authorities.

16 E. Faux, T. Legrand, G. Perez, *La Main droite de Dieu: enquête sur François Mitterand et l'extrême droite*, pp. 150-153.

7

Rheingold

Maître Korman gave me an appointment on 21 December 2000. In January I was leaving, first for a few days in Budapest then to Toulouse as assistant producer for *Das Rheingold*, the first volet of Wagner's trilogy. Subsequently, after two days in Paris, I would be off again, this time to Bilbao for Donizetti's *Lucia di Lammermoor*. It was the only possible date before March.

I started to tell him my story. I had brought the article from *L'Express* and told him of my intention to write to the magazine. I think he wasn't too sure whether to believe me or not, but my tale interested him, particularly the way I told it. By then I'd managed to collect the Nazi building permission from 1938, the extract from the Karlsruhe land registry (*Grundbuch*), my grandmother's deportation book, my own birth certificate, where it noted that Kaethe and Fritz Rosenfelder are my maternal grandparents, that of my mother who was born in Karlsruhe, my grandparents' marriage certificate and documents showing, first, that my grandfather was imprisoned in several camps and was on the deportation list from the camp in Les Milles, and second, that the Rosenfelder family had lived at 6 rue des Saussaies, in Paris. Finally, I showed him the fruits of my research on the Internet and the links I'd found between Haarfarben und Parfümerien and L'Oréal.

But all that wasn't enough for my interlocutor; he wanted still more. I couldn't hide a degree of irritation.

'I have only come to see you in order to write a letter. Please tell me if that will be at all possible. Yes or no?'

'More documentation is needed. And we can do much better than just write a letter.'

I have always mistrusted lawyers and immediately felt defensive.

'Do you want to get your house back? Yes or no?'

His suggestion was tempting, but I found it difficult to believe. He then proposed that I continue my research and find out more about the links between Haarfarben und Parfümerien and L'Oréal. How would I find such information? I didn't know where to start. I left him saying that I would think about it.

Despite all the difficulties, the conversation had rekindled my spirits. I called Angela to ask her to carry out more research. There were perhaps other facts to dig out of a library or some other institution. She was spurred on; we were now into our tenth year of investigations.

I was in Budapest when she told me that she had perhaps found something in an archive service. Fearing we would face opposition when we tried to get a copy, we acted as if we were research students. We received a document from 1961, an extract from a company register mentioning L'Oréal, rue Royale, in Paris, and Liliane Bettencourt as shareholders in Haarfarben und Parfümerien (other shareholders were listed with their respective holdings). Address: Wendstrasse 19.

It was more grist to my mill. All the more so because there was also mention of a building of great value and of the bank with which the company was working: the Dresdner Bank.

I called my lawyer to tell him of my discoveries. He then asked me to get an estimate of the building's value. That seemed a daunting undertaking as work was absorbing all my energies: *Das Rheingold* is a demanding opera that requires lots of time and energy. Rehearsals gave way to dress rehearsals, and I would never get back to my hotel bedroom in Toulouse before midnight.

Angela, whom I'd told about my lawyer's new request, called me a few weeks later. She had found a kind of figure that gave more or less the rental price of property by the square metre in Germany and by sector. But there was no such information on sale prices. So we started to research the cost of property in the district that concerned us.

Meanwhile, I had meticulously studied the deeds, noted that there were 700 square metres of land and that the house had three floors as well as a basement (My mother always said the house was 2,000 square metres). Thus, I was able to make my first rough estimates, but the price I came up with was so startling that I had to do the calculations several times over to make sure I'd not made a mistake. I like to think I'm pretty good at maths, but suddenly I doubted myself. I called a neighbour in Paris, who is an accountant; my figures were correct. I passed these figures on to *Maître* Korman. We set up a meeting for the end of February, on my return.

I had also re-established contact with Mrs V. at the Karlsruhe town hall. I wanted to know if L'Oréal still owned the building and, if not, who did. This time it was several weeks before I received a reply: the person who worked at the land registry had left but had been replaced. According to her, L'Oréal no longer owned the building, although she wasn't at all certain. She far from convinced.

'L'Oréal is still very powerful here,' she told me.

I stopped contacting her to avoid creating any more difficulties for her and finally decided to call the new person administrating the registry. It was a blessing. *A priori*, I had no idea with whom I would be dealing, I was walking on eggshells.

'I'm not the substitute, but the person now in charge of the service. How can I help you?'

Mr Müller's tone voice was quite different to his predecessor's; one sensed his courage and frankness.

'No, Madame, L'Oréal no longer owns the building. You know, it is a very large building.'

'Who does own it now?'

'The State and the Land of Bade-Würtemberg.'

'Can you send me a copy of the bill of sale?'

'No problem at all.'

On my return to Paris, I found the document in my post box. L'Oréal had sold the building in 1991 for DM5.3 million, then rented part to the new owner for the two months following the sale. What a godsend! I didn't even need to ask for expert advice: all the figures were there for the sale and the rental. Besides, a basement was mentioned and, when a building is 580 square metres at ground level, one imagines the basement is not a negligible space. I know how valuable it is to have such an extension in a coveted neighbourhood.

When I met up with my lawyer armed with these documents, I felt he took me a little more seriously. But, although he appreciated the fruits of my research, he still wasn't satisfied. I learned, after three months of interacting with him, that he rarely pays compliments in a meeting and that *Maître* Korman prefers to point his finger at the tasks still to be completed: a tactic designed to drive me mad. I advanced several hypotheses.

'That is possible, but I want proof.'

'But how will I find them? Do you realize what you are asking me to do?'

'You will find them.'

And that's all there is to it!

8

Os Gringos

My parents were gringos in the eyes of Brazilians. My mother will always retain this slightly pejorative nickname Brazilians give to foreigners: she speaks Portuguese with a French accent.

I'm not at all a *gringa*: I was born in Brazil. Nonetheless, from my early childhood, I've always felt a bit foreign. Even with the ease of communication that comes with the ability to speak several languages, this feeling continues to haunt me wherever I go.

I learned to recite the alphabet by heart in my English school. Then I went to a Brazilian school and, when I had to recite it, I'd first think it through in English before my small child's head translated it into Portuguese at top speed. I worked that way for years, 'through translation' – and not only in order to recite the alphabet; I had to adapt my behaviour continuously in order to be in step with the new realities I confronted.

Children, it's well known, want above everything to be like everybody else. At a very early age we already spoke three languages, and our mother wasn't at all like the mothers of our playmates. The difference could also be felt within the Jewish community. Several friends of my mother had also lost their nearest of kin in the camps or had been robbed. But they had all received compensation for the Shoah. Even if money were no replacement for what had disappeared, it at least had this merit: their suffering had been officially recognized. Justice had been done, and each in his or her own way had been able to turn the page.

It was quite another story with my mother. We didn't know whether her grief made her transgress the frontiers of truth. If what she affirmed was true, then why couldn't she produce documentation like other people? Why hadn't she received compensation? In the face of the doubts hovering over her, she learned not to go out on a limb, to keep quiet and pretend to be the same as everybody else. And we, her children, followed her example and in turn erected our own façades. Thus, because I felt different from my companions, I had no choice but to 'translate' in order to be understood by them.

I remember that at home our passports, together with a small suitcase, were always at the ready, to cope with any eventuality. That was how it had to be, my parents needed that to feel calm. Also the house was a real grocery store, and as soon as our reserves began to run out, my mother would rush to the shops. My brother was amused by her behaviour and couldn't stop himself from remarking ironically that we had enough to feed the whole of Napoleon's army.

My mother wasn't the only one to act in this way: all her friends who had experienced the war did the same. Cupboards and refrigerators were always full to bursting. And, as if this weren't enough, my mother would bake two or three cakes a day. But I remember the delights of her cooking as well as her compulsive behaviour. She was a real *cordon bleu*, and tasty teas always followed the French lessons she taught groups of pupils at home; her chocolate mousse and other dishes were appreciated by one and all.

Jews who didn't lose any member of their family in the Shoah don't have the slightest idea about the universe inhabited by those who weren't so fortunate. Death, for anyone who has never lost a loved one, is an abstract idea. No words can make anyone understand. The same goes for the emptiness and pain that accompany us. What a strange feeling it is to sense at your side a poignant presence singling you out from other people. It is something you'd like to throw off but will never be able to, and you wonder in the end whether one day it will in fact stop.

While I have been reconstructing my family's history, this presence has moreover allowed me to understand, not intellectually but almost physically, the causes of wars, at the risk of seeming ingenuous yet again. The reasons invoked are never those really motivating war-makers. Similarly, the 'saviours' use the pretext of coming to help those attacked when in fact they are only thinking about their own interests: in the first place money, but also fame, indirect advantage and the sharing out of power. Of course, amid the naked predators, there are fortunately people whose only wish is to serve the common interest, but their number remains decidedly small.

We celebrated Sabbath on Friday evening. My parents weren't particularly religious but, good Brazilians that we were, we liked to have a party, whether it was Jewish or not. Thus, we would pray the prayer of bread, wine and lights around the table laid with a white tablecloth where the dishes prepared by my mother had pride of place. We never answered the telephone during the meal and if one of us was meeting a friend that evening, that friend was invited to dine. We celebrated Hanukkah as it should be celebrated. The celebrations of Rosh Hashana, Yom Kippur and Passover were livelier: more than twenty guests would sit around the table when these festivities were held at our house.

Christian celebrations like Christmas, Twelfth Night or Easter gave us an opportunity to visit our friends, who were generally Catholic and came to our house for Sabbath and our special days.

My mother adored having people around her. It was her way of redressing the emptiness created by a total absence of family on her side. My father believed in God, my mother didn't. She said that if God existed, He wouldn't allow certain things to happen.

My brother and I adored one celebration more than any other: it was the Succot or Feast of the Tabernacles, because all the children living in the street were invited into our own home. On this occasion, my father would build a large hut with fruit and vegetables. We had the right to eat from it (you only had to stretch out a hand to serve yourself) and sleep there.

So our parents passed on to us certain traditions before giving us the freedom later to continue with them or not. Today I only join in these celebrations when I return to Brazil where my mother still keeps on with them. Nevertheless, in France I do go to the synagogue to say Kaddish during Yom Kippur, in memory of my father who asked me to do so from his deathbed. Each year, I make use of this moment to step outside my hectic life and reflect. I think of my father lovingly but sometimes also sadly. I ponder certain aspects of my existence, and I still experience the same pleasure hearing the sound of the shofar in the Parisian synagogue I go to. I remember how there was a resounding organ and choir in Rio. The music alone was enough to make us want to go to the synagogue: it was beautiful and moreover was played by excellent musicians.

One year, at the time of the Yom Kippur festivities, they began to read out loudly the names of all the members of the congregation who had died in the extermination camps. Each name echoed like a hammer blow in my ears. I felt I was suffocating and couldn't continue listening. I left the synagogue.

From time to time we would go to the countryside, to Itaipava, and stay in a house we rented with other families. The countryside, in Brazil, is the forest. A huge forest with exuberant vegetation. We liked to be in contact with it and feel the earth under our feet penetrating our bodies, reminding us that life was there. This closeness to the forest was a great source of comfort in periods when my mother was unwell.

Music had its place in the countryside: we performed accordion concerts for ourselves. Forty of us would play on our accordions tunes like 'La Dame aux camélias', while a young girl, dressed all in blue, carried a big basket of equally blue flowers that she threw to the audience. It was very *kitsch*, but I loved it.

9

Unterdruckverkauf

I am not the kind of person to leave things half-done. If what I've started isn't finished, it's not my style to stop mid-flow. So I read and reread the deeds and found fresh clues each time. But a few passages still eluded me.

The owner of the Internet café where I go to do administrative chores had spoken to me several times about L'Oréal's dark past. My lawyer and I had also discussed this, but without making any headway. I was advised in this respect to make contact with the World Jewish Congress. At the mere mention of the name L'Oréal, their interest was immediately aroused, but the person I had to consult was travelling. While I waited for him to return, I tried my luck with the CDJC. Perhaps I would glean some information there. I would!

'Have you never heard about the L'Oréal affair?'

'Vaguely.'

I began to read the documents they gave me. I was taken aback. The first thing that struck me was the correlation of dates. L'Oréal, through its chief executive François Dalle, was accused of 'racial discrimination' towards Jews, in the wake of a scandal – the Frydman affair[17] – which broke in 1991, the date when the group was selling its property in Karlsruhe. The first revelations in this

---

17 See Chapter 18.

scandal dated back to 1989: the same year that negotiations had begun for the sale of Wendstrasse 19.

There is one fact related to this I have yet to mention: the bill of sale Mr Müller sent me in 1991 had come together with appendices containing letters signed by a minister and members of the cabinet giving their consent[18].

I was too shocked to read to the end of the documents I'd been given. I made photocopies and went to Fayard the publishers to buy two copies of book on the affair (one for my lawyer)[19].

Each page rang bells for me. There were so many things in common between what I was reading and my family's history that they couldn't be mere coincidences. I discovered that Eugène Schueller, the founder of L'Oréal, had also been one of the founder members of La Cagoule, that Fascist, anti-Semitic organization from the 1930s which used to meet…on the corner of the rue des Saussaies. In other words, at the very time my grandmother Kaethe, her mother Emma and my mother Edith left their home on the rue des Saussaies to flee to the unoccupied territory in Allauch, near Marseille.

When I reached this point in my research, I realized that it was in 1991 that L'Oréal had sought to rid itself of a property linking it to its notoriously anti-Semitic past.

I finally met up with my adviser at the World Jewish Congress. His family was also originally from Karlsruhe. When he saw the documents I had brought, including the title deeds certifying that my family was the owner of Wendstrasse 19, he assured me that I could try to take L'Oréal to court. My lawyer and I had already discussed this possibility. My first reaction was not to go on a war footing; I much prefer peaceful solutions, and negotiation seemed to me to be much more appropriate. If we were dealing with reasonable people,

---

18 Note that the State and the Land were presenting themselves as purchasers.

19 Michel Bar-Zohar, *Une histoire sans fard: L'Oréal des années sombres au boycott arabe.*

we might be able to reach an amicable settlement. All the more so given that the anti-Semitic fervour of one generation does not condemn *a priori* the next. Besides, it wasn't my style to condemn anyone without giving them a right of reply, I told myself: 'Let's give them a chance!'

So we began to prepare a letter to L'Oréal refining the calculations of the amount of total compensation I could claim in my family's name. While so doing, I couldn't help but think of all those years my mother had spent without that money which was hers by right – and which she had sorely lacked.

But let's go back to the documentation – in particular, the title deeds – for we are still only beginning to find things out.

We noticed that Angela had made a mistake in the translation of the title deeds. She had translated 'Madischer Gemeinde' when she should have read 'Badischer Gemeinde'. In her defence, the document is barely legible at this point and I myself had confused the letters M and B[20]. Anyway, it was a reference to the Badischer Gemeinde Versicherung Verband (BGV), an insurance company working for local companies in the Baden region. It was then we realized that this firm had appropriated the house in 1938.

My lawyer asked me to reconstruct the history of this company. How could I? I was on the road again. I found it on the Internet but followed through by phone: I called Mr Müller in Karlsruhe and begged him to inform me as to the existence of a bill of sale from 1938. Yes, it existed, and Mr Müller sent it me.

The seal of the Third Reich[21] figures to the left of the signature on the deed of transfer. And, to my amazement, there is a power of attorney from my grandfather. The power of attorney authorizes one Luise Dürr to carry out all legal or juridical acts on his behalf and gives these acts the same validity as if he had carried them out himself, to dispose of all his property and even to transfer all his

20 See Appendix 1.
21 See Appendix 5.

rights to a third person. And it all remained valid after his death. Although it doesn't specify for how many generations...[22]

No one in his right mind, even less so a leading lawyer like my grandfather, could have signed such a document except under constraint. Fritz was in Paris when he signed this permission at the German consulate, while his wife Kaethe, daughter (my mother) and mother-in-law Emma were still in Karlsruhe.

There is a term in German to describe these forced concessions made under the Third Reich: *Unterdruckverkauf* – sale under constraint.

After reading these facts, what else was there to say but that it was quite obvious the story stank to high heaven. I then asked Mr Müller to send me the deed of purchase of Wendstrasse 19 by Haarfarben und Parfümerien (L'Oréal). Reading this deed, dated 1954, brought a fresh surprise: there it stated in black and white that after the war the house was subject to the provisions for the process of restoring Jewish property to their former Jewish owners. But, by the side of this observation, the Nazis who had bestowed the property upon themselves in 1938 stipulate between apostrophes that 'the case has been closed'. Everything is in order. Period.[23]

There is another quite shocking side to this document: L'Oréal gave over the war compensation to the seller, Badischer Gemeinde Versicherung Verband (BGV): in other words, to the Nazis who had appropriated the house in 1938. These indemnities should have come to my mother, the woman who inherited this house. And I just think how over the years my mother has been told when asked why she had no right to war compensation: 'It's been awarded already.' But they forgot to specify to her that it had in fact been awarded to the Nazis who'd taken her house from her in the first place. In the event, L'Oréal purchased the house for DM27,000[24].

22 See Appendix 4.
23 See Appendix 6.
24 Or some € 13,200.

We thus sent a letter to L'Oréal on 18 June 2001: the property that had belonged to them had been stolen in the Nazi era and they were still enjoying the fruits of this robbery. Consequently, we were seeking reparations for this injustice, and they were given a month in which to reply. My lawyer and I decided to make it clear we favoured the path of conciliation but that in case of refusal we would appeal to the courts.

We also wrote, of course, to the German BGV insurance company as well as to the Versorgung des Bundes und der Länder, the present owners of Wendstrasse 19.

The reply from L'Oréal reached my lawyer on 13 July 2001, five days before the expiry of the deadline. The letter, dated the twelfth, is signed by Lindsay Owen-Jones, chief executive of L'Oréal. The Shoah was an absolute tragedy as far as he was concerned, he wrote, but as a company L'Oréal did not believe it had done any wrong to Mme Edith Rosenfelder and he gave us the names of their lawyers who could provide 'a legally irrefutable analysis of the situation'.

10
Rue des Saussaies

I finally decided to see what my grandparents' apartment might
have looked like on the rue des Saussaies. Merely consulting my
map of Paris to find the nearest métro station had made me
nervous. 'Champs-Élysées-Clemenceau' had been up to then the
station where I got out to see art exhibitions at the Grand Palais.

When I came out of the métro, I noted the unusual nature of
the residential buildings in the area. I asked the man at the
newspaper kiosk for the way, and he directed me towards the
Élysée Palace, home to the president of the Republic. Convinced
he hadn't understood me, I asked several people the same question
and got the same reply. So I walked past the Élysée to the place
Beauvau, where the rue des Saussaies starts. 'Place Beauvau' rang a
bell. Under the tricolour flag of the French Republic, a group of
uniformed men was guarding a building. I asked one of them.

'It's the Ministry of the Interior.'

Of course! What a fool I was.

I crossed the street and couldn't stop shaking when I saw
number 6. I went back to the pavement opposite in order to get a
better view and saw that the Ministry of the Interior was exactly
opposite number 6. The latter is a three-storied building with
bedrooms under the eaves. I waited for someone to go in because
you needed an entry code, then I went up to the third floor and

rang. No response. I went down to the ground floor and explained to the person who had let me in that my grandparents lived there during the war. She said the flat was up for sale, gave me the details of the estate agency and allowed me to visit hers, specifying that the one on the third floor was bigger, some 180 square metres. After leaving the building, I took another look round: the Élysée Palace, then the Ministry of the Interior. In 1944, André Bettencourt worked at the Ministry of the Interior.

Shortly afterwards, I received a very kind letter from the Pyrénées-Atlantiques Regional Authorities. They had discovered a document that related to the interning of my grandfather in the camp in Gurs. It originated from the police in Lyons.

For the first time in my life I had a physical description of my grandfather: one metre eighty-five tall and blue-eyed. And a redhead like me. The document also mentioned the wounds he'd received to his right arm and leg in the First World War. I knew he had had a special violin made so he could play it with the bow in his left hand, and that his favourite pieces were the Bach Partitas for solo violin.

He also loved opera, notably Wagner and, another nod from destiny, I'd been working on a production of Wagner operas ever since that first meeting with my lawyer; and that brought me close to my grandfather again.

What a pity I never knew him. I would love us to have played together. I can imagine we'd have enjoyed some lively, passionate arguments. We wouldn't have always been in agreement as to particular interpretations or conductors, but agreed or not, we'd have compared reactions and sometimes ended up laughing ourselves silly.

Apart from music, my grandfather was fond of painting. Research I have carried out into the paintings he owned prove at least one thing: he found a place for contemporary art on his walls.

As for my grandmother, I'd seen a photo of her in a book that mentions our family in Germany and its deportation. I have the same eyes as her. Her face radiates sweetness and tenderness but also character. She was clearly a beautiful woman. She wasn't yet thirty when this photo was taken. She wasn't yet forty when she died.

When I think of my grandparents, I start imagining what our life might have been like if they were still alive. We might be in the grand rooms in their Karlsruhe villa for, if my grandfather had survived, he wouldn't have let anyone take his house from him. But perhaps we might have been on the rue des Saussaies talking politics or commenting on the actions of the successive occupants of the nearby Élysée Palace or place Beauvau. We would constitute a normal family.

On the other hand, I find it difficult to imagine what my relationship might have been with my grandmother Kaethe. I know nothing about her. My mother never mentioned her. She says she doesn't remember. Did she like music? Did she play an instrument? Did she like dancing? Reading? Was she a good cook? So many unanswered questions. A total void, nothingness. All I have to hang on to is what emanates from that photo where her gaze gives the impression that she enjoyed a rich inner life.

11

Indignation

Lindsay Owen-Jones, the then L'Oréal CEO, speaks of a 'legally irrefutable analysis of the situation' in his letter of 12 July. My lawyer had just read it to me, and he found it hard to restrain my anger:

'*Maître*, the only thing that is irrefutable in this situation is the following, that house belonged to the Rosenfelders and my mother, Fritz Rosenfelder's sole heir, never signed a deed of sale or anything delegating that to anyone else. This letter doesn't stand up, and I'm beginning to think these people are dishonest.'

'Do you know which lawyers they have hired?'

'No, you tell me.'

'*Maîtres* Jean Veil and Michel Zaoui[25]. They are the people I must deal with.'

'I'm sorry, I know the opera world, but not the world of the courts.'

'Jean Veil is Simone Veil's son.'

Of course, I knew who Simone Veil was and was astonished by what I had just heard.

'A Jew defending people who deny Jews their rights in relation to the Nazi theft of their property? I can't believe it! His own

25 See Appendix 9.

mother was a prisoner in a camp! It can't be right whichever way you look at it!'

'That's not all, Michel Zaoui is a member of the executive committee of the CRIF[26]. He was even one of the lawyers for the civil plaintiffs in the Barbie, Touvier and Papon trials.'

'Is this possible, ethically speaking? I don't know what is worse about what you've just told me. I need time to think.'

I rang the World Jewish Congress. At first, they didn't react. Then, once they'd got over their surprise, they told me that if these lawyers had accepted this job, it was to enable me to negotiate a better deal: that could be the only reason. Everyone else I spoke to gave a similar answer. Despite such reassuring observations, I felt sick and was ready to throw up.

My mother chose that moment to telephone. She sensed I was not well, and finally I told her why. She has seen every shade and hue in life and simply commented: 'Why should you think Jews are different to other people? There are good people, and people who are not so good, among Jews as with everybody else. Do you think there are no Jewish murderers, thieves or traitors? There's a bit of everything. And do you think they were all wonderful in the camps?'

'It's true, there were "traitors" in the camps[27].'

'Yes. And I'm not trying to make excuses for them – there are no excuses – but at the time those traitors were risking their lives. Today, as far as I know, nobody is risking his life. Don't let them beat you down. The directors of L'Oréal have done this on purpose; don't play their game.'

---

26 Conseil représentatif des institutions juives de France – the Representative Council of Jewish Institutions in France. I discovered subsequently that he was also president of the legal committee of LICRA (Ligue internationale contre le racisme et l'antisémitisme – the International League against Racism and anti-Semitism).

27 Jews allotted by Nazis to supervise other prisoners in the concentration camps. By agreeing to do this they saved their own lives. They often had the task of putting bodies in the ovens.

'It makes me sick! What a confusion of roles! Defending the victims in the morning and their likely executioners in the afternoon!'

'After all they've done to stop me from recovering my house, do you think they will let go just like that? You should remember that Nazi philosophy has always been to pit one Jew against another. As far as I'm concerned, those two are not Jews, at least not in the way I identify and respect those that are mine. They know that the house is ours just as much as we do. I recognize these techniques because I've lived them in my flesh. I'm only sorry you have to relive this. But the fact that L'Oréal has chosen two Jewish lawyers shows they've got a guilty conscience.'

One can defend the fact that Jewish lawyers work for L'Oréal. Life goes on, and if Jews refused to work with all enterprises which had collaborated with the Nazis or which had a dishonourable past, life would get very complicated.

What really shocks me is that these lawyers are defending L'Oréal in a case that specifically has to do with the impact of Nazi policy on Jews. Men like Eugène Schueller who are personally involved in our story have actively implemented this policy on their own behalf. He was hounded because of his past as a collaborator after the war and only escaped being sentenced because of the political connections of his future son-in-law André Bettencourt with François Dalle, a future chief executive of L'Oréal, and François Mitterand, a close friend of these two.

I spent a week recovering morally and physically. Only then could I stand back and understand what my mother had said. It restored my energy to carry on fighting.

We were at the end of July 2001, and my lawyer was leaving for his holidays. As for me, I was still waiting for this famous irrefutable proof in order to decide what step to take next: if they persisted in hiding the truth, we would take them to court.

The month of August turned out to be very fruitful.

The first days were quiet. I stayed in Paris for I had to prepare the restaging of a past production of *Rigoletto* at l'Opéra-Bastille for the early autumn (rehearsals began at the end of August).

In the middle of August, my lawyer called to say he had received a reply from the BGV (the Badischer Gemeinde Versicherung Verband insurance company which had 'bought' the house in 1938). Their letter indicated that the litigious sale of 1938 had been settled in 1951 via a Jewish organization – which no longer exists – that was dedicated to the restitution of stolen Jewish property. So the company was not implicated in the problem we were raising. It enclosed a copy of the so-called agreement with an accompanying letter that mentioned the fact that Karl Rosenfelder (my great-uncle, Fritz's brother) had signed this agreement.

But you can spend a long time looking for my great-uncle's signature on this document: you won't find it[28]. Nor will you find the least mention of the existence of my mother, the direct heir to my grandparents. How could they silence her existence or, worse, give the impression that she was dead, when in fact she had survived the Shoah?

I was indignant but had to be clear in my own mind: I faxed this document to my mother. That put her in a right state. But I persisted, risked being insulted by her and asked whether she'd ever signed a document, by proxy… Brazil is a long way from France, but I felt she was going to come down the line at me her reaction was so violent: how could I doubt her in this way?

'Mum, I don't doubt what you say, but I must confirm what I already know. To have the strength to continue, I must be sure of my ground.'

She blasted down the line: '*That house is mine*, and any document which states the contrary is a lie or the result of subterfuge. How can they pretend to know better than I what I have or haven't

---

28 See Appendix 8.

done? Isn't what they've already put me through enough? No! *I never signed a thing*, and they should stop their charades. If they think I am senile, they are mistaken. One never forgets things like that.'

I wasn't unhappy to hear her protest vociferously after so many years of resignation.

'I'm sorry, Mum, I didn't want to hurt you.'

'You're not going to get like them, are you?'

'Of course not, I just need to be sure.'

She understood me. It was becoming clearer and clearer there was something devious in this story or '*krumm*' to repeat the word used by Mrs V. at the Karlsruhe town hall. But what? And how was I going to get at it?

12

The Little She-Devil

I have always been a bundle of energy. As a child, my father found me so restless that he nicknamed me *Teufelle* or *Diaba*: little she-devil. He would say I was only angelic when asleep. That made me furious, but he never called me by my first name. Later on, the men I've lived with have had to cope with that; on the one hand, they found it stimulating, on the other I made their lives impossible.

But this excess of energy makes me feel that I exist. They say that people who have no history feel they have been deprived of the right to exist. I think it was what happened to my mother; and we, her children, have inherited her state. In order to grow, a family needs its history, as a plant needs its roots.

But L'Oréal deprived us of this vital base. I have experienced each of its negations of the truth as one more refusal of our right to exist. And I'm certain I will never regain that right until justice has given us back our property or the fruits from that property. Before the Nazis even programmed the extermination of the Jews, their policy was to take their rights away from them. If we can't reclaim our rights, it would mean they had won, in spite of history.

The word 'fruits' has a deeper sense for me. I have always wanted to have children. To no avail. Physically, everything is fine; I had every test possible and nothing abnormal was ever found but I was left feeling confused. People have told me how the feeling of non-existence might have prevented me from having children because to create them, one must exist. I am only now beginning to understand the significance of this theory.

My brother hasn't had children either. My mother did. True, but she had them before she knew she would be denied her past and that her history would be stolen from her; at that time, she was convinced she was going to recover her property after the war like the majority of Jews in her situation.

My mother has never understood why death spared her. I think the fact she survived has weighed her down terribly; she felt guilty. In her moments of anguish, she would repeat the following phrase like a litany: '*Gerichtet nein geretet*' (Judged, not saved). I only discovered much later, thanks to my profession, that this was from the final exchange in the first part of Goethe's *Faust*:

MEPHISTOFELES: She is judged!

VOICE (from on high):   She is saved!

And Marguerite goes to Heaven.

My mother never spoke to me about Kaethe before I started my research into the house in Karlsruhe. So I knew nothing about my grandmother's death. Through studying *Faust*, I understood that if my mother never mentioned her, she nonetheless knew everything there was to know. I would even go so far as to say: it was because she knew everything that she never mentioned her.

I have tried several times to broach issues to do with the war: it is astonishing how she is content to respond superficially and only mention trivial detail. As soon as I stray into a domain that is too sensitive, words fail her and she quickly shifts to something inconsequential. I then get the impression that if she took her thoughts to a conclusion, she would melt. In spite of all that, her strength sometimes surprised me.

I telephoned her shortly after I was contacted for the first time by the Prime Minister's Office. My interlocutor had asked me to try to obtain information from my mother to bolster my file.

'Mum, Marianne[29] mentioned the beautiful jewels your mother used to wear. She told me that you were rich.'

'Beautiful jewels…? How could my mother have had any…? From Sophie Schnurmann… She was a very rich woman, Monica.'

'And who was this Sophie Schnurmann?'

'She was Fritz's mother.'

'Who was Fritz?'

'My father…'

'Mum, so Sophie Schnurmann was your grandmother!'

'Yes… I think that's right.'

'So it was your family! Your family was the rich one!'

'Yes, Monica. We had a beautiful, spacious house, and Sophie Schnurmann lived there with us.'

'Do you remember the jewels?'

'I've been searching my memory for years for my mother's face. It always eludes me. I can remember my father, but my mother…'

'But you were more than ten years old when she died, weren't you?'

'Monica, doesn't the cold get at you in Paris?'

I know her abrupt change of subject was only a reflex action to protect herself from danger.

The following week, I resumed the conversation about the jewels with her. She once again avoided any direct allusion to her mother; she nevertheless recounted that when they reached the Gare de l'Est in Paris in 1938, she, Edith, was holding a doll in one hand and a bag full of jewels in the other; she had carried them as if they were playthings for her doll.

My mother is not full of hate. On the contrary, she is a good, generous woman. She has taught us to look generously upon those who are in need or who are distressed. Nonetheless, she is not

---

[29] My great-aunt, the wife of Ernst, brother of Kaethe, my grandmother.

particularly sympathetic when it is a matter of psychological suffering. Similarly, she refuses to be affected by the sight of physical injuries. She can even at times seem very hard. When I was small and hurt myself, she might go into fits of laughter and in the end I stopped showing her my cuts because her reaction would upset me. I found the way to the chemists and went by myself to get a cure. If the knock were benign, I'd treat myself, even though I couldn't stand the sight of blood: I would sometimes faint. And when the seriousness of my condition meant I had to go to hospital, my mother never took me, because she couldn't bear to.

13

The Lie Tactic

In his letter of 12 July 2001, the chairman of L'Oréal, Mr Owen-Jones wrote that the Haarfarben und Parfümerien GmbH Company, the German subsidiary of L'Oréal, 'bought the adjacent land and built an office block on the terrain'. As he didn't specify what the land adjacent to Wendstrasse 19 was, I immediately thought of Wendstrasse 17. Now Wendstrasse 19 is on the corner of Wendstrasse and Kaiserallee[30].

The land to which Owen-Jones refers is in fact situated at Kaiserallee 18 and backs onto Wendstrasse 19. My misunderstanding sent my research along a path I would certainly not have followed otherwise. It enabled me to make a fantastic discovery. Luck was on my side.

My mistake led me to discover what happened at number 17. I called Mr Müller at the land registry in Karlruhe. I asked him who owned Wendstrasse 17. He replied: 'A company by the name of Ensa.'

'What does it do?'

'*A priori* it's a perfumery.'

---

30 The sketch on p 68 merely indicates the position of the lots and doesn't attempt to represent the real scale.

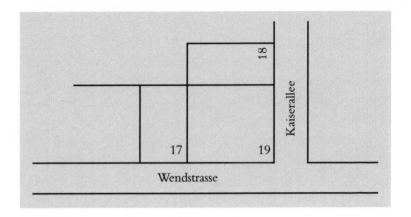

'When did it buy Wendstrasse 17?'

'In 1951.'

This company's business and the date of the sale in 1951 made me prick up my ears. 'Mr Müller, can you see who signed the bill of sale on behalf of Ensa?' I asked.

'A Mr Tondu.'

'André Tondu?'

'Yes.'

It was the same person who had bought Wendstrasse 19! He was the person mandated by Haarfarben und Parfümerien, alias L'Oréal, to buy our house at Wendstrasse 19 in 1954. André Tondu... His name appeared on the bill of sale agreed between the Badischer Gemeinde Versicherung Verband (BGV), who appropriated our house in 1938, and L'Oréal.

'Does one company sometimes hide behind another in order not to appear in public?' I asked ingenuously.

'Yes, it's called a front company.'

'I have the feeling that L'Oréal is hiding behind Ensa.'

'It could well be. Mention it to your lawyer.'

'One last thing, in relation to the date of purchase: can you find out if they expressed an interest in this lot before 1951?'

I asked the question because I'd noticed that in the 1954 bill of sale, in which the BGV ceded Wendstrasse 19 to L'Oréal, it was noted that Mr André Tondu had been already designated in 1953 to carry out the purchase.

'I'll have a look. Call me back this afternoon.'

I called him as agreed.

'Yes, something did happen in February 1949.'

'What?'

He didn't reply. I persisted: 'Mr Müller, I'm sure it was L'Oréal that bought Wendstrasse 17. I'll have to consult with my lawyer to see how I can prove it. Meanwhile, if this bill of sale relates to my property at number 19, you have the right to make me a copy, don't you?'

'I'll send you one right away.'

I telephoned my lawyer to tell him of my discovery. He asked me to research Ensa Ltd. So I contacted the company registry in Karlsruhe and asked for information on that company, as well as on L'Oréal and Haarfarben und Parfümerien GmbH.

A few days later, an official called me, rather panic-stricken: 'I started to look out the documents you requested. It's impossible to send you all this, there is just too much. What's more, it will cost you a fortune…'

I joked, to try to calm her down, and said I didn't want to cause her any problems. I then explained why these documents were so important for me. She passed me on to her boss to whom I repeated my story. We reached a compromise: she would send me the documents from the 1940s and the beginning of the 1950s; I would phone her if I needed any more.

The documents I received contained a wealth of information: L'Oréal's address was the same as Ensa's, Wendstrasse 17, and the two companies were managed by the same man, André Tondu. But I felt I was a long way from finding out the whole truth. The future would not belie my hunch.

In this same month of August, the Versorgung des Bundes und der Länder, the present owners of Wendstrasse 19 after buying it from

L'Oréal in 1991, also replied to our letter sent in June: they considered they weren't subject to our claims. In any case, the letter refrained from stating that the property didn't belong to us and referred us back to the seller: L'Oréal, as it turned out.

Autumn came and the rehearsals of *Rigoletto* began at such a hectic pace I hardly had time to think about anything but work. It was then I received details of the famous irrefutable evidence mentioned by L'Oréal's CEO. In fact, it was the document I had already received from the BGV insurance company where it says the dispute was settled in 1951 via a Jewish organization. My great-uncle Karl Rosenfelder had apparently signed this agreement, something BGV had already stated, without being able to supply evidence of his signature.

After the war, a court case was begun against BGV, accused of having stolen property owned by Jews. My mother hadn't even been informed. The signature appearing on the 1938 bill of sale of our house to BGV was that of a certain Luise Dürr. This woman, who was totally unknown to my family, disposed of the Rosenfelders' property by virtue of a power of attorney my grandfather had granted her under constraint in order to allow his wife (my grandmother), daughter (my mother) and mother-in-law to leave Germany and join him in Paris. Nonetheless, as the signature of my grandmother Kaethe didn't appear on the 1938 bill of sale, the court had supported the central indictment: BGV had well and truly stolen our property.

I had the feeling there had been an unpleasant invasion of the intimacy of our family: I was ill again. I felt sullied, couldn't think any more and spent hours in the bath. I did not understand how some people could be in possession of these documents when we, the individuals most affected, had only just discovered their existence. I later found out that they were not held in an archive that was open to the public.

I spent a week digesting this evidence. This time I said nothing to my mother; I wanted to spare her this latest insult. When I was in a state to think once more, I tried to gather together all the pieces of the puzzle: I had to get to grips with L'Oréal's tactics. Why were they acting as if they didn't know when it had been demonstrated that the property had been in the possession of the Nazis?

The tactic of sheltering behind a lie is well known. Didn't *Maître* Zaoui himself speak of this tactic during the Touvier trial when he quoted the remarks of a man called Kramer who was being tried for the responsibilities he held in an extermination camp? To the question 'What was the purpose of the gas chambers?' the Nazi criminal had replied: 'I don't know.'[31]

An irony of fate, at that very moment, the History Channel was broadcasting images from the Barbie trial[32]. *Maître* Zaoui pleads there in the name of the Jews who suffered the atrocities inflicted by their Nazi executioner. To quote him: 'Our dead cry out to us: Never forget! Never! Never!'

Yes, *Maître*, our dead cry out those words to us.

---

31 *Maître* Zaoui was quoting from an extract from the legal reports of a trial of camp leaders and their aides. This trial took place in Frankfurt from 1963 to 1965.
32 The Klaus Barbie trial was held from 11 May to 4 July 1987.

14
The Giant Octopus

L'Oréal is a large multinational conglomerate comprising a multitude of brands such as:

L'Oréal de Paris: Elsève, Elnett, Studioline, Préférence, Excellence, Open Color, Feria, Plénitude, L'Oréal Perfection;

Garnier: Fructis, Ultra Doux, Nutrisse, Lumia, Belle Color, Synergie, Ambre Solaire;

Maybelline New York: Jade, Gemey, Ylang, Colorama;

Softsheen-Carson;

Club des Créateurs de Beauté: Agnès B., Corinne Cobson, Jean-Marc Maniatis, Marina Marinof, Michel Klein, Tan Giudicelli;

Dop, Mixa, Narta, Obao, La Roche-Posay, Vichy.

The following luxury products catch one's eye:

Lancôme, Biotherm, Helena Rubinstein, Kiehl's, Shu Uemura;

Giorgio Armani, Cacharel, Ralph Lauren, Guy Laroche, Paloma Picasso.

And in pharmaceuticals, there is the *Sanofi-Synthélabo* group, controlled by L'Oréal and Total Fina Elf [33].

---

33 In 2005 the *Sanofi-Synthelabo* group became the *Sanofi-Aventis* group

Given the advertising clout that all these brands represent, it is easy to imagine the reserves of energy, and much besides, that newspapers must deploy in order to dare to publish stories like ours.

The capital structure of L'Oréal was as follows in 2003[34]:

> 53.70 per cent of L'Oréal's capital belongs to *Gesparal*. Mme Bettencourt and her family hold 51 per cent of the shares in *Gesparal*[35], and *Nestlé* 49 per cent.
>
> 46.30 per cent of L'Oréal capital is publicly held.

Other information[36]:

> The chief executive is Lindsay Owen-Jones; the vice-chair of the Board of Directors is Jean-Pierre Meyers[37].
>
> The directors include: Liliane Bettencourt, Françoise Bettencourt-Meyers, and François Dalle.

In the documentation sent by the Karlsruhe business registry, one can see that the shareholders of L'Oréal Deutschland – previously called Haarfarben und Parfümerien GmbH – both of French nationality, shared the capital as follows in 1931 when the enterprise was created, and then when it was transferred to Karlsruhe:

> Eugène Bricout held 39,000 German marks;
>
> André Tondu held 1,000 German marks.

This distribution of capital remained almost unchanged up to Eugène Schueller's death in August 1957. One wonders why Liliane Bettencourt took over Eugène Bricout's shares without any sale being noted in the business registry, at least in the documents I've been sent.

---

34 This information is supplied on the L'Oréal Internet site.

35 The person who holds 51 per cent of the capital of a firm wields total power within the board of directors.

36 Also supplied on the L'Oréal Internet site.

37 In April 2006 Jean Paul Agon became the CEO of L'Oréal and Lindsay Owen-Jones the non-executive chair of the board of L'Oréal.

Thus, in March 1958, the capital of Haarfarben und Parfümerien[38] was distributed among the following shareholders:

Mr Eugène Bricout,
resident in the region of the Seine[39]   57,000 DM
Mr André Tondu,
resident Wendstrasse 17, Karlsruhe   1,500 DM
Mr Auguste Huntzinger,
resident region of the Seine   500 DM
Mr Gaston Lechène,
resident region of the Seine   500 DM
Mr Marcel Jussier,
resident region of the Seine   500 DM

But Eugène Bricout disappeared in June 1959. The capital was then distributed between:

Mrs André Bettencourt,   80,000 + 16,000 =
née Liliane Schueller, resident   96,000 DM
Neuilly-sur-Seine
Mr André Tondu, Karlsruhe   2,500 DM
Mr Auguste Huntzinger, Seine   500 DM
Mr Gaston Lechène, Seine   500 DM
Mr Marcel Jussier, Seine   500 DM

They were all represented, with the exception of Mr Tondu, by one Henri Fèbvre, a lawyer, resident 4 rue Rodin in Paris. All this was set out and broadcast on L'Oréal headed notepaper from…1950. Besides, Henri Fèbvre was one of Eugène Schueller's seven collaborators, with whom the latter and his daughter held shares in L'Oréal, Schueller and Liliane Bettencourt being the majority shareholders[40].

---

38 Reminder: 'Colouring for hair and perfumes'.
39 His address is explicitly mentioned as are those of all the other shareholders living in France
40 Bruno Abescat, *La saga des Bettencourt*, op.cit., p. 186.

And in 1961, the date when L'Oréal *officially* appeared in the Haarfarben und Parfümerien portfolio, the group is entered as a minority shareholder, replacing the minority shareholders of 1959:

L'Oréal SA, Paris	1,1410,000 DM
Mr Henri Fèbvre, Paris	50,000 DM
Mrs André Bettencourt, Paris	80,000 DM[41]

In 1962 Orinter became the firm with majority shareholding in Haarfarben und Parfümerien. And the distribution of holdings in 1965 was as follows:

Orinter SA Paris	3,760,000 DM
Mrs Bettencourt, Neuilly-sur-Seine	107,000 DM
Mr Henri Fèbvre, Paris	133,000 DM

The figures continue to grow to 1968, but there was no change in the shareholders. And new minority shareholders appeared in 1969:

Orinter SA, Paris	9,964,000 DM
Mrs Bettencourt, Neuilly-sur-Seine	485,000 DM
Mr Dalle, Neuilly-sur-Seine	42,000 DM
Mr Lefèbvre, Brussels	42,000 DM
Mr Henri Fèbvre, Paris	3,000 DM

The following year, L'Oréal replaced Orinter, while the other shareholders remained the same.

This somewhat onerous list of names and figures shows that Mrs Bettencourt appears before 1961. Now, Mr Owen-Jones stated that L'Oréal was not involved in this company prior to 1961. However, we should recall that L'Oréal's first name was 'French company for harmless hair dyes', very similar to Haarfarben und Parfümerien's name – 'Colouring for hair and perfumes' – and one can hardly

---

41 Documents from the Karlsruhe town hall.

believe Liliane Bettencourt held shares in a German company which had the same market aims as L'Oréal (perfumes and cosmetics), and that the French company was never involved. Mr Owen-Jones can make all the chronological caveats he likes; I will continue to think he travesties the truth.

I should also add that the fact that French citizens like Eugène Schueller and André Tondu went on to found a company in Germany in the 1930s is not exactly reassuring. If they hadn't been somewhat in accord with the ideas being propounded by the Nazi regime, I doubt that the enterprise known as L'Oréal could have made much headway in Berlin. Moreover, Eugène Schueller paid a visit to the German Embassy 18 March 1942. I have, from the Frydman brothers, the copy of a document from the German Embassy. It is a report listing the people received at the embassy that day and the reasons for their visit. It records how Schueller had come to proclaim his loyalty to Hitler[42].

---

42 This information is also quoted by Michel Bar-Zohar, op.cit., pp. 57–58.

15
De-Nazification?

I kept on putting the puzzle together by looking for new pieces. I directed my research at another passage in one of Mr Owen-Jones's letters: 'In 1954 [...], the insurance company ceded the empty land (as the building was destroyed during the war) to Haarfarben und Parfümerien GmbH, the German subsidiary of L'Oréal.' This isn't totally correct: our house, bombed during the war, was on this land. What state was it in? We weren't there at the time to see for ourselves.

The reconstruction of Germany was financed by different economic aid plans, the best known of which is America's Marshall Plan. These plans allowed new buildings to be erected to replace those destroyed by bombing. It wouldn't be a total nonsense to imagine that L'Oréal could have benefited from such aid to build on the lot they had just purchased.

I needed the help of specialists to throw light on this and finally found them at the German Institute for History in Paris. I was given the names of three researchers, and one of them rang me a few days later. After hearing my story, he gave me some clues to help me in my research. Thanks to his advice, I learned that L'Oréal's financial guarantor had been the town of Karlsruhe itself and that the construction of the new building was financed by the Rheine Bank am Main. Then he advised me to contact one of his colleagues who specialized in this area. The latter gave me an appointment.

I took part of the already considerable pile of documents I had assembled so far to this meeting. My interlocutor, like others before him, was taken aback; once he'd got over his amazement, he informed me of some very pertinent facts: immediately after the war, the town of Karlsruhe was put under French aegis before being handed over to the United States. It was this Allied supervision that set in motion the rebuilding of the town. The financing came from different bodies, including banks, and everything was under the baton of a certain Hermann J. Abs. This individual, although responsible for the looting perpetrated by the Nazi regime[43], had managed to become the spokesman for the Allies in relation to the *return* of their property to the Jews. Moreover, he was director of the Deutsche Bank, until in the 1970s protests were voiced in Germany against the fact that so prominent an ex-Nazi occupied such an important post. He was called upon to resign and did so. Finally, the regional name for the Deutsche Bank was at the time…Rheine Bank am Main, and it was thus this same Hermann J. Abs who oversaw the bank which financed the construction of the L'Oréal building.

My adviser also explained to me that if the BGV insurance company had been able to take over a building as important as ours in 1938, it could only have been because its leaders at the time were affiliated to the Nazi Party; it was the necessary 'open sesame' for operations of that size. But, after the war, the game went into reverse for the majority of ex-Nazis: in order to have any hopes of continuing their work, they had to emerge immaculate from the so-called de-nazification tribunals. If they were found guilty, they lost part of their civil rights, and that could be a source of great future difficulties. Thus, a number of these ex-Nazis found a token Jew or member of the Resistance to give evidence in their favour so they would be acquitted. According to this expert, I was in my rights to demand to

---

43 See Eberhard Czichon, *Deutsche Bank Macht Politik. Fascismus, Krieg und Bundesrepublik,* PapyRossa Verlag, 2001, p. 123

see the file on the de-nazification of those in charge of BGV.

I was very moved by the generosity shown towards me by the researchers at the German Institute for History. As I lived through those moments of my life, meeting people of this calibre reminded me that good people do also exist. I have fortunately met many more, and they have been a great source of comfort. Following the advice of these researchers, I started to look for the documentation on the de-nazification of the staff at BGV. To obtain this kind of document, one has to have been a victim of the Nazis or belong to the family of a victim. It was on this basis that I gained access.

Erwin Brunner, the managing director of BGV, was definitely a member of the Nazi Party when the insurance company took over our house in 1938. He even belonged to the SA[44]. I should point out that the SA's headquarters in Karlsruhe was based in a house that had belonged to Jews – the Weils, friends of our family – and it was right opposite…Wendstrasse 19.

At the end of the war, the priority for some Nazis wasn't so much to do good business as to *prove* that they had never been Nazis. In short, it was essential to procure a whitewash: when questioned, the verbatim reports of which are in his de-nazification file, Mr Erwin Brunner stated that he 'became a Nazi and a member of the SA in order to help the Jews'. There's always a good reason for everything!

It is easy to see that his company, the BGV, urgently needed to offload a property taken from Jews, namely our townhouse. L'Oréal, through Haarfarben und Parfümerien, was a providential purchaser. The image of this company that arrived in Karlsruhe with the Allies who had fought the Nazis was perfect. It was only much later that it became public knowledge that L'Oréal had given important posts to a number of enforcers of Nazi policies or *cagoulards* like Jacques Corrèze.

---

[44] *Sturmabteilung* – storm-troopers: the Nazi Party's armed militia, which was subsequently replaced by the SS (Schutzstaffel – protection group).

I received documents from the Karlsruhe business registry attesting to the fact that Mr André Tondu worked on behalf of L'Oréal at Wendstrasse 17. I recalled that this gentleman figures first, as director-general of Ensa in the bill of sale which gave it ownership of Wendstrasse 17 in 1951, then as the representative of L'Oréal in the 1954 bill of sale of Wendstrasse 19 from BGV to L'Oréal.

A few days later, my lawyer telephoned me: 'Mrs Waitzfelder, I am rereading the documents from the business registry that you brought me, and I have just come across something that is quite incredible. Do you remember what you found on the Internet site for L'Oréal Deutschland?'

We had completely forgotten this document. It was among those I'd given him at our first meeting.

'Just listen,' he continued, 'to what they write on the presentation on the site under the rubric of "history": "*Quite the first stone of this unparalleled success was laid in 1930 in Berlin by André Tondu, when Eugène Schueller, the founder of the French firm, mandated him to conquer the German hairdressing market. The first steps taken by Haarfarben und Parfümerien GmbH were not easy. Of course, the first dyes were quickly accepted by the market, but the Berlin base was destroyed in the war and, in 1945, a new factory was to be built in Karlsruhe.*"'

What did they think we were? Backward? The chief executive of L'Oréal didn't even know what his own company's website said about its creation in Germany! André Tondu had never worked for L'Oréal? L'Oréal never had connections with Wendstrasse 17? Somewhat hard to believe!

What was becoming clearer and clearer was the goal of L'Oréal's real-estate operations in Karlsruhe: the creation of a vast holding in a well-to-do part of town. They would erect a big building (where our house was) on the biggest lot, Wendstrasse 19, situated on the corner of Wendstrasse and Kaiserallee 18, and the two adjoining lots – Wendstrasse 17 and Kaiserallee 18 – would be used as annexes, car park, garden... But the centrepiece of this complex remained Wendstrasse 19; without the latter, the whole operation would have been impossible.

Maître Korman then sent me to a court bailiff. The latter drew up a statement to attest to the existence of the information posted on the Internet by L'Oréal and of its continued link with André Tondu[45].

We resumed our scrutiny of the bill of sale of Wendstrasse 17 by Ensa. Number 17 was the object of a strange two-stage purchase: a first bill of purchase signed in February 1949 was followed bizarrely by a second confirming the first. The second bill was signed in October 1951 and was published in the property register on 5 November 1951: that is, the *very day* when BGV was reaching its so-called agreement with a Jewish organization in relation to Wendstrasse 19[46]. It was henceforth clear that L'Oréal's purchase of number 17 (via the front company Ensa) was closely linked to the forthcoming purchase of number 19. Contrary to what L'Oréal tried to make us believe, it was far from 'discovering' Wendstrasse 19 in 1954. The company had set its sights on the plot at least in 1948 but couldn't buy it before this date because the property was still subject to Allied military government law. André Tondu for L'Oréal in Germany, representing Eugène Schueller, then applied a practice that is quite usual in the world of business: discretion, nay, dissimulation – by making no public display of interest in Wendstrasse 19. The purchase of the different lots was to be achieved via different companies.

Maître Korman now told me that this was more than presumption on our part...

---

45 See Appendix 14.
46 See Appendices 7 and 8.

16

My Father

Before the war, my father was a medical student in Heidelberg. With his blond hair and blue eyes, he was like the majority of his fellow German citizens, but his origins prevented him from continuing with his studies. He had a friend, Wolfgang, whose father was a shipbuilder. When Wolfgang saw the reprisals meted out against Jews on *Kristallnacht*[47], he rushed his friend on board one of his father's ships; this ship was bound for Brazil.

Before he had barely recovered from the shock caused by this brutal uprooting, my father left for Amazonia to work for a company that dealt in precious stones. He had to work as quickly as possible and earn enough to pay for his own needs. He also had to pay a ransom for his parents who were still in Germany: he had to pay this money to the German Consulate each month in order to safeguard their lives.

Years later, my father would tell me of the cruel, humiliating game to which his father fell victim. Like other old Jews, he was

47 After an attack perpetrated by a Jew on the German Embassy in Paris and the death of the Embassy attaché von Rath, the German Minister for Propaganda, Joseph Goebbels, denounced ' a Jewish conspiracy' against Germany and unleashed a vast pogrom. Over the night of 9 and 10 November 1938, SA storm troopers, the SS and the Hitler Youth pillaged and smashed up thousands of shops and burned a hundred synagogues. Almost a hundred people were killed.

forced to spend hours kneeling in frozen streets, in the middle of winter, his torso naked and arms crossed; anyone who was unfortunate enough to lower their arms was immediately killed. And many were.

My father was a nervous man and perpetually on the move. He only calmed down when we went to the country house in Itaipava. He needed to be close to the forest; that contact with nature made him another person. And that was when he spoke to us of important matters.

He would often to talk to me about such things when we returned from a walk at twilight and took a dirt track we knew by heart and which could lead us home with our eyes closed. It was on this track that he told me that my Rosenfelder grandparents had died because of the Nazis and that my grandmother had died in a concentration camp (I'm not sure he mentioned the name of the camp). I would usually harass him with questions, but now I asked none. I didn't ask him what a concentration camp was, what my grandparents' names were or in what circumstances they died. I was perhaps too young to do so. I was perhaps aware that what he had just told me was the cause of my mother's sorrow. I too was perhaps already suffering from this. I knew nothing. And my father, in response to my silence, didn't pursue the subject.

Nevertheless, I remember that day as if it were yesterday. We started our return as the sky regaled us with the flamboyant spectacle of a Brazilian twilight. Here, in France, the colours are different at dusk: it is a palette of blue, bluish-grey with an occasional hint of orange that the eye retains. There, orange and fiery red predominate but are gradually absorbed by black after an orangey-brown phase.

Night had almost fallen when we suddenly heard a noise. We stopped and saw a peasant hitting a snake with a stick that kept breaking at every blow. There was nothing unusual about killing snakes in Itaipava. Serpents abounded, and even we children would do the same if they represented a danger to life; otherwise everyone went their respective way.

But this reptile was incredibly long, exceptionally big. It was more than two metres long with a bodily circumference of around twenty centimetres. My father took off his jacket, signalled to me to keep away while he lent the peasant a hand. It took the two men a long time to get the better of the huge snake. They finally crushed its head with the help of a big stone. Then they exchanged a few words along the lines of 'The brute put up a good fight' and 'Thanks for your help' before my father picked up his jacket, and we resumed our walk.

It was now pitch dark, but we hadn't switched our torches on. We walked on silently until he said: 'You won't tell anyone what you saw this evening, will you?'

'Why?'

'Because people won't believe you. They'll say you're spinning a tall story, and I don't want people to think of you as a liar. It will be a secret between us.'

I have always kept that nocturnal scene to myself, when I saw my father level that huge snake which today reminds me of Nazism. Later in life, I mentioned the incident to him, probably because I wanted to reassure myself it wasn't a nightmare. He was surprised that I remembered, and I was happy then to have that secret I could share with my father.

To this day, I have never spoken about it to anyone. There is no way I would want to be thought of as a spinner of tall stories.

17

Hell is Other People

L'Oréal maintains it bears no responsibility for the robbery; one should take it further back to the BGV insurance company. Despite the tragic events of which the robbery is part, I cannot help feeling it's like children bickering: 'Sir, 'snot me, it's him!'

My mother prefers to quote Sartre: 'Hell is other people.'

My mother, of whose existence L'Oréal pretended to be unaware at the time it was purchasing Wendstrasse 19... I think it's impossible they didn't know she was alive. Mr. Owen-Jones wrote on 12 July 2001, as part of his irrefutable evidence, that he only learned of my mother's existence when he read our letter of 18 June 2001. I don't believe this statement for one minute. When you buy a property, Mr. Owen-Jones, don't you check who the owner is? There must be a very poor information-flow in your enterprise indeed if your predecessors never told you where this property came from: even more so, dear sir, given that you must have known that Wendstrasse 19 was the biggest L'Oréal head office in Europe after Paris.

My mother has always kept her German nationality. From her arrival in Brazil in December 1946, she has regularly gone to the German Consulate in Rio to get her passport renewed. Moreover, as she was a minor at that time, the Jewish institutions responsible for her had supervised her itinerary and made sure she arrived safely at her Uncle Ernst's in Sao Paolo. The latter's address was consequently known, and she lived there until she married in October 1951. Additionally, after she'd left there, there was always someone living at the address that knew how to find her. In order to marry, my mother had to get a certificate of her civil status from the town hall of the municipality where she was born. The Karlsruhe public administration was then perfectly aware of her existence since her certificate of birth[48] is not followed by any death certificate, unlike her mother Kaethe's, which mentions '*deceased at Auschwitz, 27 September 1942*'. For anyone who took the trouble, my mother wasn't difficult to track down. Mr. Müller has moreover informed me that the Karlsruhe civil registry was in the same building as the land registry – and on the same floor as well!

L'Oréal and BGV pretend they were unaware of the existence of survivors among those with a claim on the house. The forgetfulness of these companies did not only relate to my mother but also extended to another survivor: my great-uncle Karl. Yet, who mentioned Karl Rosenfelder's name after the war as a supposed signatory to the 1951 agreement, if it wasn't first BGV and then L'Oréal? These companies knew there was at least one survivor since they both mentioned him.

I have equally wondered hard about the JRSO, the Jewish organization that concluded that 'agreement' with BGV. That a Jewish organization should have concerned itself with a stolen property that *a priori* had no heirs at the end of the war is fine – such was its role. But I was really astonished that *a posteriori* it had let the property fall into hands other than those of its living owners. How on earth could it have concluded an agreement detrimental to the interests of those who had the rights to the property? Did it have no other solution or did it yield to pressure?

At night I often woke up and resumed my reading. It was in the course of one of these bouts of insomnia that I reread this famous

---

48 See Appendix 2.

'agreement' between BGV and the JRSO. As I often did, I looked at the German original and the French translation side by side: I felt the need to experience two different readings of the same document at the same time.

And suddenly, after rereading the third clause of the 'agreement' of 5 November 1951, I understood its significance and implications: '*The JRSO undertakes, inasmuch as the defendant (the BGV) acts in conformity with the instructions from the JRSO, to compensate the defendant to a maximum of 5,000 DM if a situation arises where those with a priority right make themselves known and validly undermine the defendant's position.*'

Clearly, this clause means that if those enjoying ownership rights come forward, the JRSO must reimburse the insurance company to the sum of 5,000 DM: the agreement is annulled and those with ownership rights regain these legitimate rights at the expense of the robber, the BGV[49].

It all started to get much clearer in my head! Here before my eyes was the reason why they had refused to supply us with documentation from the title deeds that we had requested from Karlsruhe: these papers would have allowed us to annul this 'agreement' by establishing that we had the right of ownership of our property.

A shiver ran down my spine.

For the first time, I understood why we had gone through so many difficult years and why they had told my mother she was mad when she had repeatedly tried to ensure her rights prevailed before I even got involved. There was in effect a good reason to go mad in the face of such attitudes, and I reckoned that, all in all, my mother had stood up to them remarkably well.

By dint of hearing it repeated so often that she was imagining things, she had sometimes doubted the truth of her own suffering to the point of wondering whether the pain she experienced was

49 See Appendix 8.

really legitimate. How could she mourn for her own history if it weren't true? But at the same time, how could she resign herself to the fact it was untrue when she was haunted by so many memories?

All this wore down my mother tremendously. For years, her memories couldn't be connected to any reality whatsoever; the trauma of the Shoah prevented any individual healing, and mourning couldn't have its effect for over more than fifty years. Thus, L'Oréal had denied a whole family that had lived through this terrible experience the right to mourn those sombre years. And today, by continuing to lie, L'Oréal scorned our suffering and forced us to relive everything again. By denying what they'd done, they were very close to telling us we had invented everything.

That is why I bear such a grudge against L'Oréal, because they took everything from us. Our history as well as our home.

18

Like Father, Like Son-in-Law!

In 1991 Jean Frydman, an important Jewish businessman, entered into conflict with François Dalle, L'Oréal's chief executive at the time with whom he had enjoyed friendship and a business relationship in a film production company they had founded together[50]. Jean Frydman challenged his exclusion from the board of directors that was decided at a meeting in his absence[51]. He contested the decision in court, and François Dalle was subsequently found guilty of 'deception, misrepresentation and racial discrimination'[52]. As a result of this, with the help of his brother David, Jean Frydman began to investigate L'Oréal's past and discovered the dubious connections that linked Eugène Schueller, its founder, and other directors of the company with the Vichy government.

I devoted time to tracking down the whereabouts of the Frydman brothers. I rang David Frydman's company only to learn that he had died. Nonetheless, I set up a meeting with Jean-Pierre Pelletier, who

---

50 The Panavision Company – 75 per cent of its capital was from L'Oréal, the remaining 25 per cent from Jean Frydman, in the form of their film list.

51 For more information on this, see Michel Bar-Zohar, op. cit.

52 *Le Monde*, 7 March 2002, reports: 'François Dalle was found guilty in 1991 of 'deception, misrepresentation and racial discrimination', but the charge was dismissed on 4 December 1992 after an out-of-court settlement was reached with Jean Frydman.

supported Jean Frydman in the case that brought them into conflict with L'Oréal. Mr Pelletier gave me the warmest of welcomes. He listened carefully and looked at the documents I'd brought before he explained to me the stage they had reached in their legal action. He also gave me some very useful advice.

When I mentioned my surprise at the fact that everyone who gravitated around L'Oréal hid the truth, he responded that the Frydman brothers had met the same problem; such had always been the case when anyone took on L'Oréal.

Jean-Pierre Pelletier, a really kind, understanding man, sent me two books written by David and Jean Frydman entitled *L'Affaire Bettencourt* and *Pour la mémoire*[53].

These two books bring together documents attesting to the relationship between André Bettencourt, Eugène Schueller, leading management of L'Oréal and the Nazis.

Far from being the resistance fighter he always pretended to be, André Bettencourt – Schueller's son-in-law – was a zealous collaborator. From 1941 he wrote for a journal, *La Terre française*, which published, among other things, the speeches of Pétain, Darlan and Laval. This magazine was the personal responsibility of von Ribbentrop within the framework of the German propaganda machine and was connected to the French section of the *Propagandastaffel*. The latter was declared a Nazi criminal organization in the course of the Nuremberg trials.

At least seventy-one articles in this journal advocating hatred of the Jews carry the by-line of future minister, André Bettencourt. The strongly anti-Semitic content of these articles all made me feel sick:

> 'Jews, those hypocritical Pharisees can hope no more. It is all over for them, they have no faith. They carry within themselves no possibility of rectification. Their race is

---

53 Both these books were self-published in 2002 and were never published commercially.

eternally soiled by the blood of the just. They will be damned, everyone of them [...] The Jews of today, not in race but in thought, will be and are already vomit.'[54]

'One day, thirty years later, the Jews imagined nevertheless they were going to win. They had managed to lay their hands on Jesus and had crucified him. Rubbing their hand together, they proclaimed: may his blood spill on us and on our children. You know moreover the way in which it was spilt and continues to spill. The teachings in the eternal book must be fulfilled.'[55]

Freemasons were not spared either. André Bettencourt harboured a particularly virulent hostility towards them:

'Pimps (one could call them such since they are the real criminals, the real supporters of the rotten regime) [...] still carry out the will of the lodges, systematically loot, either from disability, or dishonesty, the coffers of France.'[56]

'Marshal Pétain has given us three keywords 'Work, Family, Fatherland'. We have already erased from the façades of our town halls the triple device of Masonic liberalism.'[57]

The above extracts were not written by a junior or peripheral contributor. André Bettencourt was the main editor of *La Terre française*, its most influential political collaborator. His responsibility for the messages of hate he distilled for the benefit of this journal is thus that much weightier.

The chapter in Jean and David Frydman's book dedicated to Mr Bettencourt's prose during the Occupation concludes on this note:

We have also showed to what extent his articles correlate with some of the most tragic periods of collaboration, particularly

54 *La Terre française* 24, 12 April 1941, 'Easter Bells'.
55 *La Terre française* 60, 20 December 1941, 'Christmas, Star of Hope'
56 *La Terre française* 33, 14 June 1941, 'Pimps'.
57 *La Terre française* 42, 16 August 1941, 'The Charter for Youth'.

successive stages in the persecution of Jews and freemasons. At the time when André Bettencourt was publishing his editorials, the psychological preparation for genocides had been put in place. The Wannsee conference, in the course of which the total extermination of the Jews was decided, took place three weeks after the publication of his prophetic article of 20 December 1941, its title so pregnant with meaning: 'Christmas, Star of Hope'. A correlation confirming, if this was necessary, that his articles were not written as random reflections but were perfectly synchronized with the orders of the Nazi authorities as conveyed by certain journals, like *La Terre française* or *L'Élan*.[58]

'Should it be a duty to inform?' André Bettencourt also wrote. 'Yes, inasmuch as this really helps the collectivity[…] Young people must be the Marshal's agents in every village, that is to say the police of the Revolution.'[59]

My mother has told me how quickly she had to leave 6 rue des Saussaies to flee to unoccupied territory after Kaethe (her mother), Emma (her maternal grandmother) and she herself were informed on. Moreover, I've never found out who betrayed them.

In the aftermath of the war, the man knew how to cover up his past. Jacques Baynac notes, in *Les Secrets de l'affaire Jean Moulin. Archives inédites sur la Résistance*: 'In the summer of 1944, Bettencourt will be able, thanks to him (the Resistance fighter Pierre de Bénouville) and Mitterand, to spend a little over a month in Geneva, thus cheaply acquiring a certificate as a member of the Resistance that he really needed in order to cover up his previous activities which were pro-Pétain or worse.'[60]

---

58 *L'Affaire Bettencourt*, op cit.
59 *La Terre française* 50, 11 October 1941.
60 Jacques Baynac, *Les Secrets de l'affaire Jean Moulin. Archives inédites sur la Résistance*, Paris, Le Seuil, 1998.

In 1947 André Bettencourt succeeded his father as chair of the Council for the Lillebonne district in Seine-Maritime. In 1951 he became a deputy for the same province. From 1954 to 1972, he went from being Secretary to the Council of Ministers, to Secretary of State for Transport, then Foreign Affairs and Minister for Telecommunications, then Industry, finally Minister with special responsibilities for the environment, and then for Foreign Affairs. The past finally caught up with André Bettencourt, and he had to resign in 1994 from the company and put a definitive end to his political career.

Schueller was fanatically anti-Semitic, anti-Freemason, Fascist and the financer of La Cagoule. André Bettencourt met him in 1938. Both evidently shared a range of ideas. In issue 58 of *La Terre française*, one reads from the pen of André Bettencourt:

'The hope of youth: to be an employer [...] my plucky young lad! I gave him a remarkable book to read by my friend, M.E. Schueller, entitled *La Révolution de l'Economie.* This is a book that all company directors of today and tomorrow should read. It is a young book par excellence...'

On 18 March 1942, Eugène Schueller proclaimed his loyalty to Hitler. After the liberation of France, he got a miraculous whitewash thanks to a man who put all his energy into avoiding national disgrace and prison. This man, who became his son-in-law in 1950, was none other than André Bettencourt. He provided shelter and protection in the heart of L'Oréal to his father-in-law and to a large number of *cagoulards* and the worst adepts of collaboration.

The past resurfaced in the 1990s with the Frydman case. In June 2000, the 'Association of Parisian Chemists for Memory', backed by a range of distinguished individuals, took the decision to change the name of the 'Eugène Schueller' lecture theatre, as did the 1961 class at the National Higher Institute for Chemistry, in order to underline their refusal to associate the school with the name of a fascist.

Jean Frydman also crossed swords with Jacques Corrèze, another old acquaintance of Eugène Schueller. The then chair of Cosmair, the US branch of L'Oréal, played a key role in excluding Jean Frydman from the board of directors in 1989. It should be recalled that before the war Jacques Corrèze was one of the thugs in La Cagoule, the pro-Hitler terrorist organization that often met at the L'Oréal headquarters on the rue Royale, and for which Eugène Schueller was both ideologue and financier. In 1948, Corrèze was sentenced to twenty years in prison.

As for Jacques Corrèze, 'he didn't knock at the door of L'Oréal by accident. He sought out the help of his old friend and supporter Eugène Schueller, with whom he shared the leadership of La Cagoule and the MSR. Schueller, the financer of both fascist movements, the founder of L'Oréal, was already by the early 1950s one of the richest men in France.'[61]

In his book, Michel Bar-Zohar mentions Jacques Corrèze's *cagoulard* past and his prison sentence for murder. He also delineates the quite strange way in which Corrèze bought the Helena Rubinstein Company on behalf of L'Oréal. He explains how Corrèze and other ex-Nazis found refuge as employees in different branches of L'Oréal. Corrèze's trajectory after the war is exemplary in that respect. He was first of all vice-chairman of Procasa, the Spanish branch of L'Oréal. Then he cropped up again in South America where he worked for a local branch of the group. It was then that he found his way to New York. Soon after he had arrived, he was appointed chair of the new company Cosmair, the exclusive representative of L'Oréal in the United States.

It was there moreover that he got to know Helena Rubinstein from whom he carefully concealed his past. He saw her a lot and managed to become a friend. Executioners will do anything to attract their prey: apparently Eichmann spoke fluent Yiddish and used this language to confuse the Jews he subsequently exterminated.

---

61 Michel Bar-Zohar, *Une histoire sans fard: L'Oréal des années sombres au boycott arabe*, pp. 56–61.

Upon Helena Rubinstein's death, Corrèze plotted cunningly and, by using pseudonyms and front companies, he discreetly bought the latter's eponymous company, all on behalf of L'Oréal. When the deal was completed, he became chairman of the Helena Rubinstein Company.[62]

During this time L'Oréal was expanding its capital in Karlsruhe. I have to hand the *Stuttgarter Zeitung* for June 14 1979 that the archive service at the town hall sent me. According to this newspaper's calculations, L'Oréal's capital by the end of 1978 totalled 4.3 billion DM. And we were still only in 1978…

62 Ibid., p. 110

19

An Epidemic of Amnesia

I didn't always understand why our adversaries strove to deny everything. I could accept they might try to pull the wool over our eyes; they were big companies and could allow themselves that luxury. Such an attitude has its limits, and when one is caught, as they say, with one's hand in the till, one should try to find a honourable solution rather than continue denying the evidence.

Our powerful interlocutors should have known that people of modest means wouldn't take lightly the risk of writing to them and that if they did take the risk it was because they had solid evidence to back their case.

In this respect, I would like to return to one of their lies: the famous signature that my great-uncle, Karl Rosenfelder, was supposed to have placed on the 1951 agreement. He never signed it! But even if they had secured it, nobody could ever accept that, in order to buy a house with two owners (Karl and my mother), a single signature would suffice. One doesn't need to have studied law to know that property belonging to two people and sold by only one of them constitutes a sale that is null and void. The 1951 agreement reached between BGV and a Jewish organization endorsing the sale of the house for 5,000 DM also contained an article number 3 that rendered it null if the legal owners appeared.

The truth is that they have no valid arguments on their side and that the only weapon they can wield is intimidation. Their arguments are fallacious; here are some more that are much more convincing – mine:

The extracts from the property register show that this house belonged to us in 1938.

The transfer documents from the Nazi era prove the transfer was obtained under constraint (that is even written into the bill of *purchase*). It was because his life and the life of his relatives were threatened that my grandfather yielded to blackmail.

The money arising from this enforced sale was never paid either to my grandparents or their heirs.

In the normal course of things, this stolen property should then have been returned after the war. They must have forgotten about us!

One bank also had an attack of amnesia around the same time. The document originating from the police in Lyons[63] contained interesting information, as well as a physical description of my grandfather: Fritz was carrying a supply of cash on him and could get money outside the camp. This had enabled him to get permission (one can guess how) to leave the Gurs camp for a few days in order to visit a cousin in Lyons. The police inspector who drew up the report states he had a sum in dollars deposited in an account with the Société générale in Paris.

I contacted the Société générale to find out about this account; they replied that the bank had no knowledge of my grandfather. How then could I explain that an official document – I didn't invent it, it exists in the Alpes-Maritimes provincial archives – mentioned that this account existed?

What I found really disturbing was that yet again any trace of my grandparents was being denied. This process has been repeated

63 See Chapter 10.

too often for me not to ask serious questions about the divulging of information by official bodies. Similarly, whenever the Drai Commission[64] pointed me to ministries in order to find information, the doors to these institutions mysteriously closed as soon as they heard my requests: they could find nothing, not a scrap of documentation mentioning that my grandparents existed. If I were to believe them, the latter never lived in France or evaporated discreetly together with the documents that related to them. Could the fact that André Bettencourt was at the head of several of these ministries be connected to this situation?

It just so happens that one of Bettencourt's friends, a director in his time of the Société générale, was implicated in the Frydman affair.

Luckily for us, there are always breakdowns in the almost reflex practice of withholding information: everything isn't entirely fixed and, by making an effort, you always finds in the end someone helpful – in this or that archive service – who will give you more or less officially the information the official organizations have refused you at least up to now...

The person in charge of research into banks for the Drai Commission, to whom I had sent the document from the Lyons police, called me soon after. The activity of the commission in relation to the Société génerale had borne fruit: the bank had just discovered a foreign-currency account in the name of Fritz Rosenfelder but was unable to say what amount was held there.

I have just received the written response that the Société générale supplied the commission. If I possess the proof that I haven't invented anything, I continue to be quite puzzled by the bank's attitude. They recognize the existence of a foreign-currency account in my grandparents' name but don't consider they need to

64 This is the commission set up to compensate victims of thefts perpetrated under the anti-Semitic legislation passed during the Occupation. The commission was a result of the Matteoli Report. When the person responsible for my dossier contacted me, on behalf of the prime minister, this commission hadn't yet been officially established.

return the sum credited on the pretext that 'it was reactivated after the war'. Well, at that time my entire family was dead, and my mother, a minor, had left for Brazil without ever setting foot back in France. I can see no other explanation for reactivating this account other than the fact that these gentlemen believe in ghosts!

L'Oréal's ability to hide the truth never ceases to astonish me. *Maître* Zaoui was also astonished: not as far as our case was concerned but during the Touvier trial, scenes from which were broadcast on the History Channel. He fulminated, in the course of his defence of the civil parties, at the Nazis' impressive ability to hide the truth: that is, to lie. He even gave a name to this skill: '*ignorance*'. He recalled how during the Frankfurt trial, Mr Hoffman[65], the head of Auschwitz, denied any knowledge of what was happening in his camp and pretended that they were only making sandbags for children...

---

65 This trial was held from 1963 to 1965. The camp commandants and their deputies were tried. *Maître Zaoui* quotes an extract from sworn statements from the trial.

20
Nightmares

The repeated denials I had to confront took their toll on my sleep; I became prey to nightmares.

The scenes were horrific. I saw things, although I'd never lived them. I see myself running from the Nazis, I see aeroplanes in flames and incinerated bodies, I see myself behind barbed wire among people who survive, although they have been deprived of their right to live, I see details of uniforms, fragments of emaciated faces, I see... I feel a sharp pain... I smell smells... I'm suddenly transported to an era that I never knew and yet it all seems real.

I have the impression that when my mother was carrying me in her belly she passed her fears on to me and that my body has retained a memory of them. This memory is all the more intense because it passes through a body exercised by years of energetic dancing.

I've slept very little for five years, as if to spare myself these nightmares. Which nevertheless don't appear by chance: they also tell stories, and I discover things I never knew.

I went to see Roman Polanski's *The Pianist* when it was released, a film bearing witness to the life of the Polish pianist Wladyslaw Szpilman in the Warsaw ghetto. I thought it was a wonderful film. From a strictly cinematic point of view, the director is undoubtedly a great filmmaker who has married technical expertise and artistic sensibility: it is a masterpiece! I felt that I was in step with the story, and seeing it did me a power of good: I had the feeling that Polanski had lived the situation from within, that someone could understand what I was experiencing. My reaction was all the stronger because I remembered my very first job at the Paris Opéra. I had been one of Polanski's assistants when he'd produced *The Tales of Hoffmann*, the opera by Jacques Offenbach. I didn't know, at the time, that he was Jewish or had a past related to the Shoah. And vice versa.

I am very happy that he was awarded the *Palme d'Or* in Cannes. It was well deserved.

I have always loved going to the cinema. The art of film enthralls and entertains me. Moreover, indirectly it helps me in my work. But ever since I started this research, I go to the cinema less and less. I find some films insipid while others suddenly really scare me, yet years ago they would have had made much less impression: I would have reassured myself by saying it's only 'a film'. Nonetheless, I think that no scriptwriter is capable of imagining the perfidious machinations certain people are able to perpetrate in real life.

All this was making me so ill that my mother at one stage asked me to give it all up.

I've already mentioned the fears expressed by friends and relatives on the dangers I was exposing myself to by setting out on such an enterprise. I was attacking something much more powerful than myself, I was entering a zone where money and collusion are bedfellows and risked losing feathers in the process. Both in France and Brazil, several friends tried to dissuade me from running such a risk.

In the light of certain facts I have gradually discovered and incidents that I have experienced personally, I have come to understand that certain things don't just happen in the cinema. I was very naïve to think France was beyond this kind of thing. Years of dictatorship in Brazil had led me to expect something different from a democracy. But too often money sweeps away beliefs it finds in its path and, as soon as it imposes its rule, it puts in place a much subtler regime than any dictatorship: the sight of money makes people bow and shut their eyes. And don't the French say that the worst blind man is the one who refuses to see? The other day, in the supermarket near my house, more than six policemen went to arrest a mildly retarded man who had stolen something to eat. The woman at the till was so shocked she offered, unsuccessfully, to pay out of her own pocket so they didn't take him off. When it comes to the poor, the law *is* applied…

Despite the anxiety that sometimes overwhelms me whenever someone asks or advises me to throw in the towel, I always tell myself: 'No! I won't give up. We are in the right. We must fight on behalf of this right. Otherwise, my family will have died for nothing. Otherwise, those who struggled to defend an ideal, the fighters in the Resistance (the real ones), the people who saved my mother, all these people will have fought for nothing. I owe it to them to show a minimum of courage.'

But I'm not the only one who needs courage, and I wonder daily whether the justice system will also be courageous. Will it dare to put a powerful multinational on trial – even if I have all the evidence to prove its alleged guilt – with all the likely political consequences that will bring?

To round everything off, L'Oréal informed us that our action would be inadmissible because the incriminating facts are invalidated by prescription. If such were the case, the prescription would serve as a pretext and not as the real reason for their inadmissibility.

The notion of prescription can be interpreted in different ways. My grandparents died in the Holocaust, which is considered to be a crime against humanity, and hence one that can never be prescribed by the passage of time. We presented an action against the receiving and retention of stolen property. As L'Oréal has kept the profits from this receiving of stolen goods[66], namely the profits from the sale of a house stolen by the Nazis, there is no prescription. But, as I have just said, there can be different interpretations. And if the legal system reckons the case is too delicate, it will find a way of seeing it off. It can judge things from the opposite perspective: an entrance can also be an exit. But you need to have the will to go in, and there lies the rub: does the system want justice to be done? Is the law the same for both the weak and the strong?

I lived under a military dictatorship for most of that part of my life I lived in Brazil. I had time to understand how dictators have recourse to violence because they have no other way of doing things.

There were certainly some ridiculous sides to the Brazilian system of repression. Everything Russian was forbidden on principle: 'Russian' meant 'Communism' and thus subversion. It was on this basis that works written before the Communist period were often banned until the censors realized they were making fools of themselves and authorized the publication of books like Dostoyevsky's *Crime and Punishment* or Tolstoy's *Anna Karenina*. But the preposterous side to censorship wasn't enough to make ordinary citizens forget the constraints imposed by the dictatorship and, in particular, the fact that it was extremely difficult to leave the country. The restriction was subtler than a simple ban on leaving the country as practised by Eastern Bloc countries; whoever wanted to leave the country had to pay out a fortune and leave a cash deposit; consequently, only well-off Brazilians could afford such a luxury.

There is something else I had grasped about dictators. They are people who are perfectly integrated into society. They are 'good

---

66 Under French law, the receiving and keeping of stolen goods is what is called a 'continuous crime' that only ceases when the property is restored. It is only from this moment that the calculation of the three-year limit begins.

fathers', married to 'charming wives' and have 'devoted staff'. Of course, people under their orders torture and rape, particularly intellectuals, but at the same time, their wives do charity work and hence put into their charitable endeavours a minute part of the money they have stolen from the people in order to bolster their Swiss bank accounts. Thus, despite the torture and pillage, they are thought to be remarkable individuals and are invited to the best dinner parties.

21

Masquerade

Mr Owen-Jones sent my mother a letter on 4 October 2001[67]. Whenever I reread it, it disgusts me. Firstly because of its oh-so-sophisticated trappings. Secondly because of its content.

When the letter arrived, I was astonished to receive a letter from Owen-Jones sent to my house since his lawyers had been in contact with ours who had contacted him. It was as if L'Oréal's chief executive thought we didn't need a lawyer!

Before I opened the envelope I drew my first naïve conclusion: they've understood! They've understood that we hold irrefutable proof and that they cannot escape their responsibilities. Owen-Jones is writing to me at home to ask us to forgive him. He must be wanting to suggest a peaceful solution in order to calm the waters.

When I started to read the letter, I didn't immediately change my state of mind; I found his tone pleasant, even friendly, and human. But I very soon realized that that was the point of his manoeuvre. In effect, his honeyed tone was only a ploy, to put my mother and me at ease.

Unfortunately for Mr Owen-Jones, I knew my dossier by heart and very quickly spotted the tissue of lies hiding behind by his

---

67 See Appendix 11.

friendly tone. This gentleman has a gift for making a travesty of truth, for making documents say the opposite of what they mean. Despite, the letter's most urbane veneer, I felt it was insulting. Far from sending us a private letter to offer his apologies, he had written to convince my mother that neither in the past nor today was L'Oréal at all responsible for the theft of our house. I was scandalized and called my lawyer:

'*Maître*, how can you let them send me a cheap letter like this?'

I felt that my fury had fazed him, even though, I think, he understood the reasons driving it.

'Madame, I understand you are angry, but is that a reason for you to lose your temper with your lawyer who, may I remind you, is on your side?'

I knew in my heart of hearts that he was right, but I wanted to hear him express his disgust. I calmed down and we were able to discuss the content of the letter and the attitude we should adopt. I asked him to wait before we reached a decision, because as always when I am in a rage, I need time to stand back and think level-headedly.

As I was rereading the letter, the documents that proved Mr Owen-Jones's bad faith paraded round my head.

I quote: 'In 1954, the L'Oréal subsidiary in Germany, in which the group bought back shares only in 1961...'

To mention 1961 is a way of locating the event at a far remove from the war and the Vichy government: as if to say, L'Oréal had no connections whatsoever with the Nazis. As if I didn't know the truth! And didn't Mme Bettencourt hold 95 percent of the shares in Haarfarben? And wasn't François Dalle, the chief executive of L'Oréal in France, also the managing director of L'Oréal in Germany? And what about André Tondu, the founder of Haarfarben und Parfümerien?

The letter sent to me and not to my lawyer was therefore an official response. And I can demonstrate its lies. Mr Owen-Jones didn't, of course, suspect that I had got the documents from the company registry. With great difficulty, it is true, and by sheer persistence, but I did succeed in the end. These documents prove, as I have already said, that in 1959, 95 percent of the capital in Haarfarben und Parfümerien was owned by Mrs Bettencourt, née Liliane Schueller.

Subsequently, I found a document from the French administration confirming that Haarfarben belonged to L'Oréal well before 1959. Today I can hold this document in my hands and state categorically that Owen-Jones, by trying to hide the fact that Haarfarben already belonged to L'Oréal in 1954 – the date when our house was purchased – and by lying so outrageously in the letter sent to my home in October 2001, is trying to protect the subsidiary from any fallout. It is what is known as 'complicity in the possession of stolen goods'.

And must we remind Mr Owen-Jones that the L'Oréal in Germany website – a fact legally recognized by a public lawyer – relates how André Tondu was ordered by Eugène Schueller in 1930 to found Haarfarben, first in Berlin and then in Karlsruhe in 1945. Schueller gave out orders from Paris. André Tondu carried them out in Germany. Haarfarben was secretly L'Oréal in Germany. And we will soon discover how André Tondu was officially employed by L'Oréal from at least 1948.

When in 1954 André Tondu bought back from BGV, on behalf of Haarfarben und Parfümerien, the house that had been stolen from us by the Nazis, he was then fully representing L'Oréal. And if the purchase only became effective from 1954, it was because it couldn't be enacted before then. In fact, as we have seen, and as I will repeat to refresh our memories, L'Oréal had coveted the house at Wendstrasse 19 at least from 1948. Under the orders of Eugène Schueller, Ensa – the front company for L'Oréal, managed by André Tondu – signed two different bills of purchase for number 17, the neighbouring house, although it only paid once. The first bill dates from February 1949, the second is signed 5 November 1951, the same day as the pseudo-agreement was signed between BGV and a Jewish association in relation to our house[68]. And, on exactly the same day, Haarfarben–L'Oréal was buying the other house contiguous to ours, number 18 Kaiserallee. To conclude the transaction that would enable L'Oréal to build its German headquarters on the three adjacent lots, the company had merely to buy our house. This series of transactions only made sense if they purchased the middle property: ours. It seems clear then, since the neighbouring properties had been bought outright, that L'Oréal was sure it was going to get Wendstrasse 19: something that the laws on stolen property had made impossible till then.

I will continue my analysis of the letter from Owen-Jones. I quote: 'In 1951, a Jewish association, legally appointed to take the place of the Jews exterminated by the Nazi regime…' Except that, in the event, we are dealing here not with a Jewish woman who has been exterminated but one who couldn't be more alive. The proof: he's writing to her. If in 2001 L'Oréal is still able to deny her existence, you can understand the difficulty my mother has always experienced in accepting she has a right to be alive.

To continue: '…and your uncle [...] signed an agreement with the insurance company…' But where is my great-uncle Karl's signature? Above all, where is my mother's signature? Nowhere to be found![69] And, as he mentions my great-uncle, he thus acknowledges his existence, and he himself makes this clear: L'Oréal knew he was alive in 1951. What Owen-Jones doesn't say – and what I've learned afterwards, thanks to other documents – is that my great-uncle not only didn't sign the agreement but also died several years later in dire poverty.

Another document exists to which I have yet to refer: an internal BGV document mentioning the Nazi lawyer[70] who was

---

68 See Appendices 7 and 8.
69 See Appendix 8.
70 I have in my possession several letters sent by Dr Sickinger that end with 'Heil Hitler!'

supposedly speaking on behalf of my great-uncle. This lawyer, Dr Sickinger, had already crossed with my family: as chairman of the group of national-socialist lawyers of the Karlsruhe district in the Nazi era[71], he was the main person responsible for banning my grandfather, Fritz – himself a lawyer – from practising. Sickinger is, by this token, the third player in this case directly linked to the Third Reich. His presence is then no chance thing; he was a very efficient ally when it came to keeping Karl away from the agreement allowing them to rob him and us. The internal BGV memo reveals this sleight-of-hand. It shows that Sickinger openly sided with BGV: 'If an agreement proves impossible, *Maître* Sickinger will renounce his brief for he has no wish to intervene against us [BGV].[72]' BGV was in possession of this document, and so was L'Oréal.

Everything was arranged in advance, so that the only outcome possible would be to turn the three plots of land into one. And this manoeuvre was carried out long after the Nazi period as if the events of history had no impact on the power of those responsible: a post-war manoeuvre that also represented a whitewash of BGV's Nazi past.

I had lulled myself with false expectations that the present generation would regret the actions of its parents. Nothing had changed.

Counter-truth followed on half-truths, and it would be too lengthy and repetitious to mention every detail. But I will quote the end of the letter. It gave me a cruel insight into the lack of respect towards my mother and made me realize that hypocrisy knows no bounds:

'I would not want you to imagine that my attitude is dictated by a wish to delay matters, that is why I am very happy to contribute towards the expenses you might accrue

71 See Appendix 13.
72 See Appendix 12.

115

in your researches in Germany and consultations necessary for the preparation of your dossier.

If you accept this offer, the aim of which is to help you in your search for the truth...'

And he concludes by inviting us to make contact with him or his lawyers.

When I read this passage, I leaped out of my chair: Mr Owen-Jones had crossed the line! Search for the truth? Documents? We already had everything. And these documents clearly indict L'Oréal. The truth is there!

What I find really indecent in his proposal is that L'Oréal deprived my mother of the enjoyment of her property and still dares to deny her: an old lady who lived the Shoah in her flesh and in her soul! Owen-Jones continues:

'A theft constitutes an intolerable attack on the rights of human beings and must certainly be redressed. I am personally committed to the group I head being above reproach.'

My friends jokingly began to advise me to take care. I think some were really worried. They asked me if I had given photocopies of the documents I'd collected to different trustworthy people. That made me laugh, and I retorted that they'd seen too many police films, even though I had in fact copied the documents and lodged them in a safe place. I was also told that I was naïve: that these people were capable of doing things you imagine impossible in a state of law.

Mr Erwin Brunner, the director of BGV who – under the Nazi regime – had taken over our house, had managed to get a whitewash from a de-nazification trial. Mr Owen-Jones – the chief executive of L'Oréal, which bought our house from BGV as if it belonged to this company – was content to write a letter and relieve his company of all responsibility, even though we had supplied him with all the documents proving that this house belonged to us, as well as evidence showing that L'Oréal had acquired a property stolen by the Nazis...

At the time I received this letter, which I was to forward to my mother, the refurbishing of a production of *Rigoletto* at the Opéra-Bastille was proving to be very time-consuming. The September 11 attacks had taken place the month before, and the psychosis gripping American airports led to the cancellation of several flights. Hence, some singers couldn't arrive on the dates agreed, and rehearsals had to begin late. I wasn't particularly distressed by this hitch in the preparations for the opera – it is something that happens frequently in my trade, and I know how to handle it – although I'd have to pull out all the stops to conclude the rehearsals on time. From now on it was the responsibility of the courts to deliver a verdict on L'Oréal's lies. No doubt I shouldn't have waited so long to take action, but now my conscience was peaceful. I had offered our adversaries every possible opportunity to reach an honourable settlement; they showed not the slightest interest. At no time did I play the game of 'an eye for an eye, a tooth for a tooth'. I always went out of my way to show respect towards them, but they showed us none. I'd given them a chance, but they had only laughed at us.

'*Maître*, enough is enough. You're right: we must take them to court!'

22
My Grandfather

My mother sent me a manuscript that my grandfather, Fritz, wrote when he was lodged in a Swiss prison after he had escaped from France. He had scrawled it on bits of paper that came his way. The style is stiff, if not laborious, and that makes the document occasionally difficult to understand. He couldn't know that after the war people would talk about the Holocaust, but you can sense his desire to bear witness, to leave evidence so people would know.

His account is extremely reserved, and certain facts are never explicitly mentioned. But the man who is writing is also afraid: he takes care never to give the real names of the people to whom he refers – to the point of travestying his own identity. Moreover, you can discern a good number of anachronisms. Was it his state of health (his stays in the camps made him incurably ill) that led him to speak of my grandmother in 1943, when she was deported and died in 1942? Or was it a deliberate intention on his part to alter the dates of certain events?

Nevertheless, what strikes me most about this manuscript is the daily struggle he engaged in, like others, to preserve his dignity as a human being. He recounts a squabble among prisoners over a potato floating in a watery soup in one of the camps he passed through. He refused to join in the squabble over a morsel of potato with people who shared his fate, even though he was as hungry as they were and had already lost fifteen kilos (he was to lose even more).

He describes moments when he is caught between his own need to survive and the help he feels he must give to those who are in a worse state and recalls that, at such moments, to think only of oneself is to abdicate from one's condition as a civilized human being and thus admit the Nazis and collaborators are right.

He speaks of his anguish in the camp at Gurs when he discovers an aunt of his, who had fallen victim to the dysentery that was rife at the time, in one of the small blocks of cabins where the prisoners were lodged. More than ten people were dying from it everyday. He bribed a guard in order to get into the female section. The critical state of his aunt and other women made him desperate.

The temperature was several degrees below zero, and he managed to gather a few men together to stop the gaps in the walls with mud as best they could so that it wasn't so cold in the cabin. One man had matches that allowed them to make a fire and warm some stones they then placed on the women's bellies like hot water bottles, thus saving several lives. His aunt, however, did not survive.

Other members of the family arrived in the camp. My grandfather recounts how he bartered in order to get a blanket for an uncle who was shivering with cold. But by the time he finally got the blanket, his uncle was already dead.

His narrative relates other similar incidents with members of the family. People were dropping like flies.

He also speaks of the decision he reached with friends to organize evenings of lectures, variety shows and concerts (there were well known artistes in the camp), so their fellow detainees didn't forget they were human beings and life didn't resign them to their condition as prisoners. These nocturnal activities enabled them to cling to life and find the strength to struggle on.

My grandfather was imprisoned several times in the camp at Les Milles, near Aix-en-Provence. Apart from his manuscript, several documents attest to this series of internments.

During his last stay there, he learned he was on a list to be deported to Auschwitz and decided to escape. He had money on him, as he had taken care not to give everything to the camp chief on his arrival. This money enabled him to get things from time to time. It allowed him to help those who had less than him, usually nothing at all.

One of his friends and fellow detainees gave him a tip-off: one guard, in exchange for money, had agreed to shut his eyes, but only at night. And that was how my grandfather's escape was organized.

The camp at Les Milles was an old brick factory and had a big chimney that was out of action. The top of the conduit had been blocked to prevent escape attempts, but the two men had spotted a recess inside, which could act as a hiding-place for my grandfather. It would be a very perilous undertaking: apart from the inevitable risk of being caught or falling, he would have to spend several days in an uncomfortable position and disregard his natural needs. But Fritz had nothing to lose and hid there while waiting for the night when the bribed guard would be on duty.

He had some anxious moments in his hiding-place, notably when the police came to inspect the chimney. He was a hairsbreadth away from being discovered, the dogs had sniffed him, and the police swept the conduit with their torches, but luckily for him, without success.

It was after this episode that his friend informed him he could come out of hiding (they'd agreed to sound a signal). Fritz and his companions had made a kind of theatre stage with scenery made from materials they'd recycled from the camp. This stage had a trapdoor that opened down to a cellar, at the end of which was the door controlled by the guard. Fritz gave him money in exchange for opening the door and thus found himself free once again, at least for a while.

In relation to this guard, my grandfather writes in his manuscript: 'He tries to efface by night the suffering he causes by day.'

My grandfather then went to Allauch, where his wife Kaethe and daughter Edith were living. When he got there, he learned the French gendarmes had just rounded up his wife and that she had been incarcerated in the camp at Les Milles. His daughter had managed to escape; she had been lucky not to be in Allauch that day; and Rosette, a young girl from the village, went to save her in Marseille, where she'd gone with her school teacher. While keeping out of sight of the French police, my grandfather went to recover his daughter. He also tried to organize his wife's escape, but to no avail.

My mother has visited me once since I've been living in France. It was in July 1988. We hired a car and went to the south east of France for a week. She wanted me to get to know this region. At the time, I knew nothing about her past, and when I saw her in an emotional state, I just put it down to her reaction to the little discoveries we kept making. I was far from imagining that it was finding herself back in this region with her own daughter that provoked the emotion. We didn't go to Allauch…

We'd agreed that, because of my work, at the end of our stay I'd go back to Paris by train and she'd go to Marseille by herself and return the car. When the time came to say goodbye, she suddenly became nervous and said in a childish voice: 'I can never drive the car by myself to Marseille.'

I couldn't understand the reasons for her distress because she had done the driving from the start of our holiday. And she knew that my international driving licence was no longer valid and that I couldn't take the wheel.

'Mum, you know I can't drive legally. What will I say if there's a police check?'

And she replied quite seriously: 'You just tell them you're with your mother and that everything is fine.'

I burst out laughing (she didn't understand why), but there was no way I could drive. We went our separate ways and, to soothe her anxieties, I promised to be near a telephone as soon as I returned to Paris, so she could catch up with me.

I'd totally misunderstood what she was going through. I even told her shortly after how I'd been completely at a loss. But at no time did she tell me she'd lived near Marseille, nor what it meant for her to go back there by herself after so many years.

I felt very guilty when I recently discovered this page from her childhood and understood why she was so anxious that day. I hope she'll be able to return to France; next time, we'll go to Marseille and come back together.

23

Media Reaction

The indictment was ready. Now my mother had only to read and sign it. I sent it to her by FedEx, but she sent it back by Sedex, a kind of Brazilian DHL. Three weeks went by, and it still hadn't arrived. It was December, the end-of-year festivities were nigh, and Sedex in Brazil had more business than it could cope with. I sent the indictment back to Brazil, and my mother finally despatched it to us by FedEx. In this way, the indictment was finally lodged on 28 December 2001.

There are moments when *maître* Korman is less available because of the other cases he has to see to. So I had to champ the bit while waiting for him to be free again. I was, moreover, intensely annoyed by the bureaucratic hold-ups that delayed the despatch of documents I had ordered. To placate my impatience, I went to the Bibliothèque nationale and asked for everything they had related to L'Oréal. But whenever one wants to consult this kind of documentation, there are special formalities to be completed at the Bibliothèque nationale. They can't be sorted in a minute, and by the time I got my pass, the library was closing its doors. I came back as soon I had some free time, and on this occasion when it was open.

The first documents that I read ranged from different ways to use hair dyes to old hairdressing magazines. Then I came across the magazine of the L'Oréal joint production committee for November 1948. This magazine, entitled *Au Cap*, carried a page on 'Our Company' which spoke of the company's different branches throughout the world including 'Haarfarben, first based in Berlin, now in Karlsruhe, with Mr Tondu as its manager as always'. It ended with the motto: 'L'Oréal everywhere, L'Oréal forever, L'Oréal always…' Indeed!

Until then all I had on André Tondu was the document I'd found on the L'Oréal website. They were still pretending Mr Tondu was not involved with L'Oréal, that he was not a company employee! The production committee magazine gives quite a different picture; and in a pile of documents I found another issue of the same magazine: this time for March 1949. There were stories on the 1948 Christmas parties, and notably the end-of-year party at Haarfarben und Parfümerien which took place on 11 December in Karlsruhe: 'We give thanks to the kind Mr Tondu, our friend as always, for sending the texts written by staff on the occasion of this event.'[73] This gentleman really had a very strange close relationship with the mother company for someone reduced to the rank of lowly estate agent by Mr Owen-Jones and his lawyers! It was quite clear in my view that he was working actively for the group, beyond the mere duties of middleman that they attempted to confer on him, and that he must really be well acquainted with the production committee (and vice versa) for the latter to dub him a friend.

Now the press had to be informed. I had no contacts in this milieu, and when I phoned the newspapers directly I got no joy. I quickly understood that you had to mention the name of a journalist in order to cross the threshold of an editorial board. Once again I turned to my friends for help. Two gave me the names of journalists to contact on their behalf. But even with this strong insider

---

73 See Appendices 15 and 16.

support, my case was far from getting a hearing.

I first met with the director of a television news team, and he welcomed me most warmly. He suggested the topic to one of his reporters. The latter meticulously reviewed my fifty-centimetre-high pile of documents. It took him almost a month to complete the task. It is true that our respective timetables didn't always allow us to meet up quickly when he needed me to explain some of the detail. I felt I was already in court because – if he believed my story after he'd read everything – like everyone else, he started out by doubting it was true. It was the beginning of February 2002. The reporter then told me that he wanted to take on the story and we'd both have to go to Karlsruhe. But before that, he had two other reports to finish. From the beginning of March, I was the one not available: I had to go and stay in Toulouse for fifty days in order to create a big opera. Nevertheless, he was the first journalist to take an interest in my case and want to work on it.

His editorial boss warned me of the difficulty of the project. L'Oréal is the premier advertiser in France, and the vast majority of the daily, weekly or television press needs this advertising manna. He warmed my heart when he assured me that, in spite of this, he would fight to get the subject on air.

In the meantime, after I'd sent a synopsis of the case to journalists, I got two appointments. The first meeting went extremely well, and the journalist promised his article would be out the following week. The second, also a journalist working for a big daily, gave me an appointment for the Thursday after our telephone conversation on a Monday. Two hours after we'd spoken, he rang back. He'd just spoken to L'Oréal by phone as his duty as a journalist required. He'd mentioned some of the synopsis, which had led to his call. L'Oréal had asked him to send them a copy. He was calling back to see if I had any objections. Additionally, even though L'Oréal did admit they were acquainted with the story, their spokesman had told him he knew nothing of any action being been brought against the group. At that moment, I leaped in: 'What are they talking about? There they go again, saying they don't know a thing! Of course an action has been started against them. My lawyer had sent a letter to L'Oréal's two lawyers alerting them to the indictment, and I myself wrote to Mr Owen-Jones to inform him that the only response his letter to my mother deserved was court action. And yet they say they have only "heard" about this story! I'm astonished at their ability to adapt reality. I can show you all this correspondence.'

The journalist was intrigued by my reactions.

'Can we meet up this afternoon rather than Thursday?'

'Of course.'

We arranged to meet in a café a few hours later. I showed him the very first letter from my lawyer dated June 2001, the one from the L'Oréal's Chief Executive and then mine telling Mr Owen-Jones we would meet in court. I started to relate my story by showing one by one the documents I had brought with me. I was beginning to anticipate this kind of exercise and had prepared a book of photos. He asked questions and wanted further explanations of certain points he found difficult to fathom.

We then went to his newspaper office to make photocopies. But I hadn't brought all my documentation. I'd already told him how extensive that was, and even if I had brought everything, he wouldn't have been able to read them all in a few hours. He also wanted to check everything. We agreed to meet again and that I'd bring him more documents. He scrutinized them all before making fresh contact with L'Oréal and their lawyers; he had questions he wanted to put to them. He also questioned my lawyer. We saw each other once more because he wanted to check some final points before the article appeared.

In the meantime, I'd called back the first journalist, who'd promised there would be an article in his newspaper the following week. But his tone of voice told me he'd had a change of mind. I work with voices, and it is rare for me to miss this kind of thing. In the eyes of my interlocutor, 'things weren't that clear', 'we weren't sure'. He didn't ask for any extra documents, and I realized I couldn't count on him to write an article for his newspaper.

After presenting his article to his superiors, the second journalist kept me up to date on its probable appearance. Every two days it was the same scenario: 'It won't be out tomorrow, perhaps the day after.' Even if he said nothing, I felt he was fighting. There were days when his voice betrayed dejection, others when I felt he was hopeful, but at no time did his tone change in relation to me. He repeated his reports on possible publication for three weeks until one day – I'd only been in Toulouse for a few days, when he called me: 'It's coming out tomorrow. We've succeeded!'

I was extremely happy. The curtain of secrecy was going to be lifted, and people would finally know what had happened.

The article, entitled 'The Daughter of Deported Parents Accuses L'Oréal of Profiting from Land in Karlsruhe Stolen from Her Family in 1938', appeared in *Le Monde* on 8 March, 2002. It was accompanied by a photo of our house in Karlsruhe. There was a second article, entitled 'Edith Rosenfelder's Long Quest to Find the House of her Childhood'. A small article referred to the Frydman affair.

I must pay particular homage to this newspaper and its journalist, Alexandre García, because it required lots of courage to publish this article. Respecting honour and ethics is a daily battle. 'It has taken men thousands of years to stand up. What would life be worth if it were conducted at ground level?' These sentences[74] would have been a perfect compliment, if they hadn't been uttered by Mrs Bettencourt, who simply forgot to match words with deeds.

I got calls from all over. Brazilian newspapers even contacted me. Those I spoke to have followed up the subject. But not a single press organ in France reacted.

L'Oréal viewed the appearance of the article as a form of blackmail.

---

74 Reported by Bruno Abescat, *La Saga des Bettencourt*, op. cit.

To be sure, I have numerous faults, I'm impulsive, I don't have an easy character, I can even sometimes be intolerable – as my detractors say – but I am thoroughly honest and would never dream of practising blackmail in order to get money.

I was married to a very rich man, and if money were my motive, I would have accepted the settlement his father offered me when we separated. But I refused it: I thought I had no right to such a thing.

You say, this is blackmail? No! We are simply asking you to give back what belongs to us, and we say that what you call blackmail is only justice.

24

My Grandmother

I did get to know Marianne, my great-aunt. Just before she died she whispered a few words to me about her sister-in-law, Kaethe, whom she had met. She spoke to me of a beautiful, very elegant women. She also told me what she felt about my grandmother's deportation. According to her, Kaethe couldn't stand more escape attempts and humiliations and simply resigned herself to her fate.

When I was given Kaethe's deportation book at the Centre for Contemporary Jewish Documentation, people encouraged me to go to the National Archives in Paris; I might come across important information there. So I went and was well received and advised on how to pursue my researches: I was given some microfilm by the man responsible for that section, who then added that the photocopier was free for victims of the Shoah and their heirs. I appreciated that gesture as a form of recognition.

I kept dropping the microfilm and couldn't manage the simple operation of slotting it into the machine. I was embarrassed, and my hands were shaking. The section head smiled and came to my rescue.

'I'm sorry, I'm really clumsy and can't keep still,' I told him. He slipped the film into the machine, showed me how it worked, then asked me what my grandmother's surname was before leaving me to my researches.

I began to process an alphabetical list of names of individuals with their age, family status and place of residence. Endless columns of men, women and children of all ages began to pass before me. Sometimes it was a whole family. These people came from all over: from France but also from the rest of Europe. What they had in common was that they'd all transited through the camp in Drancy before being sent usually to Auschwitz. I mentally pictured them saying goodbye to each other, clutching their suitcases full of personal effects which would later be confiscated. These effects were mentioned on the microfilm.

My head was in a whirl. I couldn't manage to get the machine to stay on 'Rosenfelder'. The section head came to my rescue once again, but I found I was unable to continue reading immediately. I had to get up and walk round. When I returned, I did succeed in reading: 'Kaethe Rosenfelder née Hirsch, 6 rue des Saussaies, convoy number 29.'

Although the document made no mention of personal effects, I did, however, register the epithet 'head of family'. The French police at the time was well informed: this detail was quite in order since she had become the head of family after the repeated absences of my grandfather, who was moving from one camp to another.

We looked for other microfilms related to my search, but to no avail. Anyway, my emotions on this occasion overrode my wish to continue; I had found my reference, and after thanking my saviour and making a few photocopies, I left the building so I could breathe normally once more.

I sent my brother a copy of our grandmother Kaethe's deportation book. I wanted him to share my emotions. I had taken the precaution beforehand of making him promise he wouldn't under any circumstance show this document to my mother.

Two or three days went by before he rang me on Sunday afternoon.

'Hallo, how's it going?'

'Fine…'

He started to reel off his news: he was going to work in the south of Brazil, etc. He spoke non-stop, but I felt he was going round in circles. Once he'd exhausted all the subjects that came to mind, I could only add a banal: 'Fine, we'll be in touch. Love.'

He sensed I was about to hang up.

'By the way, the documents concerning Grandmother…'

He's taken his time, I told myself. That was typical of him: he was incapable of saying they had bowled him over, and he needed to speak about the first thing that came into his head to hide his real feelings. Nonetheless, we spoke about them and finally he exclaimed: 'They must give us our house back! What do they think they're playing at? Can you take somebody's house just because you want it?'

I laughed at his way of putting it, but, essentially, it was exactly that: what did they think they were playing at by simply appropriating a house that belonged to somebody else?

In July 2002, I went to Aix-en-Provence for the annual song festival. The camp at Les Milles and Allauch, where my family had sought refuge, weren't far way. I didn't have the courage to go to the camp; that was still too much for me. On the other hand, I did go to Allauch, where the old quarter is like a very small, quite charming village in Provence. The château of Carlevent is just outside. It houses some official body or other. I didn't go in, but from the outside it looked spacious and was surrounded by a large garden. I started to imagine my family living in such a place.

When I got back to Paris, I rang my mother to tell her about my visit to Allauch and the castle.

'You know, we lived in Allauch, in the castle,' she told me.

'Why did you think I went there? I knew you'd lived there.'

'How did you find out?'

'Thanks to some documents I've found.'

And she began to tell me how Fritz's cousins, the Wolf family, lived there, that she went to the village school for almost a year and that the inhabitants of Allauch had been kind people because they had tried to hide them.

That's how it is with my mother. I have to find things out first by myself before she'll tell me how they occurred. Then slowly she will let some memories emerge, but only selectively.

Sometimes, it's the other way round and I'm the one who tells her the rest of the story: the part she could not know, which is the cause of so much pain.

25

Some Irrefutable Facts

L'Oréal reckons that it is not responsible for what might have happened before 1961. It is the weightiest argument the multinational deploys to oppose our action. Now that I have in my possession all the documents which prove quite the opposite, dated and stamped by the relevant administrative offices, I will remind you of the following facts:

• The same man, Mr André Tondu, bought Wendstrasse 17, then Wendstrasse 19 and Kaiserallee 18.

• Although he bought Wendstrasse 17 in the name of Ensa Ltd, L'Oréal is the company based at this address. Additionally, Ensa and L'Oréal pursue the same activity: perfumes.

• Mr Tondu bought Wendstrasse 17 in February 1949. He didn't pay cash but took out a loan. Now in Germany, as in most countries, it takes two to four months to get a loan, which means that the promise to sell must have been signed at the end of 1948.

• This same Wendstrasse 17 was acquired in a very strange fashion: two bills of purchase in succession for the same property. The two bills are similar and mention the same buyer and vendors. As if the only real requirement was to alter the date of sale.

• Now this second bill of sale was published in the land registry on 5 November 1951, that is the very same day when BGV signed with the Jewish organization an agreement to ratify the theft of Wendstrasse 19.

Moreover, if Messrs Owen-Jones, Veil and Zaoui have a free moment, they should dip into the archives at the Ministry for Finance and the Economy. And ask to see the file giving information on foreign companies created before 1948 with the help of French capital. There they will see, in black and white, that Haarfarben und Parfümerien has been controlled *100 per cent* since its creation in 1930 by a French firm: *L'Oréal of Paris, 14 rue Royale*[75].

This sequence of anomalies and coincidences should be enough to arouse the suspicions of the most simple-minded among us. How is it possible, from this point on, not to see anything here but the premeditated perpetration of an obscene fraud in order to bypass measures to restore a Jewish property after the war to its rightful owners? Would any of that have been possible if L'Oréal and BGV hadn't colluded?

Wendstrasse 19 couldn't have been sold before 1948 because our property was subject to military government legislation and to measures related to thefts. The first bill of sale for Wendstrasse 17 – in February 1949 – was followed by a complicated administrative process for the purchase of number 19. The presence of my great-uncle Karl didn't make matters any easier: he was cut off from his inheritance in 1951 by the 'agreement' reached between the Jewish organization and BGV.

After 1951 L'Oréal still had to bide its time before it could get its hands on our property: the necessary paperwork at the company registry, the payments of taxes etc. were dealt with in a day. And, in 1953, André Tondu reappears in the property registry, this time to purchase Wendstrasse 19: something that won't happen till the following year.

---

75 See Appendices 10 and 11.

The past caught up with me as I started on the last part of my story. I had just been called by the person within the Drai Commission responsible for researching my file on what happened at 6 rue des Saussaies[76]. I was really upset by what she told me after my recent reading of the books by the Frydman brothers.

We had been trying to find out the identity of a man my grandfather received in his apartment in Paris, opposite the Ministry of the Interior, 11 rue des Saussaies.

My grandfather's manuscript mentions that it is a diplomat he is well acquainted with. He met him when he was a lawyer working for the French consulate in Karlsruhe. He writes in detail of this diplomat, giving the exact dates of their meetings in the consulate, but never gives his name. This man whom he subsequently welcomed into his home in Paris then occupied an elevated position at the Ministry of the Interior. We wondered whether this unknown individual hadn't played a role in our case. Perhaps he'd just told the people around him of the masterpieces on the walls of Rosenfelders' Paris apartment. He had certainly visited their private townhouse in Karlsruhe.

We hadn't found anywhere documents that mentioned the paintings in my grandparents' Paris home. They had all simply disappeared. Moreover, according to a senior person at the National Archives, there were 'some bizarre things' in our file: it wasn't like most of the 8,000 dossiers checked by the Drai Commission. Consequently – and I wasn't the one who said this – everything pointed to the fact that someone in a high place who knew my grandfather had intervened at the rue des Saussaies before the Gestapo and the Vichy authorities and made a clean sweep of what was in the apartment and, in particular, the paintings.

The woman in charge of research told me of the list of French consuls in Karlsruhe where it appears that a certain Henri Guérin

---

76 The study group on the stealing of property belonging to French Jews (the Matteoli Commission) was subsequently replaced by the Drai Commission.

held this position from 1929 to 1936. She advised me to go to the Ministry for Foreign Affairs in order to find out more about this man. No sooner said than done. My heart thudded as I read his file. I won't comment exhaustively on everything I read. What stuck in my mind was how close Henri Guérin was to the powers-that-be, as evidenced by his frequent correspondence with Laval and Pétain among others. In 1939, when he had been living in retirement in Paris from 1936, he indicates to Marshal Pétain that he is at his disposal; and the Marshal writes to him in October 1939 that he wants him to go to Seville and resume his responsibilities.

Moreover, there is one name that keeps cropping up throughout Guérin's career: Camille Chautemps. Guérin owes to the latter all his promotions from the start of his career: 'my close collaborator', 'a personal request from Camille Chautemps', 'collaborator and friend of Camille Chautemps' are the terms used to support Guérin's rise. Whether they come directly from Chautemps or members of ministerial offices – several documents are on Ministry of the Interior stationery – they show the close links between the two men. I didn't know who Camille Chautemps was, and when I returned home I discovered that he was a highly influential man of politics who worked for Pétain to take power.

As chair of the Council of Ministers from February 1930, he saw his second government fall in 1934 after the Stavisky affair. He was a minister for Léon Blum from June 1936 to June 1937 and succeeded him as head of government from June 1937 to March 1938. From 1938 to 1940, he was vice-chair of the Council of Ministers in the Daladier and then the Paul Raynaud governments. From July 1940, he supported the taking of power by Marshal Pétain and formed part of his administration. In November 1940 he left to be ambassador in Washington. He was tried after the war for his acts of collaboration.

My recent reading has also confirmed that *cagoulards* actively supported Pétain's rise to power and that he had in his cabinet men like Gabriel Jeantet, who was close to Eugène Schueller. In this way, the Parisian *cagoulards* (Deloncle, Corrèze, Filliol, Schueller, Lavigne-Deville, Harispe, Duseigneur) had a bridgehead to Vichy (Jeantet, Martin, Méténier, Goussard) and rubbed shoulders with those in power[77].

In terms of my family history, when I read that Corrèze and Deloncle lived in the same apartment at 2 rue Rodin in Paris[78], the address reminded me of something else. And it was in the documents lodged at the company registry in Karlsruhe that I had come across the address of Henri Fèbvre, the L'Oréal lawyer, who acted as proxy for the associates of Haarfarben und Perfümerien (including Liliane Bettencourt), who was a L'Oréal shareholder and close collaborator of Eugène Schueller from 1936: he was based at 4 rue Rodin.

I wouldn't like my reader to think that I had lost my way and forgotten Henri Guérin *en route*. I have tried to show through this historical section that my research hasn't been linear; I've had to look in several directions at the same time while documenting for myself a period of French history. I've often followed several wrong leads. In the event, Henri Guérin wasn't the man my grandfather saw and that would soon become very clear to me.

I even made the mistake of looking for a consul when his manuscript mentioned a consular attaché. But yet again this mistake was providential. If I hadn't set my research officer on the track of consuls, or begun to take an interest in Guérin, I would probably never have found out the identity of the person we were looking for. In fact, the Ministry for Foreign Affairs could never have supplied us with information on consular attachés: it doesn't have any.

In order to pursue my research, I only had the names of Guérin and Chautemps as clues, as well as what my grandfather had noted in his manuscript about the person he received on the rue des

---

77 Pierre Péan, *Le Mystérieux Docteur Martín*, Paris, Fayard,1993, p. 205.

78 Christian Bernadac, *Dagore: Les Carnets secrets de la Cagoule*, Paris, France-Empire, 1977, p. 20.

Saussaies who held an important position at the Ministry of the Interior. So I decided to go to this ministry. The archivists at the Ministry of the Interior proved to be very cooperative and efficient. They pointed me to the Fontainebleau Archives that held the documents restored by the Russians – they took them from the Germans who had in turn taken them from France in 1941. They were General Information archives. Perhaps I might glean something yonder.

I went to the Fontainebleau Archives. There were handwritten documents from my grandfather. It was moving to see his handwriting. In perfect French he asked to remain in France; he gave the names of people who would endorse him, including a M. Eugène Faller. There were also letters from police headquarters, from the French Consulate in Karlsruhe, from Renseignements Généraux (an information department of the French police) and handwritten documents from Faller, notably a pass to allow him to visit him at the Ministry of the Interior. Eugène Faller notes there how he had met my grandfather in Karlsruhe where the latter 'was very favourably thought of at the consulate' where Faller had been 'the attaché from 1930'. We had finally found the man we had been looking for. He also worked under the orders of Chautemps (he was an aide to the Chair of the Council of Ministers office, then Secretary of State at the Ministry of the Interior.)

Back home, I studied these documents that I had photocopied. Police headquarters seemed to know everything about my grandfather, his wife and their daughter. It mentions that he owned a large house in Karlsruhe (the address is supplied) and that he was wealthy (this statement is underlined). The information came from the consulate in Karlruhe. What role had this Mr Faller played? Wasn't he my grandfather's friend? It is true the latter speaks of his great disappointment in this respect.

I pursued my enquiries in the Library of the History of Paris at the Town Hall. I discovered a file with Faller's name, with his date, place of birth and other information. He was Prefect several times, worked at the Ministry of the Interior and was promoted time and again during the Occupation. I experienced a feeling of unease and began to understand why my grandfather had been disappointed.

Subsequently, I had access to files of the Prefecture at the National Archives. The 1935–1946 files are headed: 'French Republic, Ministry of the Interior', and then everything is in German. The Faller file was in the same volume as the arch-collaborator Papon's. The latter receives barely more praise than Faller from the Germans. It is recorded that Eugène Faller carries out all their requests most efficiently and compliantly and that he is well connected in French society and in Vichy, that he collaborates with the *Propagandastaffel* and more besides. If I harboured any doubts about the fact that Faller had been a collaborator, now I had none. I also discovered that after the war he remained attached to the civil service without pay for several years, as was common practice with high-ranking civil servants who had a record of collaboration with the Nazis.

I still don't know the precise role that Faller played in the theft of our house, even though I felt there was something amiss. The day after the day in 1937 when my grandfather assigned the powers of attorney in the German Embassy in Paris, he obtained permission for his family to come and stay[79]. It is quite clear: the lives of my great-grandmother, grandmother and mother were granted in exchange for these powers. It was all well orchestrated by French and German senior civil servants, since my female ancestors got authorization simultaneously to leave Germany and join my grandfather in Paris. Did Faller play an intermediary role between the German authorities and French police headquarters?

Soon afterwards I discovered that there was a file on Faller at the Ministry of the Interior. But in order to consult it I required special authorization, which I was refused. To get it, you had to be related

---

79 See Appendices 3 and 4.

to the person whose file you wanted to see. The refusal letter really annoyed me. I couldn't see any solution that would help me get what I wanted. But, yet again, luck was on my side.

At the time I was rehearsing *Götterdämmerung* at the Toulouse opera house. A singer friend of mine saw I was in a very bad mood and invited me to go for a drink, and as we chatted about one thing and another, she managed to make me laugh. She then asked why I was in such a foul mood, and I told her about being refused access to a file – she already knew the rest of my story. She asked me a few questions about the person I was interested in, and when I mentioned his name, she burst out laughing.

'My mother's maiden name is Faller,' she told me.

This friend is American, but her family is originally from the Black Forest, like Eugène Faller. She spoke to her family, and they responded: 'If someone in our family has behaved badly, it is our duty to make amends.' And they made a request to consult Eugène Faller's file. I hope to have this document soon.

Soon afterwards, I came across a piece of information in a book that really made me shudder[80]: there was a connection between Allauch, the village where my grandparents were arrested, and La Cagoule: on 14 August, a bomb explosion in Nice put the police on the path of the murderers of Marx Dormoy. They found in the murderer's trouser pockets the name of an activist who lived in Allauch, and they immediately questioned him.

I recalled how Eugène Schueller, the founder of L'Oréal, was the ideologue and financier behind La Cagoule (the CSAR). Was it pure chance that my family, who had sought refuge in Allauch, was persecuted? Or was it related to the fact that La Cagoule had a base in the village? I continue to ask myself this disturbing question.

---

80 Philippe Bourdrel, *La Cagoule: 30 ans de complots*, Paris, Marabout, Marabout Université, 1986.

Subsequently, I contacted the municipality of Allauch. I told my interlocutor in what conditions my family had lived there. He was very moved and gave me the details of people to contact: the former mayor, a regional historian…

One of them had known the Wolfs, my grandfather's cousins, at the château of Carlevent, but he had no recollections of my family. I told him that my mother had been saved by a young girl called Rosette; I thus learned that Rosette died when she was thirty-six and that her brother had been executed by the Germans when they discovered he was in the Resistance. But Rosette had a sister who was still alive. He gave me her details, saying that I could say I was calling on his behalf. Her name was Monique Queirel, she was delighted to speak to me and remembered my mother. She was very moved and so was I. In turn, she gave me the telephone number of her very aged older sister. She also remembered my mother and my grandmother but couldn't tell me anything else.

A few days later she telephoned me: memories were flooding back. She remembered my grandfather, whom they called 'Doctor': he was very tall and very thin, with beautiful blue eyes. She couldn't remember what my grandmother looked like. But she had been at their house when she was arrested, apparently by the gendarmes. They had been looking for my family everywhere. That was all. That was already quite a lot.

I continued to call the two sisters from time to time. I liked to speak to them and find out how they were. One day Monique said she had some photos of my family. She sent them to me. There were photos of my mother when she was very young. She was very beautiful. Others of my great-grandmother and grandmother. None of my grandfather.

26

The End of the Voyage

My mother was seventy-five in July 2003. I went to Brazil so we could celebrate her birthday together. I spent more than a month over there and used the opportunity to see people who could give me an outside opinion on my file on the robbery.

First on my list: representatives of various Jewish organizations. I spoke to them about the house, the successive purchasers and about L'Oréal. I showed them the documentation. They were taken aback and gave me their unqualified support: something to which I was not at all accustomed. They were shocked and agreed to do everything possible to allow the truth to be known. I suddenly felt I was no longer alone.

Subsequently, a friend told me that her brother – a highly placed Brazilian magistrate and really trustworthy – had said he would give his impartial opinion on the file, provided I would accept his conclusion if he found I was in the wrong, if indeed that was what he decided. I met him and explained the case at length. He scrutinized the documents carefully and questioned me. He concluded it was a clear case of fraud and that it couldn't be subject to prescription because the receiving and retention of stolen goods constitute a continuous, indivisible crime.

My mother also told me about their passage to Switzerland at the end of 1942. The fisherman-ferryman they contacted had told them that it was getting more and more dangerous, that the lake was under constant surveillance. Finally, he agreed to ferry them across for a goodly sum of money. That same evening, another ferryman transporting refugees had been caught by the Nazis, and everybody was executed. The man who was to take my family to Switzerland immediately came to see my grandfather: it was too risky and he was opting out. My mother related how her lawyer father then started to plead their case in earnest by arguing that the only day when there wouldn't be any danger was precisely the day after the killings. The Nazis would think that nobody would have the courage to make the crossing after such a massacre. The fisherman was all the more easily persuaded when the money on offer was increased. They managed to cross that same night. They later learned they were the last to reach Switzerland unharmed.

On my return to France, Monique Queirel rang me to suggest I spend a few days with her so I could see the house where my family lived for some time. Consequently, I went to Allauch. Monique came to meet me at the bus station and recognized me immediately, because I looked like my mother. Then we walked slowly along the small streets of the old quarter. The weather was fine. I have always really liked the atmosphere in the small villages of Provence. We finally reached their house. You could see the château of Carlevent, on the top of a small hill. My family had lived there with the Wolf cousins. When the latter left for Mexico, my family stayed in the only hotel in the village.

Soon after, I made the acquaintance of the former mayor, who kindly offered me a book about Allauch. Monique's younger sister, Évelyne, joined us. In the course of our conversation, Évelyne told us she would never forget the day when the gendarmes came to get my grandmother. They shook her violently and kept asking her: 'Where is your daughter? Where is your daughter?'

Astonished, I asked: 'You were there?'

'Yes, both Monique and I were there. One thing is certain: they were only after your grandmother and Edith. Your grandfather was already imprisoned in a camp.'

'But why do you say they were only after my grandmother and my mother?'

'Because at the time other Jews were living in the village, and they only took your family.'

'Perhaps because my family was of German origin,' I suggested.

I knew there had been a round up of foreign Jews in the Marseille region, at about the time my grandmother was arrested. It is true that this roundup affected towns, and not villages, but you never know.

Monique replied: 'There *were* other German Jewish families. They were arrested much later, not even that year. At the time, they only wanted your family. Moreover, the gendarmes first went to the château and spoke to Mr Levi, who lived there. He was Jewish, but they didn't bother him. Then, when they went to get your grandmother from the hotel, they found the Dresen family, who were also German Jews but they didn't arrest them. In fact, your grandmother was in our house. They found her by tailing someone who was coming to warn her that the gendarmes were looking for her. It was evident that they only wanted her and Edith, for nobody else was hassled at this point. Only much later, in 1943 or 1944.'

Évelyne continued: 'The gendarmes shook her, but she didn't say where Edith was. And they took her to the camp at Les Milles.'

Taken aback, I asked her: 'And at the time did people know what would happen to the people imprisoned in the Les Milles camp? They say that at the time people still knew nothing about the deportation camps.'

'That's a lie,' replied Monique. 'Everyone knew the Jews were being brought together in camps and then deported. Those who say differently have got something to hide.'

The more indignant she became, the stronger her Marseille accent grew.

In order to lighten the atmosphere, the ex-mayor told a few jokes, and we laughed. Then I asked him if it would be possible to visit the château. He said he'd go and find out, and off he went.

Soon after, Monique came to tell me: 'Come on! We've got a date in front of the château. He's managed to get the keys!'

After the war, this château became an old people's home, then squatters lived there before it was bought by the municipality. As we walked down the path crossing the park, Monique told me what it was like when my grandparents lived there.

We went in and visited the three floors. There was no electricity but as the weather was very good: we could see even when inside. The place had become rather down-at-heel.

I thought of my family. And of all the different places they had lived. The mountains of Rio, the forest, the sea, Switzerland jostled in my head...

The day after, I looked round the village. My mother had asked me to send her photos of her school. As soon as I saw it, I heard in my head the song my mother had sung me on my last visit to Rio when she spoke to me about this school: '*Maréchal, nous voilà...*' My mother sang it through to the end, then added: 'After that, you were allowed to sit down.'

'Mum, am I dreaming or did you just sing me a song in honour of Marshal Pétain?'

She grimaced, as if she'd just swallowed something bitter.

'We all sang it. I had to be like everyone else, I couldn't stand out too much.'

This village was the last place where she lived with her mother. Even if survival was still difficult by this time, it was still possible to hope everything would be all right.

I saw the Mirador Hotel, which is now the Vesuvio restaurant. In a road farther on, Monique stopped me and pointed to the name: rue Pierre-Queirel. Pierre was her older brother. The village had thus paid homage to a great Resistance fighter who had been executed by the Germans.

'What happened to Pierre?'

'They first took him to Marseille, then to Lyon. We know they tortured him a lot because when they took him a change of clothes, the ones they gave us were torn and covered in blood.'

I suddenly thought he might have been a victim of Klaus Barbie. I didn't know what to say. I couldn't stop myself thinking that people like Pierre, like Monique's family, were the real heroes. They too were betrayed by 'respectable' people. We must never let our memories fade. We must not forget what some have done and the crimes others have committed.

We continued our walk. On each street corner, by each alleyway, I imagined my family had been there before me. I took photos. We telephoned my mother. We drank champagne. I was happy to have met these wonderful people. But also filled with melancholy at the thought of all those who had died. We could never be together. It was quite a strange feeling. But you had to do whatever you could. I preferred to try to be as happy as possible at that particular moment.

27
Memorandum

In April 2003, my lawyer finally received a reply in relation to the suit we had filed in December 2001. The ruling delivered by the examining magistrate, following instructions from the public prosecutor, concluded that there could be no trial, arguing, on the one hand, that the French legal system was not competent to judge on the matter, and on the other, that prescription did in fact exist for the crime of receiving and retaining stolen goods.

I was shocked. Soon after, we decided to appeal against the ruling.

I had already been writing the history of this robbery for several months with a view to publishing a book.

Whatever the law decides in the end – and I expect it to perform its function – it can't change anything in relation to the facts. The opposing party can try to silence the truth. But it will never succeed in overturning history. It can, at best, impose a version that some will pretend to believe, depending on their beliefs or the advantages they hope to extract. But the truth will never be changed.

The courts have been created so people don't take justice into their own hands. There should not be powerful people who are beyond the reach of the law, because as soon as the law shuts its eyes to their misdeeds, everything is possible. Impunity is a privilege that takes us back to the Middle Ages. I am certainly naive if I believe in a system of justice where the arbitrary has no place, but what is a world where only power and money count, where conviction no longer plays a part, and where justice is but a word? I dare affirm that it is a world stripped of meaning, a world that is empty.

The appeal memorandum, drawn up my lawyer in support of our case, emphasizes some authenticated facts:

'[...]the power of attorney granted by Fritz Rosenfelder is signed in *Paris* [81] on 24 May1937, and his signature is authenticated by an officer of the law at the consulate in the presence of two witnesses, one of whom is a representative of the said consulate. Quite clearly the document which lists the persons present does not record the presence of Mrs Dürr, the beneficiary of the power of attorney.'

'Evidence that has come to light after the filing of the suit (French archives taken by the Germans, requisitioned by the Soviets and recently given back by the Russians) show that the day after 24 May 1937, 25 May 1937, Fritz Rosenfelder was granted by *the police authorities in Paris* authorization papers to stay in France.'

'Mrs Dürr, equipped with this mandate, will sign in the name of Fritz Rosenfelder [...], in Karlsruhe, on 20 January 1938, the bill of sale of the Rosenfelders' magnificent property situated in Karlsruhe at Wendstrasse 19 on behalf of the Badischer Gemeinde Versicherung Insurance Company (BGV), a company that exists to this day [...]. *The amount accrued has never been paid to the "sellers".*'

'Fritz Rosenfelder was forced to carry out a second bill of sale in Paris after the sale on 20 January 1938 [...] It thus

81 Author's emphasis.

appears that, after a purchase is evidently enacted on 20 January 1938, the proxy that Fritz Rosenfelder was forced to grant in Paris on 24 May 1937 served to dispossess him of his property situated in Germany, another was enacted in Paris. Thus *two actions to extort signatures were committed in Paris* with a clear awareness that these would be used in Germany.'

'The BGV company that "buys" this property on 20 January 1938 keeps it till 1954, the date at which it sells it on to the Haarfarben company represented by its managing director, the French citizen André Tondu. *It has kept ever since the amount it received on this occasion*[…]'

'We have learned after filing our suit that, in respect of the French authorities (a document from the Ministry of Finance and Industry), but not of the German authorities (there is no mention thereof in the Karlsruhe company register), *L'Oréal had a 100 per cent holding in the shares of Haarfarben*; this fact was also known within the enterprise as is evidenced by the CAP papers from the 1947–48 joint production committee of L'Oréal where the actions of André Tondu are specifically celebrated.'

The appeal memorandum addresses the two reasons forwarded by the court of first instance in order not to open the case ('not to proceed'). My lawyer appealed against this decision. He responded in great detail, supporting himself by reference to 'jurisprudence tradition', to articles in the Penal Code, by recalling the way events were interconnected. I won't inflict upon the reader this long legal deliberation. A few sentences will suffice for even a novice to understand that there are no grounds to reject the suit.

The French courts were not competent? Well, 'the competence of the examining magistrate derives from the fact that elements

constituting an infringement of the law took place in France', and this is clearly the case in respect of:
- The extortion of my grandfather's signature.
- The instruction given for the purchase of the stolen property.
- The retention, in France, by L'Oréal, of all or part of the proceeds of the stolen property, in other words, theft, by virtue of holding on to the financial gain accruing from this sale.

Could such acts be prescribed? The suit does not focus directly on 'the extorting of a signature', but on the receiving of the product that accrued from this extortion. Thus, 'the extortion of the signature belongs to the category of crimes of the moment, whereas the receiving of stolen goods belongs to the category of continuous crimes.' In this case, 'prescription' only begins to operate from the day when the holding – or profit – has ceased', which is, of course, not the case since the sum accruing from the sale of the house has never been paid to my mother.

Moreover, alongside the supporting evidence, the appeal memorandum demonstrates that 'the L'Oréal group continues [...] to profit from the income from a property the source of which it has always known to be fraudulent.'

In recent years, both in France and Europe, after the official recognition by the President of the French Republic of the responsibility of the French state in relation to the fate that befell Jews, there has been a considerable change of attitude in relation to the theft of Jewish goods in the Nazi era. Different companies have been publicly approached by Jews who, like us, have demonstrated, with supporting proof, that their family had been robbed. Most of these enterprises have apologized, and agreements have been reached to make reparations for the damage caused. They have not tried to shirk their responsibilities, no more than they have tried to shelter behind any pretence of prescription.

I love giving presents. The offering of gifts is one of the most beautiful things in life. But I choose to whom I give presents. Neither the BGV insurance company – apart from its Nazi past, it has held on to the war compensation my mother should have received – nor the Versorgung des Bundes und der Länder (the German State), nor L'Oréal and the Bettencourt couple deserve presents from me!

I am writing this at the end of January 2004. I have just learned that our appeal has been rejected, confirming the conclusions of the public prosecutor: 'outside the competencies of a French presiding magistrate'.

I am not surprised: I have already been told that the court of appeal very rarely contradicts the court of first instance. Now, it has to go to the Supreme . This decides only on the basis of the application of the law. My lawyer has already made contact with one of his colleagues, *maître* Charles Choucroy, a specialist in appeals to the Supreme Court. And if that is not enough, there is always the European Court of Human Rights. When I think of my mother, of all her suffering and of my decimated family, I tell myself that in any case I have no right to opt out.

For a long time I have wondered: 'Why us?' Why has this family, my family, apparently without a history, inherited such a fate? Moreover, I find it very difficult to accept that I should continue to share its fate. It is because we are Jews that what I have recorded has happened. I do not forget for one moment all those, be they Jewish or not, who suffer a fate similar to ours.

I should never have been able to discover the truth about my family, but deep within me a voice whispers that if I have, it is because life appears to be stronger than all the blankets some individuals would like to use to smother it. I only hope justice can emulate life.

Afterword for the English Edition

Pressure

I had finished the book. At least that is what I thought. I had to start preparing two operas in succession at the Bastille and was immersed in work. Nonetheless, I also needed a lot of time to correct my book in line with requests from my French publisher's lawyers. Words, sentences, turns of phrase had to be changed, and then more and yet more. I had to avoid the slightest possibility that they could accuse me of libel.

At the end of June I decided to go to Brazil and spend a few weeks with my family. The book was finally at the printers. Just before I left, the magazine *Challenger* announced my book would be published in September. This news must have triggered a number of more or less hidden chain reactions, and e-mails from my publisher kept me partly abreast of what was happening. The fact is that by the time of my return to Paris in August, he had decided not to send out extracts from the book before it was published.

It came out, was sent to the newspapers, and I was bombarded by requests for interviews. I was very pleased: the case was finally going to go public. Every journalist who contacted me said he had been convinced by the book's arguments, wanted to be the first to go into print on the subject and assured me that an article would appear in the next issue of his newspaper.

The interviews took place...the articles never appeared. What was wrong? Was pressure being put on the press to stop them from appearing? It was strange: so many requests for conversations that ended in silence.

By then only *Actualités juives* had published a long article. In the two months following its publication, I continued to give a large number of interviews that led to no better outcome than before. I was then contacted by *Le Parisien*. This time an article did appear, on 25 September 2004, revealing that my case would go to the Supreme Court on 12 October. This article also quoted remarks from *maître* Jean Veil, one of L'Oréal's lawyers, stating that all this 'was ridiculous'. It reminded me of gossip that friends had mentioned to me: apparently the rumour was going the rounds that I was 'raving'.

After the article in *Le Parisien*, requests for interviews kept coming in, but with no better results. A woman friend then suggested acting as an intermediary in order to make contact with the presenter of an important television programme. The day before our meeting, *maître* Michel Zaoui, L'Oréal's lawyer, rang my friend to dissuade her from helping me. Their conversation lasted three quarters of an hour. How did *maître* Zaoui find out that my friend had agreed to help me? Apart from my lawyer and myself, no one knew who my intermediary was. My publisher and press officer had been informed of the meeting with the programme producer, but not of my contact's identity. I then felt very acutely the power of L'Oréal and its representatives when it came to finding out information – and felt very uneasy as I imagined this huge network of hidden complicities. How could I struggle, get recognition for the rights of my family, in such conditions? *Maître* Zaoui even knew – he'd mentioned it to my friend – that my own lawyer had arranged a time to meet with a Jewish institution. He knew both the date and time. Yet only my lawyer and I held this information.

It is true that L'Oréal is one of the biggest advertisers in France, that lots of the media need this advertising manna, but I thought naively that in the country of Human Rights, an ethical attitude to news would triumph over any other consideration.

I had to change my tune. More interviews…still no articles. A few journalists were polite enough to tell me of the difficulties they were experiencing in getting their articles into print but could state nothing in public. And at the same time, although I was aware of lots of things, I couldn't say anything either without risking that I myself might be sued for libel.

A few days before 12 October, the date of the hearing of the appeal at the Supreme Court, requests for interviews came fast and furious: for the eight o'clock news on France 2, for I-télé, for France info, France inter… On this occasion, the radio channels did broadcast the interviews with me: on 12 October.

My lawyer and I went to the Supreme Court. I was extremely nervous. There were lots of journalists. Louis di Gardia, the chief public prosecutor at the court, spoke and said that the law as it stood did allow a connection to be established between the extortion of my grandfather's signature, committed in France, and the theft of property that took place on German soil. Consequently, a judge who was competent to try the first crime would be able to pursue the second according to the present jurisprudence of the court.

I got the impression that he had carried out significant research and had plumbed to a deeper level legally, and consequently I was optimistic. While he spoke, tears came to my eyes. I told myself that finally the prejudice suffered by my family would be recognized, that all these years of denials would soon be a thing of the past. I thought particularly of my mother. Our right had been recognized by the most important public prosecutors in the French legal system.

Louis di Gardia made it clear that the signature extorted from my grandfather had been in exchange for the right given to his family to leave Nazi Germany and come to live in France – so that their lives would not be under threat. Louis di Gardia concluded by demanding firstly that the decision of the Court of Paris to reject French legal competency should be revoked, and secondly that the case be opened, on an understanding that the extortion of the signature and stealing of our house were interconnected. We were then informed that the appeal would be heard on 9 November.

That evening, my lawyer and I featured on the eight o'clock news. The telephone went on ringing till very late; I even felt able to answer all the calls. My mother was delighted; she even said she could now start to feel happy. I also immediately sensed that life would never be the same. I suddenly felt fine. Well, just the same as everybody else, that is. As if we had suddenly been given the right to exist. When she learned of the date when the Supreme Court would declare its ruling, my mother reminded me that *Kristallnacht*, the massacre of Jews organized by Goebbels and Himmler in Nazi Germany, took place on 9 November 1938. But that didn't sour our optimism.

The day after my lawyer called to alert me to an article in *Le Monde*: a very good, clear article, telling the facts. The journalist recalled how a few months earlier *maître* Veil had stated that this was all quite ridiculous. Now, whatever happened, nobody could accuse us of being spinners of tall stories. We had made considerable progress!

However, I started to grow anxious again. The most diverse people comforted me: how could I doubt the outcome? The court would follow the guidance of the chief public prosecutor: that should be obvious! His arguments were rock solid. The case would be opened! I replied that I was too familiar with the ways of the L'Oréal people…and that powerful people wield lots of power.

Pandora's Box

I had to spend several weeks in Toulouse, where a production of Donizetti's opera *Lucia di Lammermoor* was being restaged. My contract indicated that preparations would continue to 16

November. But I couldn't possibly envisage being away from Paris on 9 November. I had to negotiate: I should finish preparations on the seventh and return to Toulouse on the tenth for the dress rehearsal with piano: namely, a rehearsal with costumes, make-up, lights and technical support but without the orchestra, with the music played by piano.

So I didn't have very long for rehearsals. A fresh problem cropped up every day: some singers fell ill, others hadn't worked out their previous contracts... But nothing undermined my good spirits, and I felt happy in a way I rarely do. I even felt I was another person physically: I suffer seriously from asthma but didn't have a single attack.

Louis di Gardia had restored my confidence in the system of justice.

As soon as I returned to Paris on 8 November, I was yet again in demand for interviews. I was mainly contacted by legal journalists, and they were very positive in their opinions: the Supreme Court would quash the first ruling and the case would be tried.

When I arrived in the courtroom on the ninth, I felt a great unease. On the previous occasion, the Supreme Court judges had looked me straight in the eye as they took their places. This time, I had the impression that they lowered their eyes as soon as I looked at them. I told myself not to be so silly: I was being really childish! And I looked elsewhere.

And the verdict was given. I could not believe my ears! It was as if the chief public prosecutor at the Supreme Court had never spoken, had never asked for the appeal to be endorsed. My lawyer blanched. I myself felt that night had suddenly descended. I couldn't prevent myself from whispering: 'But who can have intervened?' Of course, I would never get an answer to that question. And even if I did, no interference was necessary: the judges quite simply preferred not to open Pandora's Box.

We should bear in mind that if collaboration began officially in 1940, when the Nazis arrived in France, Eugène Schueller had been actively supporting Nazi ideology from 1935 and had behaved in like fashion. And that from 1937, civil servants in the Ministry of the Interior and Prefecture of Police had straightforwardly collaborated with the German government so the abject exchange of our home could be expedited in return for a residence permit for members of my family who had stayed in Germany so they could live safely in France. They were duped by this agreement since it didn't even save their lives.

France had to wait fifty years to hear the voice of Jacques Chirac recognize its responsibility in the persecution of Jews under the Vichy regime. The country forgot, however, that some people started collaborating well before. The sores are still running, and they try to conceal them. For appearance's sake! L'Oréal is the biggest company in France, one of the country's shop windows. People prefer their shop windows clean. Nevertheless, L'Oréal's dark past is no longer a secret. But money…and power…

I had already heard the two arguments given by the court in order to throw out our appeal: the territorial incompetence of the French judiciary and prescription. Nonetheless, Louis di Gardia, the chief public prosecutor, had demonstrated very clearly before the Supreme Court that there was no basis in law for either.

This is what I call deception. The 'new jurisprudence' breaks totally with legal precedent, and my lawyers were unfairly deprived of the opportunity to voice their opposition: neither the report drawn up by Counsellor Vallat, the recorder at the Supreme Court, nor the address given by Louis di Gardia could lead one to anticipate the court's final ruling. Hypocrisy goes hand in hand with deception: before 1995, France hadn't officially recognized its responsibility in the persecution of the Jews by the Vichy government. Then in 1995 France finally recognized its responsibility. Yet, in the ensuing months, when a case should have been opened, the French justice system concluded it was too late! Before 1995, it was too soon; after, it was too late. France doesn't want to clean its doorstep. It prefers to lecture others.

I had the feeling I no longer existed. As if the refusal to open our case were a sentence against us. They were sentencing my mother to live eternally with the Holocaust, while the family and company of the people presumed responsible for these sufferings had managed to bury the case.

As I left, journalists fired questions at me. I was tremendously disappointed. I made a statement that came straight from the heart: 'We are unimportant, and the L'Oréal people are very important. I really wonder whether France is the country of Human Rights or the country of rights for those who have money and power!'

I felt that some of the journalists were shocked, or at least moved by what had just happened. They were very kind towards me. Some said don't let it stop here, take it to the European Court of Human Rights, don't let things stay as they are. At the time, I didn't know what to think: I had completely lost my confidence in the legal system.

I had to go home, pack my suitcase and catch the plane to Toulouse. But hours passed by, and I couldn't move. Friends kept ringing, but I was like a spectre. My whole body was in pain, and I felt I was living a nightmare. I decided to leave very early in the morning: I wasn't in a fit state to travel. As I closed my eyes, I recalled the words of the president of the court, and it was the face of Captain Dreyfus that came to me.

Support

In Toulouse I had to be straight back on my feet. I had to direct a hundred colleagues in an opera. From time to time someone in the choir or in the technical team would say: 'You're the only person on the radio and telly at the moment.' Some journalists had recorded my reaction on leaving the Supreme Court and had broadcast it. My spirits were raised by the people who came and said: 'Don't let it drop, you must continue.'

When I told my mother of the outcome, she also asked: 'Is there any other way out of this?'

'Yes, there is the European Court of Human Rights.'

'Well, we must concentrate on the European Court, as long as there is a way out, there's hope.'

It is at moments like this that I understand how she could have survived an experience like the Holocaust. I knew she had taken it very badly, but as far as she was concerned, we had to go on. We owed it to all those who were no longer there.

In the days that followed, more and more telephone calls and e-mails urging me to carry on. But where was I going to find the strength to continue? I had no energy left. And what was worse, I had lost one very important ally: the belief I had held till then that justice exists. This was what shocked me most. I had lived my whole life believing in values like honesty, justice and so on. How could I continue to resist if I no longer believed in them?

I needed time to gather my strength. Work was a big help: I had to get things moving. The music brought more consolation than ever before, and I was working with very talented people, people with convictions, and you could feel that in their commitment. But nights were very difficult. I got endless calls. From Brazil, from Paris, from Toulouse, from everywhere. People knew I was very fragile and didn't leave me alone for very long.

When I returned to Paris, e-mails and messages of support were waiting for me, and some suggested setting up a support committee. Members of the Culture Commission of B'nai Brith said they wanted to be behind the support committee; a website was started, and more than a thousand signatures were collected in two weeks, it still operates today: http://www.lorealapris.com

Poison

For its part, L'Oréal went back on the offensive. In an article that appeared in an American magazine, *Christian Science Monitor*, L'Oréal states that 'the family has already been compensated'. Always the same old tune to make us sound as if we were dishonest! With variations:

sometimes, the house purchase had been settled before the war; at others, the settlement was agreed by a Jewish association after the war. We should spell things out clearly.

There were in effect Jews who were forced to sell their property and who received a derisory payment in the Nazi era. Nevertheless, in such cases, the tribunals have always ruled that this property was stolen, and compensation has been paid. Now my family was paid nothing at all in the Nazi era. *Rien du tout*! Zero! *Niente*! *Nada*! Nothing!

As for the Jewish institution that we have already discussed in this book, things are also quite clear. Except that this implies that Jews were themselves responsible for the robbery: a contemptible subtext. Of course, L'Oréal is never to blame!

The Jewish organization that was indeed contacted after the war had taken care to indicate, in article three of the agreement reached with BGV, that if the previous rightful owners presented themselves, the agreement would be rendered null and void[82]. The fact is we are here. The family is the one my mother was able to create, and that was after the robbery. I was born at the end of 1953 and my brother in 1952. We are the rightful owners – everybody else is dead – and none of us has ever received anything. *Ever*.

With hindsight, one might think that this association should have undertaken the search for the rightful owners. But we ought to point out that this association was acting in an emergency situation to try to resolve all the problems flowing from the Holocaust in Germany. People who had disappeared, survivors without resources, property that had been stolen... And at the time there was no fax or Internet; even the telephone wasn't so common. Only six months! Hence, the precaution taken in article three of the agreement, so that possible lawful owners could recover what was owed to them. L'Oréal bought my family's house in full knowledge of all of this. Because I don't think it was a

---

82 See the agreement, Appendix 8.

chance thing that my mother found it so difficult to get hold of documents concerning the ownership of the house over all these years. I also recall that their contract of purchase explicitly noted that it was a stolen house[83].

In any case, today L'Oréal can no longer plead ignorance to these facts: that this house belonged to us, that its pseudo-sale is the result of blackmail and that reparations have never been made for this theft. L'Oréal nevertheless still continues at every point to search for excuses to avoid accepting its responsibilities. That is what I find most shameful. Rather than trying to find a human solution, they do everything to leave us out of account.

The only truth is that this house was stolen from us during Nazi rule because we are Jewish. And 'the family', as they say, the family no longer exists. They are dead. Only their descendants remain: we, the lawful owners.

L'Oréal prevents us from turning the page, from regaining our peace of mind, from letting all those who did not return rest in peace.

It is no use at all saying 'Never again!' and refusing to settle the dramas of the past. Problems aren't settled by speeches. But by deeds.

Europe was the cradle for all this barbarism. It has a duty to look its past in the face if it is to build its future and realize promises of a Europe at peace with itself and with others. This peace can only come with justice.

That is what I now expect from the European Court of Human Rights.

83 See Appendix 6.

Epilogue

CENTRAL CONSISTORY
Union of Jewish Communities of France
The President

Paris, 9 November 2005

Madame Monica WEITZFELDER
2, Place Charles Bernard
75018 PARIS

Dear Monica,

I would like to confirm via this letter that I am completely in support of the case you are fighting in order to recover the building situated in Karlsruhe and which was acquired at a time when the arrangements were not really clear by the L'Oréal Company situated in Clichy, near Paris.

I not only confirm that I am completely in support of your just cause but that I am ready to contact L'Oréal or other third parties to help you in this process.

Please keep me informed of the stage reached by your researches and procedure and, dear Monica, be assured of my continued interest in this matter.

Yours faithfully
Jean Kahn

Appendices

Chronology

1930. André Tondu is mandated by Eugène Schueller to found Haarfarben und Parfümerien GmbH in Berlin.

24 May 1937. Power of attorney signed in Paris under constraint by Fritz Rosenfelder in favour of Mrs Luise Dürr.

25 May 1937. Paris Prefecture grants permission to stay to Fritz Rosenfelder and to bring his family to France.

January 1938. The house at Wendstrasse 19 passes into the hands of the Badischer Gemeinde Versicherung Verband (BGV).

1945. André Tondu, mandated by Eugène Schueller, transfers Haarfarben und Parfümerien GmbH to Karlsruhe (L'Oréal Germany whose head office was 14 rue Royale, Paris).

1 January 1949. End of administrative restrictions imposed by the Allies on Jewish property stolen by the Nazis.

February 1949. André Tondu, director of Ensa, and representing Eugène Schueller for Haarfarben und Parfümerien GmbH (L'Oréal Germany), buys from Mrs Pfeiffer the building at Wendstrasse 17, adjacent to Wendstrasse 19.

5 November 1951. New bill of sale for the same Wendstrasse 17, between Mrs Pfeiffer and André Tondu for Ensa (still representing Haarfarben und Parfümerien GmbH, L'Oréal Germany). The same day BGV and a Jewish association, the JRSO, reach an agreement on Wendstrasse 19, without contacting Edith Rosenfelder-Waitzfelder and Karl Rosenfelder. Also that same day André Tondu,

on behalf of Haarfarben und Parfümerien GmbH (L'Oréal Germany), buys Kaiserallee 18, also adjacent to our house at Wendstrasse 19.

1954. BGV sells our house, Wendstrasse 19, to Haarfarben und Parfümerien GmbH (L'Oréal Germany). The bill of sale indicates that the house was property stolen in the Nazi era.

May 1991. The Frydman affair becomes public knowledge; the dark years of L'Oréal come to the surface.

June 1991. L'Oréal sells Wendstrasse 19 (our house) to the Versorgung des Bundes und der Länder.

Spring 2000. Copy of the land registry deeds of Karlsruhe sent to the Rosenfelder-Waitzfelder family.

June 18 2001. Our lawyer, *Maître* Korman, informs L'Oréal that the heir Edith Rosenfelder-Waitzfelder requests the return of the property stolen from her.

June 2001. Our lawyer, *Maître* Korman informs BGV and the Versorgung des Bundes und der Länder that the heir Edith Rosenfelder-Waitzfelder requests the return of the property stolen from her.

12 July 2001. First reply from Mr Owen-Jones on behalf of L'Oréal.

August 2001. Replies from the BGV and from the Versorgung des Bundes und der Länder.

28 December 2001. *Maître* Korman files a suit against theft in the name of his client, Edith Rosenfelder-Waitzfelder.

March 2006. L'Oréal buys the British Body Shop chain for £652 million (€940 million)

The ROSENFELDER-WAITZFELDER Family

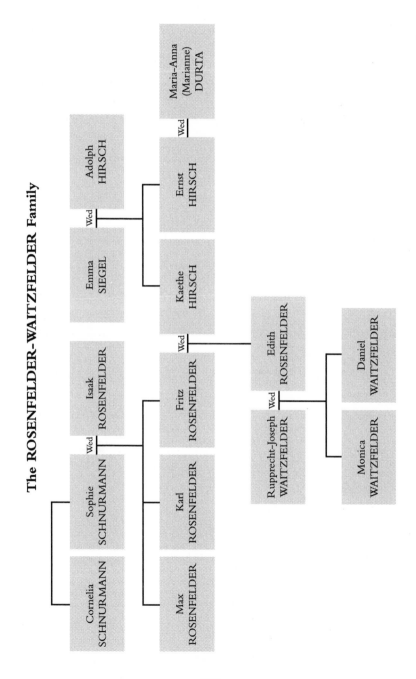

Copy of the Title Deeds in the Karlsruhe Property Registry

Abteilung

Wert.	Zeit und Grund des Erwerbs.	Eigentümer.

The name Rosenfelder is clearly legible.

3				
4	Haarfarben und Parfümerien, Ge-sellschaft mit beschränkter Haf-tung in Karlsruhe.	Aufgelassen am 9.Juni 1954 und eingetragen am 23.September 1954.(AS)		

Translation

Entry	Owner	Date and reason for purchase	Value
1.	2.	3.	4.
		Entry in old Title Deeds	Purchase Price 26,600 Marks
1.	KIRCHENBAUER [Illegible]	Volume 90, page 918,n° 123 31 March 1900, (A.S.$^{1}/_{4}$)t	Suppl. Fire Insurance: 59,000 Marks 108.100 Marks
2.	Sofia, maiden name SCHURNMANN, Widow of the private individual Isaak ROSENFELDER here	entry listed 2 April 1919 and re-entered 9 May 1919 (A.S:141//158)	Valued by the Court 19 April 1901: 88,000 Marks (A.S.19) [illegible] 136.000 Marks (cf.A.S.29)
3.	The Badischer Gemeinde – Versicherungs Verband Insurance Company Access blocked! (Section II,Number 4)	entry listed 15 March and re-entered 23 May 1938 (AS 285/86)	Valued by the Court 20 June 1904: 144,000 Marks (AS 71/V) Fiscal value 1907: 9,145,000 Marks
4.	The Haarfarben und Parfümerien, Gesellshaft mit beschränkter Haftung Company (hair colouring products and perfumery articles), Karlsruhe	entry listed 9 June 1954 and re-entered 23 September 1954 (AS 325)	Fiscal value [illegible] 345,800 Marks KV (A.S:163)
	Closed		

Extract from the Entry from the Registry of Births for Edith Rosenfelder, Dated 1952, Sent by the Karlsruhe Town Hall

Geburtsurkunde

(Standesamt ..... Karlsruhe — — — — — — — — — 1354/1923 ..... Nr. .....).

— — — Edith Karla R o s e n f e l d e r — — —

ist am ..... 2. Juli 1923 — — — — — — — — — — — — — —

in ..... Karlsruhe — — — — — — — — — — — — — — — geboren.

Vater: ..... Doktor der rechte Fritz Rosenfelder, —

Rechtsanwalt, wohnhaft in Karlsruhe — — — — — — —

Mutter: ..... Käthe Henriette Rosenfelder, geborene

Hirsch, wohnhaft in Karlsruhe — — — — — — — — —

Änderungen der Eintragung: .....

Karlsruhe ..... 30. September 2 ....., den ..... 195...

Der Standesbeamte: ..... *[signature]*

[round official seal: STANDESAMT KARLSRUHE]

[round seal: Elisabeth Lichter Dipl.-Übersetzerin, öffentlich bestellt und beeidigter Urkundenübersetzer der französischen Sprache] 20.08.1997 *[signature]*

The entry doesn't record the death of Edith Rosenfelder, whereas the entry for her mother Kaethe Rosenfelder does record hers.

Letter from Fritz Rosenfelder 22 December 1937

[...]

Fritz Rosenfelder states that he received his residence card, issued by the Police Prefecture in Paris on 25 May 1937, the day after he signed the power of attorney at the German Consulate in Paris.

Translation

Paris 8e. 22.12.37
21 rue de Miromesnil

Dear Minister,

I the undersigned, Dr Fritz Rosenfelder, born in Munich (Germany), 20 June 1894 formerly resident in Karlsruhe (Baden) Wendstr.19 and resident in Paris 8 21 rue de Miromesnil is honoured to request from you the renewal for unlimited stay in France of identity card n° 36 HC 21088 issued by the Police Prefecture in Paris 25 May 1937. This card expires 8 January next

Dr Fritz Rosenfelder

Power of Attorney Signed Under Constraint in Paris 24 May
at the German Consulate

A b s c h r i f t .

G e n e r a l v o l l m a c h t .

Paris, den 24. Mai 1937.   ))

Ich bestelle hierdurch Frau Luise Dürr, Karlsruhe
(Baden), Viktoriastrasse zu meiner Generalbevollmächtigten und
ermächtige sie zur Besorgung aller meiner Angelegenheiten.

Sie soll befugt sein, jedes Rechtsgeschäft und jede
sonstige Rechtshandlung, welche ich selbst vornehmen könnte, und
bei welchen eine Stellvertretung gesetzlich zulässig ist, an meiner Statt und mit derselben Wirkung vorzunehmen, als ob ich die
Handlung selbst vorgenommen hätte.

Die Bevollmächtigte soll auch befugt sein, für meine
Rechnung Versicherungen jeder Art zu nehmen, allgemeine und beson-
dere Bevollmächtigte jeder Art und zu allen Geschäften zu be-
stellen sowie auch die Gesamtheit der ihr nach dieser Vollmacht
zustehenden Befugnisse auf einen anderen zu übertragen.

Die genannte Generalbevollmächtigte soll alle ihnen
vorstehend übertragenen Befugnisse auszuüben befugt sein.

Die vorstehend erteilte Vollmacht soll durch meinen
Tod nicht erlöschen.

gez. Dr. Fritz Rosenfelder.

Verhandelt Paris, den 24. Mai 1937.   ))

Der den unterzeichneten Gesandtschaftsrat Dr. Bräutigam
durch Vorlage seines Reisepasses Nr. 2508, Polizeipräs. Karlsruhe
8.VII.33/38, ausgewiesene Reichsangehörige Dr. Fritz Rosenfelder,
z.Zt. Paris, gegen dessen Verfügungsfähigkeit kein Bedenken
obwaltet, legte das vorstehende Schriftstück vor und erklärte mit
dem Antrage auf Beglaubigung, dass er die darunter befindliche
Unterschrift Dr. Fritz Rosenfelder zum Zeichen der Genehmigung
selbst geschrieben habe.

Translation

<u>Copy</u>

<u>Power of attorney</u>

Paris, 24 May 1937

I designate herewith Madame Luise DÜRR, Karlsruhe (Bade), Viktoriastrasse, as my legal representative with full powers of attorney authorising her to deal with all my business.

She is thus authorized to sign any legal paper that I could sign myself and for which the law authorizes her to represent me legally and to act in my name, giving these papers the same validity they would have if I had signed them myself.

My representative is thus equally authorized to contract, on my behalf, in whatever way, to give general or special powers to any legal representative in order to sign any legal act, as well as to transfer all the rights that issue from the present letter to a third person.

The representative designated herewith, having powers of attorney, is authorized to exercise all the above-mentioned rights.

The power of attorney will remain valid after my death.

Signed Dr Fritz Rosenfelder

Made in Paris, 24 May 1937.

The present document was presented to the delegated legal officer signed here below Dr BRÄUTIGAM, on the presentation of passport n° 2508, issued by the *Polizeipräsium* [police headquarters] Karlsruhe 8.VIII.33/38 belonging to the citizen of the Reich Dr Fritz ROSENFELDER, presently living in Paris and in full possession of his legal rights; Dr Fritz ROSENFELDER has stated, when requesting the legalizing of this document, that the signature 'Dr Fritz ROSENFELDER' placed at the end of the document endorsing its approval has been written by his own hand.

Bill Ceding the Rosendfelder Property, Wendstrasse 19,
to the Badischer Gemeinde Verband (BGV),
Issued Under the Nazi Regime

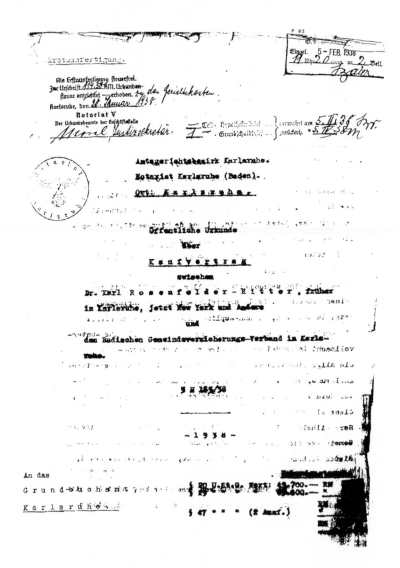

Die Übereinstimmung vorstehender Abschrift mit der vor-
gelegten und wieder zurückgegebenen Urschrift wird beglaubigt.

Karlsruhe, den 20. Januar 1938.

Notariat 5

Justizrat   ,als Notar.

Last page of the bill of concession to the BGV in 1938 complete
with the swastika of the Third Reich

Transfer of the Property on 29 June 1954 from the BGV
to Haarfarben, Signed by André Tondu

A u s f e r t i g u n g .

Amtsgerichtsbezirk Karlsruhe

Notariat Karlsruhe (Baden)

Ort: K a r l s r u h e .

Öffentliche Urkunde

über

K a u f v e r t r a g

zwischen

Badischen Gemeindeversicherungsverband, öffentliche
Körperschaft in Karlsruhe

und

Firma Haarfarben und Parfümerien, Gesellschaft
mit beschränkter Haftung in Karlsruhe.

— IV H 789/54 —

- - - - - - - - - - - -

Jahr 1954.

An das
G r u n d b u c h a m t ,
K a r l s r u h e

eingetragen:
Badischer Gemeindeversicherungsverband in Karlsruhe.

Reichsmark-Rechte wurden nach dem 20. Juni 1948 in der III. Abt.
nicht gelöscht. Eine Hypothekengewinnabgabe ruht somit auf dem
Grundstück nicht. Bezüglich des Eigentums des Grundstücks war ein
Rückerstattungsverfahren anhängig, das erledigt wurde, sodaß der
derzeitige Eigentümer voll verfügungsberechtigt ist.

[...]

Die Ansprüche aus Kriegssachschaden verbleiben in voller Höhe dem
Verkäufer.

[...]

gez. Wilhelm Krause
"   André Tondü
gez. Kammer.

Translation

is registered under the name of:
Badischer Gemeindeversicherungsverband in Karlsruhe.

According to section III, the rights to convert the Reichsmark were registered
after 20 June 1948. Consequently, the terrain is free of any tax on profits from the
mortgage. A restitution procedure was begun concerning the ownership of this
property: the file has been closed, so that the present owner is fully entitled to
dispose of the property.

[...]

The compensation rights owed to victims of the war remain entirely within the
possession of the vendor.

[...]

Signed Wilhelm KRAUSE
Signed André TONDU
Signed KAMMER

[...]

Bill of Sale of the Lot Contiguous to Wendstrasse 19, 25 February 1954 on Behalf of Ensa, Renewed 5 November 1951

– A u s f e r t i g u n g –

Amtsgerichtsbezirk Karlsruhe

Notariat Karlsruhe (Baden)

Ort: K a r l s r u h e

Öffentliche Urkunde

über

A u f l a s s u n g

u.a. zu Kaufvertrag vom 25. Februar 1949 ✓))

zwischen

der Firma "Ensa G.m.b.H. für Chemie und Kosmetik"in Karlsruhe,

u n d

Frau Lina N a g e l geb. Pfeifer in Karlsruhe.

– I H 2516/51 –

Jahr 1951.

An das

Grundbuchamt

K a r l s r u h e

nebst 6% Zinsen nach näherer Massgabe der oben für das Restkauf-
geld festgelegten Zahlungsbedingungen, zu Gunsten von Frau Lina
Nagel geb. Pfeifer.

S c h l u s s :

Ausfertigungen sollen erhalten:

a) die Beteiligten,

b) das Grundbuchamt Karlsruhe.

Hierüber Urkunde,

auf Vorlesen von den Anwesenden genehmigt und von ihnen und
dem Notar, wie folgt, eigenhändig unterschrieben:

gez. André Tendu

" Dr. Friedrich Nagel

gez. Deimling, Notar.

— — — — — — — —

Diese Ausfertigung der amtlich zu verwahrenden
Urschrift ist richtig.

Ausgefertigt für das Grundbuchamt

K a r l s r u h e

zum Eintrag gegen Vollzugsanzeige.

Verzichtserklärung des Finanzamtes Karlsruhe vom 21.12.5o ist ange-
schlossen.

Karlsruhe, den 5. November 1951
Notariat I Karlsruhe

Oberjustizrat   als Notar.

Translation

Copy

District of the Court of First Instance of Karlsruhe

Office of the Karlsruhe notary (Baden)

Place: Karlsruhe

Official note

concerning

the entry into the property register

among others concerning the bill of sale of 25 February 1949

between

the company "Ensa Gm.b.H. für Chemie und Kosmetik" at Karlsruhe.

and

Mrs Lina NAGEL, née PFEIFER, at Karlsruhe.

IH 2516/51

Year 1951

A: Property Register
Karlsruhe

188

as well as 6% interest according to the conditions of payment of the outstanding sum of the purchase price defined above, in favour of Mrs Lina NAGEL, née PFEIFER

Conclusion:

A copy will be sent:

to those party to the contract,
to the Property Registry of Karlsruhe.

Bill established,

Read, approved and personally signed by the persons here present as follows

Signed André TONDU,
Signed Dr Friedrich NAGEL

Signed DEIMLING, notary.

This copy of the original co-signed bill is complete.

Made for the property registry
of Karlsruhe

to be entered on notification of completion.

The statement of waiving of rights from the Ministry of Finance (the treasury office) of Karlsruhe of 21 December 1950 is attached.

Karlsruhe, 5 November 1951*
Notary's Office of Karlsruhe

Legal officer [illegible signature], as notary.
[Stamp of the Karlsruhe notary's office]

[Stamp of the Karlsruhe notary's office]

[handwritten: illegible]

---

* French translator's note: This bill begins with the declaration 'Made in Karlsruhe, 26 October 1951', whereas the date of the signature on the present page is 5 November 1951.

Document Concerning the Settlement on 5 November 1951 Between a Jewish Organization and the BGV Authorizing the Latter to Dispose of Wendstrasse 19

Amtsgericht Karlsruhe   Karlsruhe, den 5.November 51
Schlichter f.Wiedergutmachung

Resi E (IRSO) 1045

Gegenwärtig:

Landgerichtsrat Hempel   In Sachen
als Schlichter,
                                        der Jewish Restitution Successor Organi-
Justizangestellte Harder   zation, Inc., New.York, (IRSO)
als Urkundsbeamter
                                                        Antragstellerin –
                                        (Verf.: Dr.Fritz Rosenfelder und Dr.Karl
                                                Rosenfelder-Ritter)

                                                        g e g e n

                                        den Bad.Gemeindevers.Verband-öffentl.
                                        rechtlicher Körperschaft in Karlsruhe

                                                        Antragsgegner

                                        wegen Rückerstattung des Grundstücks
                                        Lgb.Nr. 525 oe, (Wendstr. 19) in Karlsruhe

sind erschienen:

1.) für die IRSO Herr Dr. R i e d e l aus Mannheim als Allge-
    meinbevollmächtigter der IRSO

2.) für den Antragsgegner Herr Dir. Wilhelm K r a u s e aus
    Karlsruhe, Barbarossaplatz 2,

eine Bestätigung über seine Vertretungsbefugnis vom 21.8.1950
zur Einsicht vorlegend.

Die Beteiligten nahmen Bezug auf die Sitzungsniederschrift v.
26.5.1951 und einigten sich hierauf im Wege des

                                    V e r g l e i c h s

gütlich dahin:

1.) Der Antragsgegner verpflichtet sich, an die IRSO zur Abfindung
    deren Ansprüche 5000,— Deutsche Mark umgehend nach Rechts-
    wirksamwerden des Vergleichs zu bezahlen.

2.) Im Hinblick auf diese Zahlung verbleibt der Antragsgegner im
    Eigentum des Grundstücks Wendstr. 19.

3.) Die IRSO verpflichtet sich, den Antragsgegner bis zur Höhe von
    5000,— Deutsche Mark schadlos zu halten, falls sich noch
    Besserberechtigte melden sollten, die den Antragsgegner mit Er-
    folg in Anspruch nehmen, vorausgesetzt, dass der Antragsgegner
    sich den Weisungen der IRSO entsprechend verhält.

4.) Etwaige Ansprüche gegen das frühere Deutsche Reich oder seinen
    Rechtsnachfolger wegen Kriegssachschädenansprüchen verbleiben
    dem Antragsgegner.

5.) Durch diese Einigung sind sämtliche Ansprüche der Beteiligten,
    soweit sie mit dem Erwerb oder Rückgewähr des Grundstücks im
    Zusammenhang stehen, abgegolten.

                                                            ./.

6.) Die außergerichtlichen Kosten werden wettgeschlagen.

7.) Die IHSO behält sich Widerruf dieses Vergleichs bis 5. Dezember 1951 vor.

Vorgelesen,   genehmigt,   unterschrieben:

gez. Riedel   gez. Krause

gez. Hempel

gez. Kärcher

Ausgefertigt

Karlsruhe, den 6. Dez. 1951

Schlichter für die Wiedergutmachung
beim Amtsgericht Karlsruhe
Der Urkundsbeamte der Geschäftsstelle

(Just.Angest.)

Gemeinde Versicherungsverband

Karlsruhe

There is no Rosenfelder signature.

191

Translation

<u>Agreement</u>
<u>Copy</u>

Karlsruhe Court of First Instance   Karlsruhe, 5 November 1951
Negotiator responsible for Reparation Affairs
<u>Rest</u> <u>K</u> <u>(IRSO)</u> <u>1045</u>

In the presence of:
Mrs Hempel, Member of the High Court
acting as negotiator

Marder, court employer and recorder
In the case opposing
The Jewish Restitution Successor Organization, Inc.,
New York (JRSO)
- claimants -
(victim of persecution: Dr.Fritz Rosenfelder and Dr. Karl
Rosenfelder-Ritter)
to the:
Bad. Gemeindevers.Verband, legally established company,
in Karlsruhe
- defendant -
for the restitution of the property entered under land
register number 525 a (Wendstr. 19) in Karlsruhe.

there appeared:
1. for the JRSO: Dr. Reidel, from Mannheim, in his position as general agent for
   the JRSO;
2. for the defendant: Director Wilhelm KRAUSE, residing in Karlsruhe,
   Barbarosatzplatz   2;
   who presented a statement certifying his capacity to represent, dated 21/08/1950.
   Those present, referring to the minutes of the hearing of 26/06/1951,
   reached a settlement by means of an
Agreement
as follows:
1. The defendant agrees to pay the JRSO, as soon as the agreement has become
   legal and binding, the sum of 5000 German marks as compensation.
2. Consequent on this payment, the defendant retains ownership of the land on
   Wendtstr.19.

3. The JRSO agrees, provided that the defendant acts in accordance with the instructions of the JRSO, to exonerate the defendant to the extent of 5000 DM, if the case arises where the legal owners should make themselves known and validly contest the defendant.

4. The possible rights against the former German Reich, or its successor, in terms of war compensation, fall to the defendant.

5. The present agreement relieves the parties of all their interests in relation to the purchase or restoration of the land.

6. The non-legal expenses will be paid between the parties concerned.

7. The JRSO reserves its right to withdraw from the present settlement to 5 December 1951.

Read, approved and signed:

Riedel   Krause   Hempel   Harder

Agreement reached
in Karlsruhe, 6 December 1951
Negotiator responsible for Reparation Affairs
at the Karlsruhe Court of First Instance
Secretary
[signature]

The settlement is null and void if the legal owners appear as set out in the conditions in clause 3.

9

Letter from Lindsay Owen-Jones 12 July 2001 to Edith Waitzfelder's Lawyer

L'ORÉAL

Clichy, le 12 juillet 2001

M. Charles Korman
Avocat au Barreau de Paris
66, avenue Kléber
75116 Paris

Maître,

La lettre du 18 juin 2001 que vous m'avez adressée à la demande de Mme Edith Rosenfelder, veuve Waitzfelder, a retenu toute mon attention.

Après m'avoir rappelé le sort subi pendant la dernière guerre par la famille Rosenfelder, juifs allemands persécutés par le régime nazi, vous m'exposez que la société que je préside aurait bénéficié d'un avantage indu que vous chiffrez à 60.556.726 DM (soit plus de 200.000.000 FF).

Vous précisez qu'en 1938 les parents de Mme Rosenfelder ont été contraints de vendre un immeuble à la compagnie d'assurances Badischen Gemeindeversicherungsverban. En 1954 (16 ans après la spoliation et 10 ans après la chute du 3ème Reich), la compagnie d'assurance a cédé le terrain nu (l'immeuble ayant été détruit pendant la guerre) à la société Haarfarben und Parfümerien GmbH, filiale allemande de L'Oréal. Cette filiale a acquis le terrain voisin et fait construire sur l'ensemble un immeuble de bureaux. Elle a revendu le tout en 1991. Vous analysez ces faits comme constitutifs d'un recel en France comme en Allemagne. L'Oréal SA aurait, selon votre opinion, commis ce délit du seul fait de sa perception des dividendes versés par sa filiale allemande.

Au-delà des accusations que vous proférez sans aucune réserve et qui me blessent personnellement, la demande que vous formulez sur un ton comminatoire inhabituel pour un avocat suscite de nombreuses questions, tant de fait que de Droit, qui ne sont, ni de pure forme, ni dilatoires.

A défaut de paiement au plus tard le 18 juillet 2001 de la somme de 200 millions de FF, vous m'indiquez avoir d'ores et déjà reçu instruction de déposer, entre les mains de M. le Doyen des juges d'instruction près le Tribunal de grande instance de Paris, une plainte avec constitution de partie civile pour recel d'extorsion de fonds à l'encontre de notre société et de ses filiales.

La Shoah représente pour moi, comme pour toute personne soucieuse des valeurs humaines, la tragédie absolue et ma compassion à l'égard des victimes est totale. Il est légitime que ces dernières demandent réparation, mais cela n'autorise pas à poursuivre sans fondement une personne physique ou morale. Or ma plus grande conviction est que L'Oréal n'a causé aucun tort à Mme Edith Rosenfelder. Aussi, ai-je demandé à vos confrères Michel Zaoui et Jean Veil de nous représenter et de procéder avec vous à une analyse juridiquement incontestable de la situation.

Je vous prie d'agréer, Maître, mes sentiments distingués.

Lindsay OWEN-JONES

Translation

L'ORÉAL

Clichy, 12 July 2001

M.Charles Korman
Lawyer at the Paris Bar
66, avenue Kléber
75116

Maître,

The letter of 18 June 2001 that you sent me concerning the request of Mrs Edith Rosenfelder, widow Waitzfelder, has exercised me greatly.

After reminding me of the fate suffered in the last war by the Rosenfelder family, German Jews persecuted by the Nazi regime, you tell me that the company I head must have benefited from an unwarranted income that you estimate at 605,567,26 DM (or more that 200,000,000 French francs).

You note that in 1938 the parents of Mrs Rosenfelder were forced to sell a property to the Badischen Gemeindeversicherungsverban insurance company. In 1954 (six years after the robbery and ten years after the fall of the Third Reich), the insurance company ceded the empty land (the building having been destroyed in the war) to Haarfarben und Parfümerien GmbH, the German subsidiary of L'Oréal. This subsidiary acquired the neighbouring lot and built an office block on the extended lot. It resold everything in 1991. You analyse these acts as constituting a theft both in France and Germany. L'Oréal would have, in your opinion, committed this crime via the simple act of receiving dividends as paid by its German subsidiary.

Apart the accusations that you make without any reservations whatsoever and which hurt me personally, the demand you formulate in threatening terms unusual for a lawyer suggest numerous questions, in matters of fact and law that are not purely a question of form, or of deferment.

If there is no payment at the latest by 18 July of the sum of 200 million French francs, you indicate that you have been requested forthwith to lodge with the Chief Public Prosecutor in the Paris Court of First Instance a law suit in terms of the receiving, retention and extortion of funds against our company and its subsidiaries.

The Shoah represents for me, as for anyone concerned with human values, an absolute tragedy and my compassion for the victims is unreserved. It is legitimate for the latter to seek reparation, but that gives no authority for the unwarranted pursuit of a physical or moral person. My deepest conviction is that L'Oréal has done no wrong to Mrs Edith Rosenfelder. On this basis, I have requested that your colleagues <u>Michel Zaoui and Jean Veil</u> represent us and proceed with you to a legally irrefutable analysis of the situation.

Yours sincerely,

Lindsay OWEN-JONES

10
Document Obtained from the Ministry of the Economy, Finance and Industry Where One Can Read: 'Haarfarben und Parfümerien GmbH-L'Oréal, Paris, 14 rue Royale – a 100% French company'

[...]

HAARFARBEN – u. PARFÜMERIE GmbH   L'OREAL,Paris,I4 rue Royale   20.000   I00 %
lin – Steglitz

Translation

PRINCIPAL INFORMATION IN ALPHABETICAL ORDER ON GERMAN COMPANIES WITH FRENCH INVESTMENT CREATED BEFORE <u>19 JUNE 1948</u> (MONETARY REFORM)

[…]

Haarfarben u.Parfumerien GmbH, L'Oréal, Paris, 14 rue Royale 20000 100%

11
Letter from Lindsay Owen-Jones Addressed to Edith Waitzfelder

L'ORÉAL

Clichy, le 4 octobre 2001

Madame Edith Waitzfelder

c/ Me Charles Korman
66, avenue Kléber
75116-Paris

c/ Madame Monica Waitzfelder
2, place Charles Bernard
75018-Paris

Madame,

Me Charles Korman m'a écrit en votre nom le 18 juin 2001 pour attirer mon attention sur votre situation et me demander de faire verser par le groupe que je préside un montant de 60.556.726 DM afin de vous indemniser de la spoliation dont vos parents ont été les victimes du fait du régime nazi.

Comme vous le savez, j'ai demandé à nos avocats de se rapprocher du vôtre pour prendre connaissance du dossier afin de pouvoir m'éclairer.

Je comprends que les faits qui sont à l'origine de cette affaire concernent l'achat en 1938 par une compagnie d'assurance allemande d'un immeuble situé à Karlsruhe en Allemagne et appartenant à vos parents alors citoyens allemands. En 1951, une association juive, légalement désignée pour se substituer aux juifs exterminés par le régime nazi, et votre oncle, rescapé de la Shoah, dont vous êtes l'héritière, ont contesté judiciairement cette acquisition puis ont signé avec la compagnie d'assurance une transaction qui a été homologuée par le Juge allemand des Restitutions, juridiction spécialisée mise en place par les Alliés après la guerre.

En 1954, l'agent de l'Oréal en Allemagne, dont le groupe a racheté les actions en 1961 seulement, a acquis le terrain qui portait les bâtiments détruits par les bombardements. Ce terrain a été intégré dans un ensemble plus vaste, revendu en 1991.

J'ai découvert cette situation à la lecture de la lettre de votre avocat et j'ignorais jusqu'à cet été que notre groupe avait détenu de 1961 à 1991 un immeuble construit sur des terrains dont l'un avait été la propriété de vos parents. Une spoliation constitue une atteinte intolérable aux droits de la personne humaine et doit certainement être réparée. Je suis personnellement attaché à ce que le groupe que je préside soit irréprochable. Dans le même temps, le mandat dont je suis investi m'interdit d'utiliser les fonds sociaux sans fondement et vous comprendrez certainement que je ne puisse envisager le paiement d'une somme de plus de 200 millions de francs au vu d'une réclamation dont tous les éléments n'auraient pas été préalablement vérifiés.

200

L'extrême complexité de la situation résultant de l'ancienneté des faits, de leur déroulement en Allemagne, de ce que trois propriétaires se sont succédés depuis la vente de 1938, de l'intervention passée d'une juridiction allemande statuant en droit allemand dont les règles me paraissent devoir continuer à s'appliquer, m'interdit encore de formuler une opinion définitive.

Pour me permettre d'apprécier votre demande, des vérifications et des consultations s'imposent. Il me semble notamment que les dossiers et les explications que pourraient fournir la compagnie d'assurance allemande, dont je présume qu'elle est également et en premier lieu votre interlocutrice puisqu'elle a détenu l'immeuble de 1938 à 1954, devraient permettre de mieux comprendre la situation.

Je ne voudrais pas que vous imaginiez que mon attitude est dictée par une volonté dilatoire, c'est pourquoi, c'est bien volontiers que je vous propose de participer aux frais que pourraient entraîner pour vous en Allemagne les recherches et les consultations nécessaires à l'instruction du dossier.

Si vous acceptez cette proposition qui a pour objet de vous aider dans votre recherche de la vérité, ce que je souhaite de tout cœur, vous voudrez bien me le faire savoir, soit directement, soit par l'intermédiaire de nos avocats respectifs qui auront pour mission d'en faciliter la mise en œuvre.

Je vous prie d'agréer, Madame, l'expression de mes sentiments distingués.

Lindsay OWEN-JONES

Translation

L'ORÉAL

Clichy, 4 October 2001

Madame Edith Waitzfelder

c/Me Charles Korman
66,avenue Kléber
75116-Paris

c/Madame Monica Waitzfelder
2, place Charles Bernard
75018-Paris

Madame,

Maître Charles Korman wrote to me in your name on 18 June in order to draw my attention to your situation and ask me to pay you on behalf of the group I head a total of 60,556,726 DM in order to compensate you for the robbery your parents were victims of as a result of the Nazi regime.

As you know, I asked our lawyers to contact yours in order to become acquainted with the case and be well informed thereon.

I understand that the actions that give rise to this affair concern the purchase in 1938 by a German insurance company of a building situate in Karlsruhe in Germany and belonging to your parents who were German citizens at the time. In 1951 a Jewish association, legally appointed to take the place of the Jews exterminated by the Nazi regime, and your uncle, a survivor from the Shoah, whose heir you are, legally challenged this acquisition and then signed an agreement with the insurance company which was endorsed by the German judge for Restitutions, a special judicial process put in place by the Allies after the war.

In 1954, the L'Oréal subsidiary <u>in Germany, in which the group bought back shares only in 1961</u>, acquired the land which included the buildings destroyed by bombing raids. This land was incorporated into a larger complex, and resold in 1991.

I have learned of this situation on reading the letter from your lawyer and I was unaware until this summer that <u>our group had owned from 1961 to 1991 a building</u> constructed on plots one of which had been your parents' property. A theft constitutes an intolerable attack on the rights of human beings and must certainly be redressed. I am personally committed to the group that I head being above reproach. At the same time, the mandate with which I am charged prevents me from using social funds without proper reason and you will certainly understand that I cannot envisage the payment of a sum of more than 200 million francs on sight of a claim in which every element has not been previously checked.

The extreme complexity of the situation resulting from the past nature of these acts, from their taking place in Germany, from the fact that there have been three owners since the sale in 1938, from the intervention made under German jurisdiction based on German law the rules of which I think must still continue to apply, prevent me from reaching a definitive conclusion.

In order to be able to consider your request, I need to check and consult. I believe in particular that the files and explanations that could be supplied by the German insurance company with which I assume you are also and primarily in contact since it owned the building from 1938 to 1954, should allow us a clearer understanding of the situation.

I would not want you to imagine my attitude is dictated by a desire to delay matters, that is why I am very happy to contribute towards the expenses you might accrue in Germany in your researches and consultations necessary for the preparation of your dossier.

If you accept this offer the aim of which is to help you in your search for the truth, which I sincerely desire, would you be so kind to let me know, either directly, or through the mediation of our respective lawyers who will be charged with putting this in place.

Yours sincerely,

Lindsay OWEN-JONES

BGV Internal Memorandum

BGV.   Karlsruhe, den 4.Juni 1951.

I. Aktenvermerk: Betr.: Hausgrundstück Wendtstr. 19.

Am 2.6.1951 teilte Herr Rechtsanwalt Dr.Sickinger fernmündlich
mit, dass Herr Dr.Karl Rosenfelder z.Zt. in Deutschland weile
u. ihm beauftragt habe, seinen Rückerstattungsanspruch aus dem
Hausbesitz Wendtstr. 19 gegen uns zu verfolgen. Er erkundigte sich
nach dem Stand der Angelegenheit und ich gab ihm Auskunft über die
Ablehnung der IRSO. Herr Dr.Sickinger wird veranlassen, dass Herr
Dr.Karl Rosenfelder sich umgehend mit der IRSO in Verbindung setzt
um zu erreichen, dass diese die Angelegenheit an ihn abgibt. Dann
soll gemeinsam die Frage geprüft werden, ob eine vergleichsweise
Erledigung angebracht und möglich ist. Sollte es nicht zu einem
Vergleich kommen, wird Herr Rechtsanwalt Dr.Sickinger das Mandat
gegen uns niederlegen, da er nicht gegen uns auftreten will.

II. Z.d.A.

Translation

BGV.

1. Memorandum for file

Subject: land built on Wendtstr. 19

On 02/06/1951, Mr Sickinger, lawyer, informed me by telephone that Dr Karl Rosenfelder presently resided in Germany and that he had charged him with establishing, against us, his right for restitution in relation to the property situate Wendstr, 19. He enquired how advanced this matter was, and I informed him of the rejection on the part of the JRSO. Mr Sickinger will make sure that Dr. Karl Rosenfelder gets into contact as soon as possible with the JRSO so that the latter can deal with the matter. Then it will be necessary to examine the whole business to decide if the settling of this issue by negotiation is opportune and possible. If an agreement proves impossible, Mr Sickinger will renounce his brief, for he has no wish to intervene against us.

II. attached to file

Letter Signed by *Maître* Sickinger,
Dating from September 1934 and Bearing the Swastika

Bund National-Sozialistischer Deutscher Juristen

Gau Baden ✦ Landesgerichtsbezirk Karlsruhe

Bezirksfachgruppe
Rechtsanwälte Karlsruhe.

S/He.

Anschrift
Bezirksfachgruppenleiter
Rechtsanwalt Dr. Sickinger
Karlsruhe, Kaiserstr. 199

Karlsruhe, den 11. September 34

An den

Vorstand der Badischen Anwaltskammer

Herrn Rechtsanwalt Brombacher

K a r l s r u h e .

..., nimmt aber neue nur auf

seinen eigenen Namen an .

Gegen das Verhalten von Dr. Krämer dürften hiernach
Bedenken nicht bestehen .

Mit kolleg. Hochachtung

Rechtsanwalt .

Affidavit Made by Process-Server on 19 September 2001
on the Content of the L'Oréal Internet Site

3

Elle propose l'arborescence suivante : "l'OREAL DEUTSCHLAND".

Je clique sur ce lien et j'arrive sur une page contenant la mention « PORTRÄT », que j'imprime sur deux pages et constituant l'**annexe 2**. Cette page d'accueil comporte un menu vertical, faisant apparaître les rubriques suivantes :

- GRUSSWORT
- ZAHLEN UND FAKTEN
- GESCHICHTE
- UMWELT
- QUALITATSSICHERUNG

Je clique sur la rubrique "GESCHICHTE" et apparaît à l'écran une page intitulée " GESCHICHTE " que j'imprime pour constituer l'**Annexe 3**.

Je reproduis littéralement le premier paragraphe de cette page :

« Den Grundstein dieser einzigartigen Erfolgsgeschichte legt André Tondu 1930 in Berlin, als er von dem französischen Firmengründer Eugène Schueller beauftragt wird, den deutschen Friseurmarkt zu erobern. Dabei sind die Anfänge der Haarfarben und Parfümerien GmbH (HUP) nicht leicht. Zwar finden die ersten Colorationen schnell Anklang, doch das Berliner Werk wird im Krieg zerstört, und 1945 muß in Karlsruhe eine neue Fabrik gebaut werden. »

Je me connecte ensuite sur le site Internet http://www.atendo.de

Une page de présentation du site apparaît que j'imprime et constituant l'**annexe 4**.

Société Civile Professionnelle
Maurice ESKENAZI ~ André HADJEDJ
Et Didier BENHAMOU
Huissiers de Justice associés
2, Rue de la Roquette
75011 PARIS
☎ 01 49 23 81 00

Translation

She suggests the following connection: 'L'ORÉAL DEUTSCHLAND'

I click on the link and reach a page containing the mention 'PORTRÄT', that I print out on two pages and that constitutes Appendix 2. This welcome page carries a vertical menu, where the following headings appear:

GRUSSWORT
ZAHLEN UND FAKTEN
GESCHICHTE
UMWELT
QUALITATSSICHERUNG

I click on the 'GESCHICHTE' heading, and a page entitled 'GESCHICHTE' appears on the screen that I print out and which constitutes Appendix 3.

I reproduce literally the first paragraph from this page:

'The foundation stone of this unparalleled success was laid in 1930 in Berlin by André TONDU, when Eugène Schueller the founder of the French firm charges him with conquest of the German hairdressing market. The beginnings of Haarfarben und Parfümerien GmbH (HUP) are not easy. Certainly, the first dyes are quickly accepted by the market, but the base in Berlin was destroyed during the war, and in 1945, a new factory will be built in Karlsruhe.'

I then went to the Internet site http://www.atendo.de

I print out the page introducing the site and it constitutes Appendix 4

Société Civile Professionnelle
Maurice ESKENAZI – ANDRÉ HADJEDJ
Et Didier BENHAMOU
Huissiers de justice associés
2, Rue de la Roquette
75011 PARIS
TEL 01 49 23 81 00

**Extract from the Magazine of the L'Oréal Joint
Production Committee Dated November 1948**

La HAARFARBEN, d'abord à BERLIN, maintenant à KARLSRUHE, avec son manager de toujours, M. Tondu, l'OREAL-HOLLAND, l'A-B-OREAL-SUEDE à STOCKHOLM où Marcel Stein s'est installé, l'OREAL-CANADA.

En Afrique du Nord, la Société AZURVILLE à ALGER et l'U.F.C.I. à CASABLANCA pour laquelle M. Raymond a quitté Pantin.

Et dans tous les pays du monde, les agences OREAL sont installées et travaillent : en AFRIQUE DU SUD, en ANGLETERRE, en AUTRICHE, en AUSTRALIE, en BULGARIE, au CHILI, en COLOMBIE et à CUBA, en EGYPTE, en PALESTINE, au PEROU, au PORTUGAL, en URUGUAY.

Partout l'OREAL, encore l'OREAL, toujours l'OREAL...

Translation

The HAARFARBEN, first in BERLIN, now in KARLSRUHE, managed as always by Mr Tondu, L'OREAL-HOLLAND, L'A-B-OREAL-SWEDEN in STOCKHOLM where Marcel Stein is in place, L'OREAL-CANADA.

In North Africa, the AZURVILLE Company and the U.F.C.I. in CASABLANCA for which Mr RAYMOND left Pantin.

And branches of L'OREAL have been set up and are working in all the countries of the world: in SOUTH AFRICA, in ENGLAND, in AUSTRIA, in AUSTRALIA, in BULGARIA, in CHILE, in COLOMBIA and CUBA, in EGYPT, in PALESTINE, in PERU, in PORTUGAL, in URUGUAY.

L'OREAL everywhere, L'OREAL for ever, L'OREAL for always...

Extracts from the Magazine of the L'Oréal Joint Production Committee Dated March 1949

Le 11 décembre 1948 avait lieu la fête de fin d'année de la HAARFARBEN UND PARFUMERIE à KARLSRUHE.

Nous devons à la gentillesse de M. TONDU, notre ami de toujours, d'avoir les textes qui ont été écrits par le personnel à l'occasion de cette manifestation.

M. ZORAYAN, de l'usine de La Courneuve a bien voulu nous en faire la traduction et nous l'en remercions.

La place nous manquant pour reproduire tous les textes, nous avons reproduit les différentes maquettes qui illustraient ces textes.

Hommage rendu à l'OREAL pour ses fabrications, l'ouverture disait en substance :

La devise de la firme reste toujours :
« Le meilleur pour la femme. »

Après une évocation de la teinture, en faisant spirituellement appel à la sagesse... animal, les tableaux défilaient tour à tour sur la Chimie, la Physique, la Science, la Technique oratoire, l'Astronomie.

L'affirmation finale rejoignait la première :

IMEDIA teint toujours merveilleusement :
Toutes nuances pour tous cheveux.

Et nous citons le chant de la firme qui n'a, malheureusement pas la même saveur dans la traduction :

Dans tous les pays et dans toutes les régions,
Partout où les hommes habitent, en entend
La mère dire à son enfant,
Le père à son fils avec enthousiasme,
Dans tout le monde, enfin, un seul écho :
« Tous, nous n'utilisons que l'OREAL ».

Bravo, M. TONDU et merci d'avoir bien voulu faire cette liaison KARLSRUHE PARIS.

Translation

On 11 December 1948 the HAARFARBEN UND PARFUMERIE in Karlsruhe held its end of the year party.

We give thanks to the kind Mr Tondu, our friend as always, for sending the texts written by staff on the occasion of this event.

Mr ZORAYAN, from the factory in La Courneuve translated them for us, and we thank him for that.

Since we don't have the space to reproduce all the texts we reproduce the different designs that illustrate these texts.

Homage is paid to L'Oréal for its products, the opening says in substance:
> The motto of our firm remains as always:
> 'The best women can have'

After evoking their dyes, and making a spiritual appeal to animal...wisdom, the scenes parade by in focus on Chemistry, Physics, Oratory technique, Astronomy.

The final statement returns to the first:
> IMEDIA always dyes wonderfully:
> Every shade for every hair.

And we will quote the company song that unfortunately doesn't have the same flavour in translation:
> In every country and in every region,
> Everywhere where men dwell, we hear
> Mothers their children tell,
> Fathers their sons excitedly,
> Throughout the world, in a single echo:
> 'We all use only l'OREAL'

Bravo, Mr Tondu and thank you for wanting to make this KARLSRUHE–PARIS link.

Tract from the MSR Executive Committee

REFAIRE LA FRANCE

Chef : EUGENE DELONCLE.

Chef adjoint et remplaçant du Chef :

JEAN FONTENOY.

Comité executif (réunissant les chefs des grands services, conseillers techniques pour l'exécution des ordres du Chef et du Chef adjoint).

Président et dirigeant de toutes les Commissions techni-
ques et Comités d'études .. SCHUELLER.

Service de renseignements .. FILLIOL

Région parisienne ....: CORREZE (à la Légion)
CHARBONNEAU

Organisation territoriale .... FAURAN

C. E. R. F. A. T. .... SOULES

Propagande, Presse .... CHRISTOPHE

Pour tout ce qui concerne le Secrétariat général, s'adresser, provisoirement, sous cette rubrique, au 80, rue Saint-Lazare.

Des précisions seront fournies à nos amis et aux sections dès la semaine prochaine.

Comité exécutif du M.S.R. ▬▬▬▬▬▬▬▬▬▬▬▬

Translation

REMAKING FRANCE

Head: EUGENE DELONCLE.
Joint head and deputy head: JEAN FONTENOY

Executive committee (including heads of main services, technical advisers for the carrying out of the head and joint heads' orders).
Chair and leader of all
Technical Commissions
and Research Committees.... SCHUELLER
Information service.......... FILLIOL
Paris Region.............. { CORREZE (At the Legion)
CHARBONNEAU
Territorial organization....... FAURAN
C.E.R.F.A.T............... SOULES
Publicity, Press.............. CHRISTOPHE

For anything concerning General administrative business, provisionally write, under this rubric, to 80, rue Saint-Lazare.
More details will be supplied to our friends and sections next week.

Executive Committee of the M.S.R.

Newspaper Cutting Mentioning Eugène Schueller, Chairman of the MSR Technical Committee, the Secretariat of Which was Based at 14 rue Royale

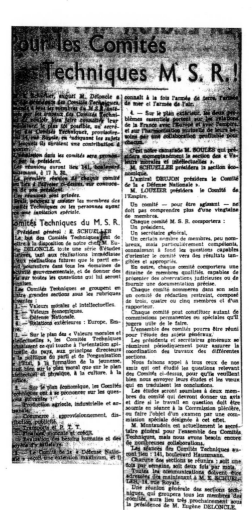

Translation

For the M.S.R. Technical Committees!

Mr E. Schueller, to whom Mr Deloncle has entrusted the chairmanship of the Technical Committees asks all M.S.R. members involved in the work of the Technical Committees to communicate as soon as possible their candidacy, to the secretary of the Technical Committees, provisionally at 14 rue Royale, indicating the subjects on which they would like to make a contribution.

Membership of the committees will be decided by the chair.

Meetings will take place at 141 boulevard Haussmann, at 17.30.

The first meeting of each committee will take place at the above address, convened by the chair.

These meetings are private.

Only members of the Technical Committees or specially invited people may attend.

Technical Committees of the M.S.R.

General chair: E. SCHUELLER

The aim of the Technical Committees is to put at the disposition of our head Mr Eugène DELONCLE a whole series of studies related as much to immediate as to future endeavours that the party will pursue in every domain of government activity, and to give help on all issues it faces.

The Technical Committees are grouped in four important sections under the following headings:

1 – Moral and intellectual values.

2 – Economic values.

3 – National Defence.

4 – Foreign relations: Europe, Empire.

1 – In the area of 'Moral and intellectual values', the Technical Committees will define what concerns the spiritual orientation of the country, the main lines of the policies of the party and the organization of the State, the training of the youth, morally, intellectually and physically, culture and justice.

2 – In the area of economics the Technical Committees must give a lead on the following questions:

Agricultural, industrial and craft production.

Trade, supplies, distribution, advertising.

Transport and Telecommunications.

Finance, money and credit.

Evaluation of human needs and ways of satisfying them.

3. – The Committee for National Defence is all encompassing and includes the army, air force and navy.

4 – On external issues, the two main areas concern France's relations with Europe and with the Empire and the mutual harmonization of their needs for a collaboration that will be profitable for each party.

It is our comrade Mr SOULES who will for the moment chair the section for 'Moral and intellectual values'.

Mr SCHUELLER will chair the economics section.

Admiral DRUJON will chair the committee for 'National Defence'.

Mr LOUZIER will chair the Committee for the Empire.

A committee – in order to function – must not comprise more than twenty members.

Each M.S.R. committee will comprise:

A chair

A general secretary

A few members – not too many – but who are particularly competent to understand the relevant issues and able to direct the committee to tangible, appropriate results.

Moreover, each committee will have ten qualified members able to provide judicious opinions or necessary documentation.

Each committee will appoint a small editorial committee comprising three, four or five members and a rapporteur.

Each committee can constitute as many permanent or special commissions as it thinks useful.

All committees can be brought together to study general issues.

Chairs and general secretaries will meet regularly to ensure the coordination of the work of the different sections.

We appeal to all those of our friends who have studied the relevant issues for the above mentioned committees, to send us their analyses and the conclusions that arise from them.

The studies will be submitted to two members of the committee who will give an opinion and say whether the study in question should be put before a plenary session or should be the object of an examination by a special commission designated to that end.

Mr Montaudoin is currently the general secretary for all the Technical Committees, but we need many other collaborators.

The Technical Committees will meet at 141, boulevard Haussmann,

Each of the sections will meet once a week, that is twice a month.

All communications must be addressed from now on to Mr E.SCHUELLER, 14 rue Royale.

A general meeting of the technical committees bringing together all the members of the committees will take place shortly under the chairmanship of Mr Eugène DELONCLE.

Acknowledgements

Monique Queirel; Évelyne Queirel; Paulette Queirel; Anne Schuchman; Domique Missika; Sylvie Vormus; *maître* Charles Korman; *maître* Charles Choucroy; *maître* Charles Morel; *maître* Bernard Jouaneau; Christian Poslaniec; Jean-Marc Heller; Angela Kohler; Jérémy Fiedler; Bernard Monge; Diane Kuperman; François Giustiniani; Aude Gillon; Jean-Pierre Pelletier; Jean Frydman; the World Jewish Congress; *maître* Serge Klarsfeld; Beate Klarsfeld; the Centre for Contemporary Jewish Documentation; Nicole Yardeni; Bruno Abescat; Diane Kamienny; Jean-Marc Dreyfus; Karine Vidal; Thal Bruttmann; Vincent Frank; Alexandre Garcia; the editorial board of *Le Monde*; the research department of L'Opéra-Bastille; the research department of the Théâtre du Châtelet; Charles Ageorge; Carlos Proenza; Sylvie Dubois; Pierrette Chastel; Tino Müller; Csaba Airizer; Frau Fetzner; Dr Koch; Philippe Sprang; Alexandre Ifi; Mathias Widmaier; Didier Benoit; Helio Limoeiro; Camille Bonamy; Amanda Dalton; Mme V.; Jean Kahn, President of the Central Consistory Court; Dominique Verdeilhan; Philippe Délerac; Marie-Amélie Lombard; Martine Archambault; Agnès Gardet; Jean-Philippe Deniou; Nicolas Marut; Michel Zerbib; Sebastien Laugenie; André Darmon; Eugène Leiba; Joelle Perelberg; Arielle Lellouch; Laurent Léger; Helène Keller Lind; Laurent Valdiguié; Niels Klawitter; Sue Hoppough; Sarah Wildman; Amelia Gentleman; Jack Gee; Commission Culture B; BBF; Gérard Ulmo; Charles Leselbaum; Arno Klarsfeld; Michel Chetrit; Joseph Hattab; Loge Ben Gurion; Thierry Lascard; Rodolph Cahn; Yaël König; Ilan Katz; Robert Bader; Martinianne; Wizo; Monik Kern; Laurent Kern; Pierre Levy; Barbara Lèfebvre; Cécilia Gabiizon; B'nai Brith France.

I would equally like to thank all the friends who have given me such support.

THE
KINGDOM'S
DAUGHTER

'You can be a hero.'

THE
KYNGDOM'S
DAUGHTER

DANIEL JP HARRIS

Dear reader,

It's no secret I've made Jesus my Lord (you only need to check my socials to see that!) If Jesus isn't for you that's okay, I hope you enjoy this book as something cool and inspirational, but if you want to know the truth here it is. There are many reasons I wrote this book, some I'm just understanding now, and others I'm sure I'll come to understand. Most of all though, I believe this is God's reminder that despite what we feel, we are his – his son and his daughter – and in him, we are capable. It's his encouragement to us to do what is scary, even if that looks like a double suicide, and trust he has a plan. If you're in an impossible situation right now, I pray you receive this as his word to you: 'Child, I know this seems lost. Just trust me.'

The story doesn't end here.

EPISODE I

OATH'S ORIGIN

THE PAST

CHAPTER I
BREATH OF DEATH

WHAT FEELS LIKE forever ago now, in the late winter afternoon, I was sitting beside a river. It was cold and on the verge of freezing over. My mother had made me a sheepskin jacket over the summer, so I was warm. It was my early Christmas present, because like her, I never coped well with winter, and we couldn't afford central heating. Jedidiah, a British refugee I'd known from three years old, was trying to kill time before his birthday banquet and had taken me to fish with a spear he crafted from illegal wood. No one is allowed to cut the trees where I'm from, so we rarely had firewood through the winter either. Though he was fourteen, two years older than I was, Jedidiah had the strength and stature to rival the eldest boy in our village. I watched him, amazed by his skills. He caught his first fish in minutes, and he brought it to me.

"Here."

He placed the fish in my hands, which were equal in size to his, but otherwise our attributes were north and south: He had short mousy hair, mine was long and gold; he had bright eyes, mine were deep and dark; and he was built like an athlete, I was petite and frail. Our skin color differed too, but not for the right reason. His family was unanimously pale, but he was born with a warmer tone. My relatives were all olive, so my snowy complexion was a shock to everyone.

Naturally the fish slipped through my fingers the instant I received it, but he caught it. He looked at me with his wonderful smile.

"What was that?" he teased, nudging my shoulder.

"Shad*daap*, you're used to it," I beamed back at him. He brought the fish closer to me again, only this time he held onto it.

"It's beautiful, isn't it? When my dad first showed me one of these, I was speechless. Nothing like what you see on land."

The late sun sprang from its scales. It shimmered in his hands.

"You're right. It's amazing."

Grabbing my hand, he pulled me from the grass, leading me closer to the river.

"Come on. I'll show you how to catch your own!"

I just laughed. There was no going back, for the next hour I'd be fishing regardless of how foolish I looked, but at least he didn't care.

"Alright! *Alright*, I'm coming over!" I squealed.

He handed me the spear and attempted to direct my hands in the correct position, but I was useless.

"You just look down the middle right here…there you go."

With effort, I managed to adopt the right stance, but he propped up the spear from behind me because it was too heavy to hold steady.

"Aw, where are they? I think they've all gone to sleep."

"Don't be silly, Allie, here's one now. Look."

His finger directed me towards a murky patch a few feet from us, but the sudden break in the clouds revealed a silvery glint.

"There! There it is!" I fought to contain my excitement, fearful of frightening it. It felt like years waiting by that river in the plummeting chill, but in reality, it was a couple of minutes.

"Ok, now just keep your eye on it, and when you're ready... strike."

"How do I hit it?" I panicked, jerking back to him. But he turned my face around.

"Don't look at me, look at the fish! Just imagine you're throwing a dart, but the dart stays in your hand."

I was good at darts. My father was gifted a board during his childhood so I found myself throwing at it on the regular. So, listening to everything Jedidiah instructed, I watched, waited for the right moment, and struck the fish with all my might. But I still missed, and it shot off down the river. What I *did* get however was a drenched face – the water shot straight up and splashed all over me. I screamed.

"That was brilliant!" Jedidiah shrieked, rolling on the ground. He even cried.

"Uck, that's nasty! I might have fish pee on me now or something!"

He wiped his eyes and sat up.

"Don't worry. I didn't expect you to catch anything first time."

He waved his hand for me to come closer, so I sat opposite him, my cheeks burning.

"Do you want to know a secret? The trick is to aim slightly below the fish."

I wrung out my hair.

"Why?"

"Refraction. What you're seeing isn't actually what's under the water, because of the way light bends. The water distorts it."

"How?"

"I can't remember exactly, but we covered it in science not too long ago, and my dad was telling me about it, too."

My hair had almost dried, but my clothes were still soaked, so I took off my jacket and laid it out to dry. Jedidiah saw what I was doing and also took his jacket off, shuffling over to put it around me. It was miles too big, but still warm.

"No, no, you keep it on!"

"Don't worry about me. You're still wet, and I'd hate for you to get a chill on my birthday."

He went on to light a fire with nothing but a few twigs, like his father Hamza taught him, and we cooked his fish and ate together, something we hadn't done in many years, because he would always leave to train with his father after school. As we ate, exchanging satisfied glances, all I could think was how grateful I was to have him in my life.

"How's the fish?"

"It's amashing, thank you," I moaned, my words muffled because I hadn't even finished my mouthful.

"You'll get there. Keep trying, and one day you'll have enough fish for everyone in the town to try some."

"I guess. That's if I had a spear to start with," I sighed, which was met with a chuckle. "What?"

"That's why I brought you out here to try it. I was hoping you'd enjoy it, because that spear is for you."

I bolted upright, the fish frozen at my lips.

"No…no Jed, you can't do that for me."

No one had ever done anything like that for me.

"You worked so hard on it, it's a lovely spear! You can't just give it to me – it's *your* birthday today, not mine!"

The spear was beside him, so he took it with one hand and laid it over his lap. I tried to continue, but he cut me off.

"It *is* a lovely spear, but it's only that way because I wanted you to have it. All along, honest."

I simply stared.

"I don't care if it's my birthday. You're always telling me you wish you could come and do what I do with Dad, so it felt right for me to make you this. Now you can try it for yourself, without me ever having to be there. And look-" He turned the spear over to the other side and pointed to the far end, where the spearhead was. "I even engraved your name into the wood, so you know it's yours...'Allie Mirabel.'"

"Come here," I whispered, arms open for his embrace.

Wasting no time, he got up, pulled me from my feet once more and hugged me tightly, mouthing tenderly into my ear...

"Thanks for being my friend."

When we got back home the sun had almost disappeared from the sky, leaving the faintest pink trail in its wake. The moon was visible. I knocked on my door and waited, still holding my damp coat. Hopefully Mom wouldn't ask what had happened to it – it was getting harder and harder to lie about going to Kingdom-restricted areas on our own. My father's footsteps diverted my worry, and I could tell they were his, because he always walked around so loudly. Sometimes it was annoying; other times, it was quite funny. The door opened.

"Where have you two been? Come on, we've all been waiting for you!"

I was eager to tell him about the spear.

"Dad! Guess what Jedidiah did for me!"

"Tell me about it once you've got your shoes off. And what's that you've got all over them? Where have you been, a swamp?"

My shoes got filthy walking through the woods, most of it was marshes. Thankfully Jedidiah quickly spoke over us.

"Good evening, Mr. Mirabel, I hope you're well. Sorry we came so late."

My father really liked Jedidiah, probably more than me sadly.

"Ah, the man of the hour," he laughed, as he punched Jedidiah's shoulder like he always did. "We were just finishing the goat so you've come in good time."

"Don't keep hitting him, Dad, you'll hurt him."

My father just stared, put his hand on my head like I was a leaning post, and proceeded to mess up my hair, badly.

"Oh, don't you worry about him sweetheart, he's growing into a real man now. Soon you will, too."

He winked at Jedidiah, and they both cracked up. I'm sure sometimes he forgot Jedidiah wasn't his actual son, but no one told him that.

"So do you want to hear what I got?" I could've almost burst – my shoes flew off my feet.

"Go on then, Aletheia. Tell me your big news."

"Jedidiah made me a *spear!*"

"What spear?"

"That spear!" I cried, pointing to the one Jedidiah was carrying. It was even too heavy for me to carry back, not to mention almost as big as I was. My father looked at it curiously.

"Oh…that spear. A bit big for you, isn't it?" he chuckled again.

He was his own comedian. He really was.

"I'm only messing, sweetheart. That was a truly lovely thing to do for her, Jedidiah."

"Ah, well, I know how much Allie's into the whole idea of learning what Dad taught me, so I hoped you wouldn't mind me making one for her…?" Jedidiah was good at being subtle.

"Of course, we don't mind!" His hand returned to my head. "It looks like you've made one girl very happy today, so it's only right we return the favor!"

My father cheerfully led us into the kitchen where my mom was, working hard on the vegetables from our little orchard, dicing them up ready for a quick boil. The goat smelled incredible, I was already drooling. Jedidiah handed me my spear as we walked in to show my mother. Hamza was also there, keeping his eye on the goat.

"There you guys are," Hamza sighed, as we walked in. "I was just going to try and find you."

"Mom! Jedidiah made me my own spear to go fishing, look!" I cried, hurrying to her. I knew she wasn't keen on the idea of me using anything sharp, but I saw a hint of a grin. "Now I can catch fish for everyone!"

"That's lovely Aletheia, now go and take it upstairs and get ready for supper. We'll be serving once these vegetables are boiled," she snickered, throwing the last of the vegetables in the pot. I'm sure she was laughing *at* me, but I didn't mind. I was going to become the town's fish merchant, and I couldn't wait for her to see it.

Rushing out of the kitchen with the spear, I shot up the stairs and into my bedroom. There was a small mirror in my room my mother bought for me when I was seven, and from looking into it briefly, I noticed my dress was still a little damp and dirty, so I opened my closet and got changed into something fresher. As I returned to the mirror, I heard a knock on the door.

"Who is it?"

"Jed."

"Oh, come in."

He wandered into my room and sat on the bed, so I joined him.

"Wow, I haven't been in here for a while. You finally changed your sheets, too."

He found that amusing, because not long ago I slept with a very small sheet which used to belong to my mother when she was young. It was too small and the bottom of my feet poked out of it.

"Actually, Mom spent the fall knitting me a new one. She wanted to make sure it would cover me even if I had a growth spurt."

"Well…that's unlikely," Jedidiah winked.

I pushed him, and he fell back onto the bed.

"Stop it! I'll grow eventually! Look at you, all tall and strong."

"And handsome," he winked again.

"*Quite* handsome. Still a bit of maturing to go, I think," I smirked. "So, what do you want?"

"Just to let you know dinner's going to be ready in five minutes, and your mom really wants you to hurry up. Seriously, how long does it take you?"

"I was just about to come down...I had to change first, that's all."

At *that* moment he noticed my dress, which was typical of him.

"Ah. Nice dress."

"Thanks. I was saving this one for your birthday. I bought it with one of the new piglets I bred."

"Aw, you didn't have to wear anything special." His smile had vanished, replaced by something even more precious. A mouth void of words.

"I know I didn't, but I like looking special, and this time I have a reason to," I shrugged.

Suddenly Jedidiah became serious, looking at the spear I'd set in the corner of my room.

"I do want you to use that, you know."

I was amazed he didn't believe I would.

"Of course, I'm going to use it! Whenever I have the time, I'll be down that river fishing, don't you worry!"

"You'll become the best spearfisher who ever lived if you keep using it," he sighed reflectively. "Just promise me you'll use it when you can."

I nudged his shoulder with my own so he'd stop looking at the ground.

"Jed, I promise. Happy birthday."

⌇

Thump. Thump. Thump.

I snatched the clock beside my bed, awake and bolt upright

from the incessant pounding on our front door. *Almost midnight? Who could need us at this hour?* I pondered, but I already knew the answer. I just didn't want to believe it. Before I could put the clock back the clamor ceased and was swiftly followed by an eruption of shouts and one final crash – it slipped from my hand and broke.

I leapt from my covers and out the bed. My family's distress enclosed me, blended with the fury of unfamiliar voices. I reached for the door knob to get out of my room, but I froze. Entirely froze. I could only feel my lungs, my breath agitated and heavy as I urged myself to be still. Fear had shrouded my sense of reason, paralyzing me at the doorway. My mother screamed, but I couldn't lift my arms to hold my ears – rather I screwed my eyes shut, hoping it wasn't real, and I'd wake up. Her scream pierced my mind in such a painful frequency I can still hear her in the quiet. Whenever I'm alone, my ears still ring.

There was another almighty crash and shrill of shattered glass. And silence. I drew one last breath and let out a scream of my own as I forced my door open, so loud I scared myself, I wasn't aware my voice could carry so far. My mother must've heard me, she rushed from the living room to the bottom of the stairs, hysterical.

"Aletheia! Get back in your bedroom *now!*"

I was terrified of her.

"Mommy, what's happening? What's happening? What's happening?"

"Just get back in your room!"

As she climbed the stairway Hamza flew out the living room with a Kingdom guard beneath him – they landed at the bottom of the stairs where Hamza threw hard punches to his head repeatedly. He had the man pinned, but another officer jumped him from behind and locked their elbow around his throat, allowing the other to rise and beat him with his baton.

"*Hamza!*"

My palms trembled on the handrail.

My father appeared from behind the man strangling Hamza, pulled him off and threw him against the wall with a bone-crunching thud. All the men were a state. Mom tried to rush and help my father, but more officers stormed into the hallway. Our door had been kicked down. They took both Hamza and my dad, beating them brutally.

I ran down the stairs to help – they had my mom. As I got closer, I saw from the entrance into the living room Jedidiah fighting three men by himself, using everything within reach: plates, jugs, a candle holder. And he was winning. Our table was in two, where one of the officers had fallen, and Jedidiah was the one striking them down. I screamed at them.

"Jed! Stop! Jed!"

He saw me, and looked up.

"No-Allie! Get-"

They didn't let him finish. That distraction was all they needed. A baton struck his temple, and he fell motionless. There were too many men in front of me to reach him, I could only watch as two of them picked him up, restrained him with cuffs, and led his limp body out of the house where our fathers lay. The officer confining my mother pushed her toward my father, and she collapsed in tears. I galloped for the doorway.

"Jed! *Jed!*" I screamed so loud my voice broke. "Je-*Jed! No!*"

One of the men who wasn't holding Jedidiah stopped and grabbed hold of me.

"Get out of here!" he yelled.

I didn't care about him, I tried to push past him. But I was less than half the size of him.

"Jed! You can't-*No!*"

∽

I clenched my numb hands, my body clothed in a bitter breeze. We all stood in a line, my family, gazing at the graves of Hamza and his wife, Olivia. A cold silence cloaked their burial ground, making me shiver with hate. I had a bandage over my left eye from where the officer struck me with his icy weapon, frosted by midnight's breath. Its tip met my forehead like a bitter kiss, leaving a perfect stripe of frozen blood in its wake. But with no pain.

'Hamza Cadman ~ whose roar was silenced' read his stone. As I walked out from my parents to kneel by his resting place, my lip quivered. He was, to me, like family. Whenever I saw Jedidiah, I always looked forward to meeting my uncle Hamza with him. Now the only other family I'd known were gone: Hamza and his wife, and Jedidiah with them. A reality that stung my heart, and with every beat…agonizing anger gripped my body. It threw me to the foot of my uncle and auntie's grave, and it kept me there, head to the ground.

Behind me, my parents held back their tears, sniffling and attempting to appear strong, presumably so I would cry no longer. But such a painful weight crushed me beside Hamza's grave: the thought I could've done something to stop the officers, or even if I stayed in my room Jedidiah wouldn't have been taken, and he could've saved his father. These questions racked my mind until I was nothing. Nothing but a remnant of someone who once laughed, and was happy. My mother stroked my neck as she tried to get me up, but I stayed where I was, sobbing. Not giving her any thought.

My awareness returned to the crunch of snow-dusted grass beneath my parents' feet, which grew more and more distant, until it had faded to the back of my mind. I was truly alone now, so I looked up, and my neck ached. My fingertips were sore, but with them I touched the rough granite of Hamza's memorial. I pulled them down the slab so I could feel the cracks. And again, and again…until my nails were chipped and throbbing. The wind had locked my watery eyes closed, and my legs had lost all feeling. Drops of tears gently prodded the snow beneath me, my only warmth being my breath which I tried to catch in my hands and cling to, but every time I did a strong gust would carry it far away. And there I would remain, cold. This heaviness was too much to bear; it had compelled me down, but I knew there was only one person who could raise me up.

Me.

With one last gaze toward the grave, the earth below me heated up, and burned to a thousand degrees. But I wasn't seared by its strength, rather its power charged through me, pulsating around my body like fiery blood, melting away the remorse and awakening my sleeping passion for revenge. My teeth gritted; my eyes pierced the grave like molten swords, ready to impale whoever stood against me. The cold air around me broke and dispersed in terror from me. Only the heated hatred was left. It had consumed me, and all else was irrelevant.

My body glowed in the red mist.

"I promise you both, I *will* find your son. I *will* find Jedidiah," I snarled, and I arose reborn, a woman I remain. Allie Mirabel died that day. She died alongside Jedidiah's father.

But even death can give life.

CHAPTER II

SHARED FATE

THE SUN HAD almost bled from view when I got back from my afterschool hunt, leaving behind it a beautiful reddish glow like the ones in summer. This day was a tough one for me. I waited around in the waters for hours before my first sighting, but I still managed to catch two fish before the sun had gone. I opened the door to a glorious warmth. Around this time of year, we had a fire going in the living room, which we could afford now, but only when needed. Outside was getting brisk, on the verge of chilly, and after a whole day out in the town, by the river and in an unheated school, it was so wonderful to have a place where I could heat up my hands. If there was a fire going, that was always the first thing I did.

"You're back pretty late today, honey. Did it go well?" Mom was resting beside the fire as she was nearly always cold. I dropped my sack in front of her.

"Two fish for supper. Yeah, it wasn't too bad, just took a long time to find my first one."

"That's good. You know I don't like you out when it gets dark."

"Don't worry, neither do I," I smirked, remembering the night I almost burnt myself with a makeshift torch because I'd spent too long trying to catch my first fish. Over three years ago now, and Mom still didn't know about it, thank goodness. "Would you like me to cook them tonight? You look tired." My eyes hung on her. She was paler than usual.

"That would be lovely. Yes, please, Aletheia. If you don't mind."

"I don't mind. Is something wrong?"

"I just woke up feeling a little under the weather, that's all. Must be the last of that winter bug going about."

"Probably." My eyes veered to the fire. "Would you like me to stop by the market and pick up some more firewood before this goes out?"

"Why don't you just go and look for some in the forest?" She didn't sound amazing either. I looked through the window.

"No. It's getting too dark now, and it could take me a while before I get back. I don't want you to get cold."

She looked at me warmly and opened her arms.

"Come here."

Tentatively, I got up from the fire, my hands very toasty now, and shuffled over to Mom. She stroked my cheeks; her hands were still cold. "You're a fine and beautiful young woman, Aletheia. Bless you."

That's so touching, I thought, as I left to get my coat again, and yet, all I could do was give her a smile and say 'I'll be back soon.' I wanted to kick myself. I wished my mother knew how much I loved her.

"Don't forget your key!" she croaked from the living room, remaining still.

"I won't!" I hollered back, still wishing I told her how I truly feel. Since Jedidiah's capture, I'd never been one for sharing my thoughts.

The market was soon to close, so I hurried down the streets passing much destruction on my course. My heart dropped. It had been weeks since the blizzard, but its effect on me hadn't changed. The scale of desolation was vast, and it had wrecked our normal way of life. Now a lot of people were either homeless or living in cramped accommodations with their loved ones whose homes survived the storm, in rooms which were never intended to house them. I felt like crying, but I didn't. I reminded myself I was a grown woman, and I needed to leave those childish emotions behind me. That's how broken I'd become, yet I did not know it.

Around me the old folk were leaving the late market sale. I knew I still had ten minutes or so to get there, so it wasn't like time was in my favor, but it sure was easier than searching for the firewood myself.

Everyone was smiling at me.

Since I started selling fish, I had become a familiar face, and I had a soft spot for the elders. They were the ones who always seemed most appreciative of what I did, and encouraged me even if I hadn't caught much. I waved to them as I passed, watching them all huddle together to keep warm. *If only I was good at knitting too,* I sighed.

Across from the market at the far end stood Mr. Milano, who was a Kingdom-certified wood supplier of all kinds, including the illegal ones used to craft durable weapons, like spears, practice swords, and bows. Not that the Kingdom knew that part, of course. I was never taught how to make those, so I always carried the same spear around, always making sure to take the low routes where the Kingdom couldn't see me. Everyone else in the market was busy packing away their stalls, but Mr. Milano always stayed later. He was a good friend of my father, so I always got a discount, too. He opened his arms wide. He was one of the few Italians in our town, which was mostly full of immigrants trying to escape the civil wars of their nations. The other Italians were hard to tell apart from the locals, but this man lived up to the stereotype.

"Bella! So good to see a pretty girl in this place again!" he cried out to me, kissing me on both cheeks as he always did. It made me giggle every time.

"I was here this morning, Mr. Milano!"

"And I've been counting the hours for your return, *signorina*," he grinned, smoothly as always.

"Do you have any firewood leftover?" I laughed, shedding the embarrassment.

"You're in luck!" he exclaimed, producing the wood from nowhere. "Will that be all for you today?" He pressed closer to me.

"No, that's everything." I tried to hold him at arm's length, but it still didn't stop his advance. Buying something from him was always a spectacle.

"Very well. As you blessed me with your fish this morning, shall we say ehh, split the cost? Fair and square, yes?"

Bless him. He was always generous to me, and everyone else that approached him in the market, but that's because he only had his regulars. Everyone else was slightly terrified of him.

"How much is it?"

"This much wood, uhhh, I sell to you for twenty credits only," he smiled, waving his hands at the word 'twenty.'

"That's fantastic. Thank you, Mr. Milano."

In response he touched my cheek, running the back of his hand slowly down its curvature.

"Anything for such radiant beauty as yourself, Aletheia."

What I now held was enough wood to last us tonight *and* tomorrow. *From now on, I'm always collecting the wood,* I thought, amused, but the joy was as momentary as turning my back. The ground rumbled, only not to a quake, but noise. Like the sound of boots – imminent.

And great in number.

A squadron of officers stormed through the town and into the center, some smashing into people's houses as they had when they took Jedidiah. I noticed one of them take a classmate from her house, dragging her out from beneath her arms. The screams of tormented families soon swallowed the clamor.

"It's the Kingdom! They're taking people away! Aletheia, run!" Mr. Milano yelled, his signature smile lost to terror.

My heart beat as fast as it did the evening Jedidiah was taken. Swirls of fear and anger rushed back at once, as if I was reliving the moment in a terrible nightmare. I couldn't breathe.

"Aletheia!"

They reached his stall and, drawing their batons, smashed his supplies, and tipped over his shelves. I wanted to go back to help him, but there were too many officers – in their hundreds, which is something I'd never seen.

I had to get my parents out the house.

With all my strength, I sprinted ahead of the mayhem, the cries of innocent people overflowing in my mind. They were not going to hurt my family. I would not let them.

"Hey you – stop!" one of them bawled, bringing two others to chase me. I turned in panic. They were on my tail, and they were fast.

Gasping, I weaved through the labyrinth of part-standing homes and rubble, throwing myself down the street where our house sat, screaming. My father, who was tending to our sheep, ran to me, probably hearing my voice a mile off. His face was horror.

"Get Mom! Get Mom! Get away from here!" I shrieked, desperate for him not to come to my aid and get killed. *Praying* he'd take Mom to safety.

"What's happening?" he wailed. I had almost reached him as I yelled again.

"Just run! Get Mom and *run!*" My throat hurt from screaming, and I couldn't think straight. There had never been such a vast attack on our town like this. What had we done?

My father grabbed me tight, hurting my arms, watching as the men neared us. Racing like hunters, and we were the hunted. Looming like spears…and we were the fish. I couldn't move, he wouldn't release me. Our eyes met as I looked at him in utter urgency to get Mom, but he kept staring, coldly. Not making a sound.

"Stay where you are!" they barked, only a few feet from us.

I could only manage a whisper.

"Dad…don't do it."

He threw me to one side, and I almost lost my footing, stumbling dreadfully. I stretched out my hand to keep my balance, and refocusing to Dad, I saw the very thing I dreaded. An officer was on the floor.

Dad had rammed him in his skull.

The other two pulled him off, but my father was a good fighter. He regained control of his right arm, yanking at one of the officer's shoulders and dropping him to the ground in front of him. The one holding his other arm swung out his baton. It collided with my father's head, but he didn't fall.

"No!" I yelped, watching stunned as my father took another thrust to his ribs. And again to his chest. He caught the baton on the fourth time though, and plunged his thick fist into the man's stomach, flooring him. My father looked a state, the blow to his head had drawn blood. It gushed down his nose and chin, and onto the weathered concrete.

All three officials were on the floor, and it looked like he might have done it. But as he looked back to me one of the men by his feet catapulted himself at Dad's legs in a sweeping tackle, bringing Dad down with him. Head first.

I ran over to him. I didn't care anymore; I wasn't thinking straight – those fiends weren't killing my father. I was never taught to fight, especially to Dad's extent, but it didn't matter. Rage was enough. And it was all I needed.

The officer continued to strike my father to no end, merciless and inhuman. He saw me run at him, but I gave him no time. Using every ounce of my effort, I cut through his face, kicking his head up and off Dad with nothing held back.

I wanted to kill them all.

Grunting, I hauled his full weight off the floor and kneed him in the groin, and as he crouched, I struck his jaw. His face landed right into it.

"Don't *ever* touch my dad!" I roared, leaping onto him and tugging at his padded vest, passionately lashing him with punches as I did. He tried to shield his face as I beat him, but I was forceful, and now his nose bled, thick and black. I wasn't going to let up – if I could kill at least one of those monsters that would be one less officer. One less in the town.

But I had to stop.

A cold and prickly sensation shot from my head to toes, and my joints went stiff. My body dropped to the officer's side, shuddering violently. There, above me, stood one of the men who had managed to get back up and take aim at me with a pulsing gun. I panted for air, my lungs closing in. My dad lay not too far from me, clutching his bloody head.

Endless tears flowed down my face and splashed amidst the red-stained floor I lay on. I wanted to crawl to my father, but a hand grabbed my collar and pulled. My mother rushed out from the house as they took me, the other guard lifting me from my feet, carrying me to a place I could only imagine as hell.

"Mom! Mom, go back inside! Go back-" I was silenced by a grubby glove. There was nothing I could do.

More officers arrived from up the street, two of them hoisting the man I'd hurt. My mother cried out to me, but I was unable to respond. She ran over to my father on the floor, only to be flung off him by the guards and escorted back into our home. I tried to wriggle from their hold, but I was truly restrained. And as if my eyes were suddenly submerged in water

...everything blurred out.

CHAPTER III

MARK OF A HERO

OUCH! I WINCED, trying to rub my head, but I couldn't move my arms; the harder I pulled the deeper something cut into my wrists, which were secured above me. Empty faces gazed back at me, their bodies rocking to the sudden jolts that slammed me awake. None of them dared to bleat a word, but if they had, I would've been hard-pressed to hear them. A loud noise consumed the room around me, which once I could focus, I realized was chockfull with girls.

Frantically, I snapped my head left and right, suddenly more aware of the situation. Each girl had been bound to the wall, arms up, some with their head drooped as they slept. The room itself was bland, with only a doorway and one big blank wall at the far end, but the other three were full to the brim of helpless young bodies, all younger if not slightly older than me. The youngest-looking was a petite ginger girl, whose soft face and frightened eyes told me she was about twelve or thirteen. Maybe even eleven.

One of the girls next to me was awake, so I whispered to her, "Where are we?"

She didn't respond, but instead kept her eyes fixed to the floor. Reluctantly, I tried again.

"Excuse me. Where are we?"

"Don't speak!" she warned, finally returning a glance.

"Why?" I flinched, head buzzing from confusion. And the drugs.

"*Shhh!*"

I tugged at my arms to get an idea of how strong the cuffs were, and if it were possible to break out. They were unbearably tight. Pulling at them was only bruising my wrists, so I had to stop. *Why is no one talking?* I studied the wall in front. *Maybe she's too nervous,* I concluded, so I tried to grab the attention of the girl opposite me instead.

"Hey! Hey! Do you know where we are?" I kept my voice just loud enough to be heard, but even that was too much. The doorway slid open, retracting into the wall in a sci-fi manner, and out walked a large brute of an officer, baton in hand. I looked around. No one was giving him eye contact, except for me. He marched over, assessing me with eyes that screamed with hunger.

"You're the bitch who kicked one of our lads' head in," he snarled, pointing his baton at me. "Well, you've got guts, sweetheart, and that's just what we need."

He came right up to my face, spitting his words.

"But now you're on *our* turf, and you follow *our* rules. And in case you haven't noticed from your friends around here, there is to be *no talking!*"

His rage was met with gasps, but I gazed back at him silent, swallowing my resentment for his worthless life, because I knew it would only endanger the girls if I provoked him. He tried to intimidate me, grinning stupidly as his baton stroked my cheek, but that only added to his pitifulness.

"You know, you remind me of my daughter. Very headstrong. That look in your eyes which told me she hated me, and she could do better."

I didn't realize he could get any closer, but now I could smell his breath, which was salty.

"Where is she now?" he rambled on. "She's a slave along with her ma, just as you'll be, sweetheart."

My stomach stirred as he stroked my hair, baton still close to my nose. I tried to shake him off, and he stepped backward.

"Oh, don't like that, do we? Well, don't worry. That's not how the Kingdom punishes slaves."

He grinned at me, and my palms moistened. My eyes were fixed on his baton.

"We punish them like this-"

He swiped me.

The baton struck my skin with a sharp snap, tearing a striking long wound across my face. The sting jarred me, heating my cheek to a feverish intensity which oozed to my chin. I cried out, but with several quick gasps dragged my focus back to him, flaring with anger. He laughed at me.

"How does it feel to be on the receiving end, girl? Don't serve what you can't eat!"

Another strike followed, connecting with my head, almost dropping me to the ground as it did. Only my cuffs kept me from falling. And again, to my ribs, and again in my stomach. I hung by the bonds brutalized, my strength escaping me. My muscles strained by my own dead weight.

"*Stop!*" cried one of the girls opposite me, her eyes welling. The guard turned on her, raising his baton.

But I couldn't let that happen.

"I thought a big man...like you would pack...more of a punch," I spluttered. He snapped at me.

"Oh, you've got *big* guts, sweetheart! We're going to have *a lot* of fun with you!"

I took one sharp breath before the imminent blow – there was only time for one – and braced myself. His baton flew fast, slicing the air, which was directed at my face again, hitting the exact same area on my cheek as before. He must've practiced daily, his accuracy brought on searing pain. Floods of tears rushed my vision, and I could no longer stand. Instead, I sagged there, by my wrists, moaning. The stress of my bodyweight burning at my shoulders, until my muscles were hot coal.

"You've got a big day ahead of you, so rest up!" the man sniggered, and with that he was gone, and the room was silent again.

Coughing, I tried to heave my body up. My legs had gone limp, shaking uncontrollably, but I managed it. Blood splattered the floor from where the now-deepened gash on my cheek leaked. I sighed, still breathing heavily. At least it was over, for however long that would be.

For the remainder of the journey, I stood there in the same position. My head was dizzy, my upper body throbbed, and the sting on my cheek was so intense it was as if someone was repeatedly cutting away at it. Some of the girls were trying to get some sleep, as we had been in the room for a long time. None of us knew how long exactly, but it must've been several hours. As I scanned the room continuously, occasionally my eyes met with another girl, and they would stare back almost compassionately. I must've looked terrible.

Eventually the endless routine of staring at each wall, one after the other, was disrupted by a sudden rattle of the whole room, awakening every girl. My torso quaked, along with my wrists, which jolted uncomfortably between the cuffs. Finally, the mind-numbing drone cut silent.

All of us moved our heads anxiously, unsure if we'd be freed. A tiny click shot everyone's attention to the blank wall, which lowered down and out, forming a platform. It was a hanger door, for a Kingdom deployment ship. We'd been transported through the sky.

As the door gradually lowered, we were drowned by a bright light. It bore the warmth of a thousand suns and, though harsh, it evoked memory. It reminded me of sitting closely to the fire like I did while talking with Mom, and warming my hands. It was soothing, like a gentle kiss. Consoling, like my mother's touch. For a second, I thought of her, looking at me with gratitude for suggesting more wood, and telling me how much she loved me. That I was beautiful. At least that memory was something no one could beat out of me.

The guard from earlier, as well as several others, stormed through the doorway and back into our room. They carried between them a long chain. I didn't want to imagine what they'd use it for, so I slipped my eyes away. Their footsteps came to a halt in the middle of us, and the officer from earlier proceeded to shout again.

"Listen up, and listen well! You are now property of the Kingdom, and you obey everything we say. In a moment, my colleagues will release you from the wall, then, in single file, you will walk outside and wait for us to instruct you further, understood?"

A majority of the girls nodded, but no one spoke. Dropping the chain where it was all the guards dispersed and proceeded to shoot at our cuffs with some kind of ray gun, which released our arms from the wall but still kept the bonds in place. Fortunately, I was released by a different guard. I knew the other one, the one I presumed was the leader, would most likely beat me for looking at him now.

One-by-one the girls stepped down the platform, at which every one of them would shriek. I still couldn't figure out why even as I reached the ramp, but the moment my foot left it, the reason became all too apparent. All of us had been stripped of our footwear, forced to walk wherever we were headed barefoot, and below the platform stretching until you couldn't see any further was sand. They were offloading us in a desert, where the sun beat down like a rain of fire, heating the sands to a scorching intensity. Stepping onto it was like touching a saucepan after it had roll boiled for hours. I winced, and reluctantly lowered my other foot. Everyone stood in a large crowd waiting for the officers, restlessly treading around on the spot. Quickly, I paced over to the rest of them, my mind silently screaming.

Once we had all been rounded up on the desert floor the guards rose from inside the cooler, now much more attractive ship, with the chain back in their grasp. I hated the noise it made as the steel jittered and clashed between itself. It worsened my anxiety, spreading shivers from the hairs of my arms to my neck. Gazing around the desert confirmed there wasn't an escape in sight. That much was obvious, but the guard still reminded us. His face emanated pleasure.

"Ladies, you are now standing in the African wilderness. Miles away from civilization, and even *further* away from freedom, because even if you *did* reach the Kingdom alone, you'd be executed immediately. Now, luckily for you, we know exactly where we're going, and if you *follow* us and reach the Kingdom *with us*, you won't be executed. Let me assure you, your deaths will not be quick, whether through execution or starvation, so I recommend…"

I was too concerned about my feet to care for what he was saying, so most of it was noise.

"Look around you," he gestured, reclaiming my attention. "Nothing but dry hell everywhere you look. So, if you honestly think you have a chance of surviving, there's your exit."

Each of us eyed each other. We all knew it was hopeless.

"Good," he laughed. "At least you all have common sense. That will benefit you down the road!"

My blood boiled, though not from the aggression of the sun or the scalding sand.

"Now, we are about to unravel this chain. It's long enough to accommodate all of you. We will lay it out fully, and then, in turn, you will stand over it, where we tell you to, so we can secure your cuffs to the chain. Then you will walk and sleep together for as long as required, *each day*, until we reach the Kingdom."

Now he had my attention, and his words made me queasy, almost vomit. But I held it back. Already thirsty, I gnashed my teeth from the cry of my feet, the pain of my torso and ribs and the relentless headache from the pounding I took earlier. How could I possibly survive this for days? And why was this happening to us?

None of us cried what our hearts pleaded us to, and all of us were secured to the chain spread carelessly on the red sand. They attached us to the chain in the exact same way they pried us from the wall in the ship, which had taken off and left us for dead. As its engines ignited it threw hotter air in our faces, making me pant. With every girl secured to the next, and led by the callous chief as his men walked alongside us, we set off into the midst of the oven.

Our chain was deliberately loose by our feet so we could walk, but no one could attempt to run, or walk faster than the person in front of them. The trek was arduous, and the first couple of hours seemed to last forever. I kept jumping from toe to toe to avoid my skin searing, and now the chain was red hot; at times it would welt my leg and leave a sore gash in its place. There was no food in sight, not even water, and already my stomach groaned. Every time I swallowed the dryness of my throat jabbed me like a blade.

Eventually I lost track of time, only gathering a sense of the hour when the sun finally lowered, an incredibly welcome sight. We were all drenched in sweat, which only made my thirst worse, especially when I was forced to watch it flow down the body of the person in front, reminding me of the running water we had at home. With nothing else to watch, I continually observed where the sun stood in the sky, willing it lower and lower as every exhausting minute passed. Once it disappeared entirely however, the desert almost immediately changed.

I trembled from the cold breeze, but my feet sighed in thankfulness. The sand had cooled. Regardless of the fact it was so dark that none of us could see more than a couple of feet forward, the guards drove us onward. *At least we'll reach the Kingdom faster*, I sighed, trying to rub my shoulders warm, only the cuffs prevented me from warming both at once. I grew increasingly weary and nauseous as we walked, until even the simple task of walking became a struggle; I would either lurch into the person in front or drag into the one behind. A guard near to where I stumbled saw what was happening and swiped my arm with his baton. It knocked some sense into me, at least. I was convinced I'd crumble into a carcass at any given moment.

"Fall here!" cried the chief, at last. I couldn't see him because he led from the far front, and I was around a quarter from the back. His voice echoed through the midnight air. "We sleep here tonight, and resume at sunrise! Now fall!"

I didn't need any encouragement to drop. It was the first proper chance to rest since I last slept at home, without hanging from a wall by my wrists. Silently we all crouched down, and I sprawled across the sand, head pointed to the stars, and the guard who marched beside us made his way up to the front, where the other guards were. We were alone.

The desert murmured to the sound of various insects and creatures while I laid there, gazing up at the moon. I admired how majestically it sat there, watching over the earth.

"I wonder how many stars there are?" whispered a tiny voice, lying to my left. It was soft and soothing to the ear.

"I've never tried to count them." I shifted my head and squinted. I could just about see her face, and she looked a couple years younger than me. She giggled to herself and looked back.

"No, I don't think anyone has." She focused on my eyes. "What's your name?"

"Aletheia. What's yours?"

"Olivia."

"That's a pretty name," I sighed, fighting my memories of Jedidiah's mother, Aunt Olivia.

"Thank you." She contemplated for a moment. "Aletheia. Like the legend?"

She was referring to a Greek myth about a woman with the power of a god who freed her people from captivity. My parents adored it.

"Yes. Actually, that's who I was named after." I forced a smile to put her at ease, but in reality, I felt as dark inside as the surroundings out.

"It's a very good story," she nodded.

"It is," I nodded back, hoping she would leave me to sleep. I understood her motivation though. At this point even small talk was a comfort.

"I saw what happened to you, in the ship. I'm sorry." Her eyes shifted to my cheek, which I could still feel as if I'd taken the thrashing five minutes ago. I wanted to cry.

"Don't be. It wasn't your fault," I grimaced, struggling to ignore the anger.

"You're brave. You took one last hit so the other girl wouldn't."

I didn't want her to think highly of me. I wasn't in the position to help any of them, so I tried to hush her. She didn't listen though, and continued to express how admirable she thought it was to do that, to take a hit for someone I didn't know. In my mind, it was only natural. No one wants to see another person get hurt, even if that means you might come off worse. That's how I had been brought up at least, but this Olivia was making it out to be a big deal. In the end, I tried politely asking her to let me sleep, not wishing to carry on the topic, but she took offense. Curling over to the opposite side of me she closed her eyes and blanked me out, apologizing for being so interested. I tried to get her to turn back around, lightly pushing at her shoulder, but she wouldn't budge. *Great going, Aletheia,* I rebuked.

I was the last one awake. The officers were up for hours, but even their voices had died out by the time my eyelids drooped. I wished I had Jedidiah to hold me as I slept. He always used to rest my head on his lap if I ever got too tired to play, but now I had to make do with a bed of unsupportive sand. *It doesn't matter. At least they're letting us sleep,* I reminded myself, trying to stay positive. That's what he would have done in my shoes, and I repeated it aloud until I could hear him saying it – until my tears ran dry and I was lulled into the dreams where he awaited me. It had been years since I let myself do that, and I knew if I met him there it would only hurt worse the next morning, but I couldn't resist, his grip was too tight, pulling me in to be with him where he could sing sweetly, over and over...

It doesn't matter.
It doesn't matter.
It doesn't matter.

CHAPTER IV
HEART OF A HERO

"RISE AND SHINE, bitches! What a beautiful day!" the chief snickered, shaking girls awake as he progressed down the line. I groaned. Getting up took tremendous effort, as my legs were both achy and sore from the burns of the chain. I gazed up to the sky and saw the sun was rising. I knew it would soon get unbearably hot so I was keen to keep moving. Olivia was the girl bound behind me, and as we journeyed into the heat of midday, I planned carefully what I would say to her.

The day battered away at us, and each hour grew increasingly difficult to endure. We were all famished and parched, but we weren't even offered a drink. Everything blurred into one feeling – pain, pain, pain – and the line slogged onward. The noise, never ending, of the chain striking wounded legs. The shrieks of girls as it did, only contested by the sobs of those brave enough to express themselves. Methodical, consistent. A melody of sorrow. It should never have changed.

But it did.

"Did I tell you to stop? *Why aren't you moving?*"

The chief again. Hearing him reminded me of those cliché drill sergeants in movies, which I was always grateful for not being real. Now though, I was living it.

"What's going on?" he hollered again, marching up the line. Everyone was confused and anxious to know what was happening, including me. I stepped out from my place and peered out. Several girls up from me was the answer.

A girl had fainted, barely able to keep her eyes open. The officer locked his hands around her hair and heaved her up, and she wailed.

"What's your name?" he jeered, still clutching her tousled locks.

She moaned louder.

"*What's your name?*"

"Jenny!" she bawled, tears gushing from her eyes.

I couldn't take it anymore.

"Leave her alone!" I howled, stepping entirely from the line so he could see me. I wasn't afraid.

"You again," he scowled, at which he waved down the men who had already encircled me, batons drawn.

"She can't walk, so let her go!" I got as close as my chains would let me. Adrenaline seized my senses.

"That's not a bad idea. She can't walk so she's no use to me, we don't need her."

The officer reached for his ray gun and shot her cuffs, releasing her from the chain. He dropped her on the sand where she collapsed in a heap, like a body with no bones.

"She can die there."

I wanted to ram his head into the rocks.

"No!" I cried. "I'll take her! I'll carry her!"

Every girl turned to me, all of them startled at what I was doing.

But what am I doing?

I kept my focus on the officer, whose eyes told me he was also alarmed. Suddenly his face lit up, and he grinned at me.

"You're interesting," he nodded. "If that's how you feel, take her." He eyed the girl. "Fall behind at your own expense, understood?"

I didn't respond, but continued to gaze into his cold, soulless eyes as my cuffs were released from the chain. Biting back the urge to lunge at the officer who freed me, I followed him to where the girl was slumped, directly below the chief. I walked right up to him, and my eyes didn't waver. He didn't own me, and I wanted him to know it. No matter what beating I could've taken.

"She's all yours," he sneered, gesturing me to pick her up.

I looked down at her, she was writhing in terrible pain. Thankfully, I'd been shown the 'fireman's carry' back home by my father, in case I had to carry someone who was injured from various Kingdom beatings. Dad told me it was important to learn, because it relied on technique more than strength. I bet that was something the chief didn't expect me to know. His smile was gone when I rose back up, the girl wilting neatly over my shoulder.

Now I had a new motivation: not to survive but to preserve someone's life. That was my responsibility, and despite the voices telling me I was emaciated, the breath of the girl spoke louder. Her restless groans drove me deeper into the plains, and I walked on, hypnotized by exhaustion. *It's only the second day.* I had to keep reminding myself, knowing many people in the past endured worse than me. Whenever I was hungry at home, or our well dried during the droughts, Dad would always explain there were many brave people who survived even when they had no food or water for several days. One story he used to tell me frequently was in the Bible, where Jesus resisted temptations from the devil, and with nothing to eat and drink for forty days and nights. It was hardly plausible, however he told me that wasn't the point, that the story can encourage us to forget our pain when we look to something greater than ourselves. Jesus was preparing to die for the world. The least I could do was get another girl to the other side, and ignore everything else, because I think that's what my father was trying to teach me all along.

Her weight buried me further into the sand. It seared at my ankles, grabbing me tight and trying to keep me there, like it was willing me down to hell. I couldn't watch my feet anymore, I had pictured the devil from Jesus' trial, raking my legs with his rugged nails.

You're just tired.

I knew it wasn't real, but regardless, it plagued my mind. It consumed everything, until demons were all I could see. Stalking me. Waiting for us to fall.

Occasionally, as the hours dragged into the late afternoon, I needed to lower the girl back to the ground to recover my strength. Each time I did, I would check her pulse, and what started as a weak heartbeat became a stronger, healthier one. She was out until the sun had gone, yet another day of pain. When I heard her cough to consciousness, however, the day made sense.

"Hey. You're awake," I smiled, carefully bringing her down so she could see me. I reckoned we were the same age, and she had straight black hair flowing all the way down to her midriff like me, just without the waviness.

"What happened? Who are you?" the girl whimpered erratically.

"You passed out," I hushed, turning my head to make a note of how far the line had moved. Several girls gazed back at me, coldly. "I carried you over my shoulder. We've got to keep moving, okay?"

She nodded, still dazed. I didn't think what I'd said even registered with her, but she allowed me to help her up. There I walked her next to me, her arm flung behind my neck. It took a ton of stress off my body, but I had to urge her on so we didn't fall behind the line.

At times, I needed to assure her we were almost ready to camp. Her eyes were welling up again, and her legs had grown less stable. It got so dark that once again it was impossible to see, so I had to keep us close to the line to ensure we didn't get lost. When the time came to fall and sleep off another brutal day, still with no food or water, the girl felt better and had a handle on her emotions. I helped her down, trying to keep the strain of her weight as I did, and we lay there, lost in the night.

"How are you feeling?" I checked her temperature. She felt hot, but not as bad as she had midday.

"Better now. So thirsty though. How do I feel?"

"Cooler," I assured. "At least the air will cool you down."

She nodded at me. I assumed she was tired, trying to save her voice, however as I continued to count the stars, it came back.

"Thank you. For what you did. Thank you so much."

The girl was lying next to me, facing me, so I rolled over to her side. Even though the breeze was icy and my teeth were chattering, the cold stopped affecting me at her comment.

"Hey, I wasn't going to let you die," I smiled, fighting the tears.

"Why?"

I loved her eyes, the moonlight danced in her large pupils.

"So, your name's Jenny," I snapped back, trying to shift the topic.

"You know?" She clearly couldn't remember much, so I eased her in.

"You told the officer your name when he grabbed you, and I heard it. I'm Aletheia."

"Oh, yes. It's Jenny Auburn." She appeared to be contemplating something, her face screwed in hard thought. "Your last name?"

"Mirabel."

A sudden realization wiped her face, and she smiled.

"You were Jedidiah's friend, weren't you?"

I was half asleep until she said his name, which shot my head up and my eyes open sharply. How did she know about Jedidiah? Who was this girl?

"How do you-?"

"Sorry, I should explain," she interrupted. "Jedidiah was my cousin. He used to come with his dad to my place with the food they caught on the weekends."

That makes sense.

"Every Sunday," she continued abruptly, as if assembling her fragmented thoughts. "And they even caught us a little extra, for the week ahead, because we don't have much."

"Nobody has much," I muttered, as I shut my eyes.

"He always spoke highly of you." She nudged my arm. "He told me you were his girlfriend."

I couldn't ignore her, I had started to weep, missing him painfully. Wiping my tears, I turned my head to her and laughed quietly. That was *so* Jedidiah: lying to people that he had a girl-friend because he was about as popular as, well, me.

"I'm not his girlfriend."

Jenny observed my happiness intently as I thought back to his quirks, and giggled herself.

"I didn't think you were."

Her eyes were watery, too.

"He always used to make himself out to be bigger than he was. He even told me this one time, he caught this big-"

"One-hundred-pound salmon," we stated at once, and we both proceeded to laugh the tears from our eyes. I was practically burst-ing with gratitude for meeting Jedidiah's cousin. How, of all the people I could've met, did I manage to find her? Still, having her around was almost like staring Jedidiah in the face. It hurt too.

"I miss him," I sighed, resting my head down.

"So do I." Jenny curled up closer to me, and I reached my arm for her, wrapping it around her front as she rested on my lap.

﹌

Morning dawned, and the wind was still fresh. The guards rallied us up as before and quickly we were moving again. I wasn't sure how much longer we would have to walk, or if we'd see the end of this day before reaching the Kingdom, however knowing I had such a close connection with Jenny made her weight ever easier to bear. She was like a sister I was never given: one who I could talk to, and who understood me. I couldn't do that with my real sister, not least because she was six years younger than me. She and my brother lived with my grandparents in another state, because my parents were committed to feeding those who relied on our farm's produce. I called them the JJs: Jacob and Joselyn. We could only see them at Christmas, if we could afford it. The sun rose and beat us like stones, but together we trudged forward, arm in arm, not once falling behind the line. Until the unthinkable happened. Everyone stopped, as if I was reliving yesterday.

Another girl had collapsed.

When the chief guard saw it, and stormed over to where her body lay, his haunting grin came back, making me ill. I wasn't far from where she'd fallen, but I couldn't see her, the girls chained to her front and back were too tall. Suddenly I burned, not from the heat of the desert or the chains lashing at my legs, but from an indescribable rage. I hadn't harbored anger to this extremity since the night of Jedidiah's capture. I gritted my teeth so hard it felt like they would shatter – shooting pain through my gums – and I watched, in silent torment, as the guard shot the girl from her chains and tossed her body to the side. Before he marched back down, knowing full well my eyes were driven to him, he shouted back.

"Looks like you couldn't save this one, *hero*."

"Don't!" Jenny begged, tugging me back as I tried to pursue him. I was free – no chains or anything – and one last strike to his repulsive face was enough to die for. That's what my head told me, but resting my eyes on Jenny was enough to snap me back to sanity. She was my responsibility now.

Falling at the girl's body I sobbed, and Jenny knelt beside me, holding me. I shook the girl hysterically, shouting at her, but she didn't respond. I tried pumping at her chest, still wailing at the top of my voice, but she was truly silenced. I cried more, hitting my fists against the ground, the desperation engulfing my voice until I couldn't manage another word. I could only cry.

"You can't save us all Aletheia," Jenny soothed, clutching me firmly. She was right, and I knew it, but it didn't make a difference. I couldn't save Jedidiah, and because I hadn't paid attention to the line, I failed this girl, too.

"It's my fault," I groaned, as Jenny broke me away. "It's my fault!"

CHAPTER V
A HERO'S WELCOME

"STOP. STOP CRYING," I repeated, clutching my ears in a feeble attempt to shut out the weeping around me. It was quiet at first, but soon my mind amplified it to a piercing level. Sleep was impossible. "Stop crying! Please...*stop crying!*"

"Aletheia, *shhh*, it's okay. Aletheia!" Jenny hushed.

More tears flowed, violently.

"Aletheia, look at me. Look at me!"

Jenny sat up and grabbed hold of my shoulders, shaking me. I also sat upright, panting heavily. She brushed my eyes dry.

"It's okay, you're with me. We're fine."

This wasn't the girl I'd salvaged, tearful and frightened. She was composed, her face angelic.

"It's okay. It's okay." She took me in, cradling me. I gasped. My throat had constricted.

"What's happening?" I spluttered, watching my hands as they shook. My heart was coming through my chest.

"You were having a panic attack," she whispered, rubbing my arms. "You're dehydrated, so that doesn't help. Just focus on me. I'm not leaving you, okay?"

Suddenly, I was being mothered. I wasn't in the right state to look after anyone.

"Ok," I agreed, pressing my hands against my forehead as I tried to claw back some sense. Ever since the girl's death that afternoon, I hadn't been myself. "I want to go h-home." I had become the same sobbing kid the night Jedidiah was taken.

"Try and get some sleep. I'll be right here. I won't sleep until you do, I promise." Jenny ushered me back down so I could face the stars, resting my head across her own body this time. Gently, she ran her fingers through my hair as I lay there, which I didn't mind at all. I wasn't shaking as much now, and my heart rate had slowed. Jenny's chest was warm, like lying on a soft fabric which had spent hours in the sun. I didn't feel myself drift off, but sure enough night melted into day. I opened my eyes to see the stars I admired gone, and Jenny asleep.

Already sweating, mostly from angst, I assured myself this would be the last day, that *we would* reach the Kingdom, surely. We had no food, and more crucially, there was only so long we could go without water. I didn't want to think of water, it only made the sandpaper texture of my tongue plainer to me, but I couldn't shake the memory of my last drink by the well, how it flowed down my throat as sweet as honey, for water was all I craved.

"Time to rise! Get up and move it!"

Please God, be the last day.

My voice was charred, and the inside of my mouth was like bone. Even the slightest pressure on my foot brought on screaming pain, it blazed up my leg and cramped my stomach. I could barely concentrate. Now even the task of walking was too complicated, and I had to think hard about how to step forward.

Around me girls dropped like flies, tossed into the smoldering sand to breathe their last, and be buried by the gusts at nightfall. But I didn't have room to worry about them. I was faint, and with every step, I became giddier, until my whole body was an iron weight lugging me down.

"Aletheia! Aletheia, stay with me!" Jenny yelled, tugging at my arms. I had collapsed to my knees.

I could see her, but she was moving all around me, up and down and everywhere, flickering and distorting like she was submerged in electric water. The pounding of my head was unbearable, but I got a fraction of what she said.

"Aletheia! We're almost there, come on! Look! It's in sight."

My head reeled. I was disorientated, and couldn't stop it, but I was still able to guide it upward and across to where the line was headed.

And there it was.

A grand and humungous wall towering high in the deserts, hiding within it the Kingdom of Old Africa, just as my mother described. Above its blindingly high wall poked the top of various buildings which reached all the way up to the sun, so it was impossible to look at them for more than a second. Despite the fact I was utterly exhausted, the sheer scale of what lay ahead was enough to leave me awestruck.

"Wow," I croaked, through withered vocals. "It's. Beautiful."

"Come on," Jenny groaned as she dragged me up. "Stay with me!"

Hurling ourselves closer, we gazed at the scene unfolding. I was a young farm girl who knew nothing but farms and forest, and a relatively small town which tallest building was no more than four times my height. This was a whole new league of exciting, and yes, somewhere inside, I was genuinely excited. And terrified.

I couldn't express how thankful I was to Jenny, literally because I could barely talk, but it went without saying. She'd been there for me just as I had for her, pulling me forward as we unburdened our weight on each other's shoulder, taking turns to switch and let the other person recover. I was dazed, and not even sure what time it was, but I still managed to smile at her as we reached the Kingdom wall, and she smiled back.

"I won't leave you," I uttered, under my breath.

"Stand still!" the guard ordered, back to his drill sergeant persona. "Well."

I just knew he was about to give one of those tedious speeches.

"Congratulations," he smirked, as he paced up the line. "I didn't believe half of you would get this far. Lord Hane is going to be very proud, you resilient women!"

Hurry up, I pleaded. My legs trembled.

"Today, on the fourth day of your trial, you have done yourselves and your nation proud. Well done. But, this was only the *first* phase," he added. "And ahead of you, you shall prepare for the biggest moment of your lives."

He jabbed his finger at us as he spoke. They looked gruesome, plagued with sharp, chipped nails.

"*Far* tougher than a mere four-day trek in the Kingdom's backyard. You'll be wishing you could do it all again as forfeit!" His eyes had lit up again, the other guards laughed in sync. "But, should you survive the challenges ahead of you, and I have *every* confidence you will…"

We locked eyes, but I couldn't tolerate it for long.

"Your reward will be *so* great, and you'll be elevated to *such* high honor, you will be bowing in gratitude for the opportunity."

Come closer, I frowned, clenching my fists.

"Any questions?"

You could hear a pin drop.

"Then let us…proceed. Break the gate, and expose the glory," he cried to the sky, outstretching his arms.

Below us, the ground shook violently. A few girls tumbled from the shock, including me, but I managed to stretch out my hand to break the fall. In front of us, the large stone wall collapsed into itself, folding neatly into the sand like it never used to be there. Struck by a sight so incredible, I forgot for a moment where, and how desperate for water, I was. A bit like my worries had fallen away, along with the great weight of the wall. Taking each other in our arms for support, Jenny and I followed as the Kingdom officials led the girls inside the perimeter, still keeping them in strict formation as they staggered into the great city.

My eyes were lost in its extravagance. I could move my head, but I was breathless. Around us, standing as tall and mighty as gods, were the most advanced and complicated towers I could never have imagined even in my wildest dreams. We were entering a *gargantuan* city, which appeared to stretch on endlessly, like the desert, and everywhere I looked were people: smartly dressed, beautiful, and well-groomed. They gawked at us all like we were a new breed of animal, but they couldn't come near us – to our left and right shimmered strong force fields, keeping the civilians away from the road. A road leading us from the desert to what looked like, from what I could see, the center of the city. I clung to Jenny to avoid falling in front of them.

It was a bizarre sight. Everything was high tech and mind blowing, many buildings were afloat, but at the same time the city adopted an ancient feel to it. Decorative stone pillars adorned the road on either side, and there were statues of men – famous officials – and lions, which were stunning. Some were roaring, and others were eyeing us silently, like they were waiting to pounce. Even fountains emerged near the busy center, their waters glimmering in the midday sun, as if crystalized. I yearned to run to one, and dive in its hydration, but it wasn't possible. They were all behind the force fields.

The floor below us was paved, like the square of my town, but it was perfectly smooth to the touch. It still burned to walk on; it was in direct sunlight, but that didn't concern me anymore. The soles of my feet had withered away, and I was stepping on nothing more than blistered numbness, only slightly able to feel the pavement with what was left of my toes. My neck also ached terribly, so for the remainder of our journey, I kept my head down, regardless of how keen I was to embrace the new scenery. I forced myself to look up again though, one last time, to see the city square.

Many Kingdom officers were lined up alongside us, kitted with various armor, animal skins, and weapons to hand. Not far away from them, and us, stood what appeared to be an arena, or colosseum, like the ones we learned about at school from the Roman times, and aside to it, overlooking us from a low balcony were three people: two Kingdom guards – one man and woman – and in the center of them a youngish man wearing a suit, vastly distinctive from the many thousands around us. They watched us from a powerful-looking tower, the summit of which stretched so high I'd seen it from the desert. The buildings around it were plotted in such a way that they gave significance to this one, as if all part of one towering fortress.

I wanted to stop and keep watching the three people – the woman met my gaze – but there was no opportunity to take it all in. I was pried from Jenny by another guard, each of us individually bound with our wrists magnetized together, sealed at the front. Simultaneously, I found myself being led into the confines of the Colosseum, until the sun was shut from view.

Inside the atmosphere was dark and murky, yet still muggy and unbearable to breathe in. The walls were stone, and it looked like I had been sucked into one of my old textbooks, gazing at Ancient Rome from within the building. The corridors were incredibly long, even while inside we endured an arduous trek to the final room. I had to keep encouraging myself that they couldn't keep us walking forever.

As we were shoved into the last room, we were all instructed to get into what looked like pods, which were almost too tight to enter. One-by-one the guards broke us free from our cuffs. My bands had never been released, only separated so I could carry Jen, so my wrists were still as sore as everyone else's. Even if only briefly, it was nice to feel them again. They did however, promptly secure us again as the pods all had their own cuffs, positioned by our wrists and ankles, and a strap fastened our torsos.

I wasn't being forced to walk anymore, so I was able to keep calm and think, taking in my surroundings a little better than before. We were inside a laboratory of sorts, and wherever my head turned was advanced, brain-puzzling equipment, gadgets, and technology, all of it flashing or making noise. Most of the officers left, leaving only a few behind, but they stood there firm, and blank, as if inhuman. I tried to keep facing the other direction, but the puff of the door retracted my attention to the entrance, where the guards were.

From the entrance emerged more elegantly groomed men and women of the city, only this time they were in white coats. Unlike the Kingdom guards they didn't appear threatening whatsoever, but my mind raced ahead of me, leaving logic in the dust. Were they going to run tests on us? Experiment on or torture us? I flinched, picturing wads of voltage pulsing through me, charring my insides, my body convulsing in inescapable constraint. No escape. No escape.

My legs were so worn down, I could barely stand; they were giving out beneath me as I continued to envision the worst, the difficulty of straightening them growing steadily unbearable. My torso dropped further to the ground, and an immense strain tore at my arms as the cuffs pressed deeper into my bone. One of the white coats hurried over to me, but as my head fell, I could only make out her feet through my squint.

"We're losing this one!"

Her colleague also rushed up to me, handing her a small capsule.

"Eat this!" she demanded, holding a strange gel-like chew in her hand. It looked as though it contained an ocean, raging majestic within the pill's shell.

"What's…that?" I uttered weakly. She forced it into my mouth.

"Chew! Chew it, girl!"

With every effort I could muster, I clenched my jaws across the capsule, my teeth sinking deep into the gel as its outward shell cracked, snapping loudly as it did. At the same time, the mighty roar of the sea bellowed down my throat and rushed into every fainting area of my body. I gasped desperately, choking, as if I was drowning, but in that miraculous second all feeling came back – my muscles no longer withering, my eyes wide open in eagerness. The taste of exhaustion once bitter on my tongue, flushed away, and with it the sandy texture that tormented my throat. All aspects of my dehydration gone, all in that instant. I couldn't believe it. I stood there, bound in my pod, panting.

"What-what was that?" I gaped, mesmerized by my restored power. The strength that left me in the desert, suddenly pumping through me again like it never left. Like travelling in the desert was a dream, and now I was awake.

"A hydration capsule," the woman smiled. "It's full of the minerals your bodies are lacking, but unlike other consumables it's absorbed immediately. That's why you feel so alert."

I looked around. The others were being treated with it, too.

"You have just experienced the revival phase. Your body will be in a lot of shock – it's a bit like rebooting software. You need to adjust to the reboot, so you'll feel frequent cramps specifically close to your stomach and chest. You'll sweat, and it will get difficult to stay upright. Don't worry." She cupped my hand. "This is normal. It's your body trying to fight the process because it's so unnatural, and it thinks it's under attack. We have to keep you awake though, which is why we've secured you like this, otherwise you could die."

I nodded gingerly to her explanation, but for some reason, I trusted her. She was only trying to help.

"Unfortunately, the energy shot you need can only be applied during the final phase of your hydro consumption, but once your body starts to relax and the sweating ceases, we can inject a concentrated burst of all your deficient nutrition, and then we'll have you up and running just as you were. Until then, there's nothing more we can do. I'm sorry."

It looked as though the woman truly pitied my situation, but I was capable of a smile back.

"Thank you," I mouthed, at which she left with her colleagues, leaving only the guards by the doors.

Silence flooded the room.

CHAPTER VI

THE KINGDOM TRIALS

I LEAPT UP from my pillow as the guard opened my cell, because this time he wasn't holding any food or drink, something that hadn't happened since I was first taken from the lab and locked in. We were ordered to stay quiet, but all of us were guided out of the dungeons and lined up at the back wall. This was the first time I'd seen the other girls since the day we were strapped to those medical pods, a thought that sent shivers down my aching spine, because the night that followed our treatment was the worst of my life. None of us slept through the withdrawal phase.

I could just make out Jenny's face in the dim light of the torches behind us, but I had learned my lesson. I didn't call out to her, fearful of yet another beating. All of us stood there, not muttering a word, hoping the guards would finally take us out of the dreary cellar. They didn't give any verbal orders, but instead signaled us to follow them, silently, and sure enough we walked up the same steps that led us to lonely confinement. I couldn't remember what the Colosseum looked like until its hallway greeted us again. This time it appeared grander, but I guess anything would after spending that long in darkness.

All the hope and relief that budded up from being outside immediately withered and died when I saw who was waiting for us: the chief. I couldn't look at him without trembling, so I tried to watch the other guards instead. He played with his baton as we gathered, smiling at us. Other girls gazed at me; they knew what happened to me before. Their eyes were fixed to my head, staring at a wound I still hadn't seen for myself. If I'm honest, I didn't want to. I knew what I looked like before everything else happened, and that's how I wanted to picture myself. 'Beautiful' like my mother told me I was.

"Well, ladies…"

I even hated his voice.

"Over the past month, you have recovered from your trial, which you all survived. You are the strongest we could find, and you should all be proud."

It didn't surprise me a month had passed, but my cheek was still sore.

"Now, the time has come for you to meet your king, Lord Hane, who out of his generosity will give one of you the opportunity to enjoy all the goodness the Kingdom has to offer for the rest of your life. You are ready, rested and recovered, to begin your preparation for what the Lord has in store. In a moment, you shall meet him, and your future advisors, who will play a great importance in your survival. So I recommend you keep silent, and do as you are told."

With their batons drawn, more guards appeared from around the corner, shoving us into formation again. Jenny managed to edge her way closer to me during the chief's speech, but just as our fingers connected, she was torn from me again, dragged to the front of the line. The chief flashed me a grin as he tugged her away.

When we were first led into the city, into the center where I saw the Colosseum, I couldn't comprehend how big it was. Partially I'm sure due to my drunken state of emaciation, but looking back I was too distracted by the woman on the balcony – I was certain our eyes met – so there wasn't enough time to appreciate anything else. Here though, as I walked the seemingly endless passageways of the Colosseum, I realized it must've been three or four times bigger than it first appeared. *Why is it so big?* I pondered this question for a while, and I had plenty of time to do so. There was a laboratory, a dungeon, and clearly some type of arena. *What else is in here?* We came to some archways which we were redirected to follow, but even that led to more hallways and archways. It was like a stone maze – everything around me was of pale cream brick, with yet more threateningly large statues and pillars planted in and around the walkways. Ancient. Fascinating. Surreal.

At last, sunlight glowed through one final archway. I looked at my presentation. I was still in my school uniform, but now its white cotton was an ugly grey, and dark smudges suffocated the floral stitching at its hem. The threading around the neck and sleeves was loose and tattered, and in various places, the fabric had ripped entirely, exposing my burned legs further. I knew I was in no condition to meet important people, particularly those who could ensure my survival. Who would care about *this?* I looked awful. I grew more self-conscious the more I thought it through, already sentencing myself to a hopeless end. There wasn't time to focus on myself for long though…for my point of the line had reached the entryway.

The sun filled the atmosphere gloriously, like an enormous spotlight. Though I was still without footwear, the soles of my feet had crusted into an unattractive mixture of dried blood and dead skin, so walking was painless. I was no longer starving or thirsty, nor faint, so this time I took care to observe everything. There were various apparatuses positioned around the court, which was paved in creamy grey granite. I wasn't sure what most of the apparatuses were, but they were all large. Some had hanging ropes, some monkey bars, some looked like tall climbing frames, and others had rings to grip. Around it all sat boulders and various weights and equipment, like sacks and large tires which people used for cars, until they were all scrapped Year Zero due to their impact on the environment. There was also a section littered with bars and dumbbells, as well as benches, squat cages and safety catch bars to use them. Equipment once banned from the outside nations, piled everywhere I looked.

Inside the court awaited hundreds of Kingdom officers, armed and focused on us, but that was the least shocking discovery. Hundreds of other girls had also been rounded up, with more pouring in every second, their vast assortment of shapes and bobbing heads resembling multihued streams filling the world's largest basin. They had been lined up in rows, which we were added to from the far left. My eyes stalked the chief as he walked up the aisle where the groups parted, toward a line of decorated guards at the front.

Sobs filled the air, which I could hear even though most of the girls were trying not to draw attention to themselves. I felt so helpless. I wanted to move from my place and embrace all of them, but there was no point in trying. None of us were cuffed, but there was no possibility to move from where we were, from our place in the line, as fencing us in on either side stood a trail of guards so far up the court I couldn't see its walls, and beside each line stood a guard at both ends.

Silence befell the court.

Encompassing us were many empty bleachers, which parted at the front, rear, and sides for wide steps that led up to an archway. Emerging from the darkness of the front archway, and walking down the steps but remaining in the midsection so they were in view, appeared the mysterious suited gentleman accompanied by the man and woman I spied before, the day I was dragged into the Colosseum. It left me breathless, and fearful, the sight of these magnificent beings, all three of whom made the guards surrounding us look like something they'd scrape off their shoe at the end of the day. The young man's suit clutched his body firmly, tailored perfectly to his chest and shoulders to reveal a powerful physique. He made my father look scrawny, that much I knew even though he was clothed, but his two escorts were even more impressive. Both were the embodiment of beauty, shimmering in their armor in the same way fish dazzle in the midday sun. They appeared as if they could kill us with a penknife, especially me. In fact, I reckoned they could've singlehandedly slaughtered every officer in that court, including the chiefs. Their weapons, particularly the mystifyingly radiant spear of the woman, gave me chills.

Finally, the suited man spoke. His voice shook the court like thunder.

"Good day, ladies, and welcome to the Kingdom. I imagine you are all keen to know why you are here, and what happens next. Well, as I'm sure many of you are too young to know, allow me to first introduce myself. I am Hurtis Hane, Lord and ruler of the Kingdom, and of your nations, and *this* shall be your home, which I give to you, in the years that lie ahead.

"I apologize for the treatment you bore upon arrival, and I hope you will forgive me, truly. But…it was necessary as part of the process I have envisioned to build a new world, and a new culture. One where there will no longer be risk of losing loved ones to war, where brother is forced to kill brother to settle pitiful disagreements. We shall be one people! United for the first time since this wretched earth gave life, and through one of *you* – the Kingdom's Daughter – we will have peace.

"The pain you have suffered is admirable, and will not go to waste, for you are now ready to be a part of the greatest movement humanity has known. I have decided, therefore, to give the young, the weak, and the irrelevant, a chance to prove their worth and rebuild earth's future as the cornerstone of its new foundation.

"In Ancient Rome, gladiators were more than just entertainment, they embodied honor. They gave their lives to the cause of the Empire, to fight, humbling themselves before the Emperor, even if that fight was to be their last. Not only were the gladiators brave, they were true warriors, and through the games Rome gave rise to some of the greatest heroes in history: men who denied themselves, so they may serve. And thus, it occurred to me there is no greater warrior than one who has pledged themselves to a cause. Ladies, I aspire to raise an army. One of freedom, comprised of the strongest warriors this world will ever know. And for that, I need you. In this place you shall be trained, and when you are ready, you will fight each other. As gladiators you will fall, and the woman who remains, the strongest, shall have the privilege of mothering my army, leading it by the strength within her, giving rise to a Kingdom that will abolish crime, and bring an end to evil. Dear ladies, history will remember this…as The Kingdom Trials!"

I couldn't comprehend what I was hearing. Gladiators? Us? My palms and forehead sweated at the word, which kicked and screamed in my mind like Hane was stood next to me, shouting in my face. It was increasingly difficult to breathe, each breath grew shorter than the last. Stumbling, I reached for my neighbor's ebony hand, a hand I'd never felt in my life, or whose eyes ever crossed mine amongst the sea of girls at school. She caught me, holding me tight so I wouldn't fall, absorbing the tremors of my body into her own. Every last memory of my mother, my father, my brother and sister, grandma and grandpa, Mr. Milano, and Jedidiah played over in my thoughts on repeat. Taunting me with the reality those memories would be my last, that the last my mother would see of me is her desperate daughter screaming at her to get away. My father, too, watching half-conscious on the street as they take me to my death, which would be presented in a colosseum full of spectators, all cheering. My lips parted.

"*This* is the Ludus. In the spirit of the Roman games, I have provided you a school, and around you stand my advisors, whom I give to you as a gift. They are experts in combat and war, and in a moment, each of you shall be allocated one of your own. They will work with you like their child, giving you every ounce of knowledge they can offer so you may live, and in doing so exceed your own expectations.

"In the ancient days, gladiators were forced to live with their opponents: train, eat and sleep with them. But not you. We are a civilized community, and we will never force you to kill a friend. Therefore, you shall train and live in your groups, within your respective nations, but the opposing groups will be your adversaries, and you will be kept separate from them. It is through unity, which brings forth strength, that man can overcome the greatest obstacles. Befriend each other, *learn* from each other, bring out the strengths of *each other*, and you will find victory.

"Brave women, I welcome you to the Iron Court. Complete with the same equipment that has trained our past warriors, its efficiency has stood the test of time, shaping the gladiators before us into the resilient fighters they were. In the hope that you may flourish, I give you these grounds, these tutors, and to further ensure your success the Gymnasium. A room that lies beneath the court ready to assess your fitness, equip you with skills, and discover your hidden gifts, until you emerge the champions you are.

"Hidden within you is the potential for greatness. Use both sources of training provided, listen to your advisor, and your efforts will serve you well. You have each been given the honor... to be slaves to a cause."

CHAPTER VII

THE HERO'S HERO

No one dared to whisper. You could've cut the tension not just with a knife, but the tip of your fingernail. A thousand hearts pounded in unison – soon to be a thousand silenced, but one. How? How was it possible to create such a cruel fate for the innocent? I looked around the court, searching for the answer, but all I could see for row after row of girls as far as my eyes would allow was the sickly sheet of blood-drained faces.

I wanted to break away from the line, run down the aisle and up toward the steps where Hane stood. Every bone in my body wanted to grapple him to the ground and pound his chest until his lungs gave out. I didn't care if it meant my end, I was dead anyway, the least I could do was bring that fiend down with me. I bit my lip hard, so hard my teeth pierced the skin, drawing blood. I wouldn't make it. There was a whole gathering of chiefs below him, let alone his escorts.

How do you sleep at night?

I ran my tongue along the open wound, glaring intently upon his dark, grinning expression. I had never killed anything more than a fish, but should anyone had given me a moment with that man alone, I wouldn't have hesitated to rip his head from his spine.

My anger was diverted by a bizarre floating orb, which shot out of nowhere and came to Hane's side. It had what looked like a camera piece on the front, and there weren't any engines or thrusters from where I could see, so it was anyone's guess how it stayed in the air.

"Because my advisors vary in skill and experience, and only *eight* lucky ladies can train with my chiefs, it's only fair we determine who pairs with them, as well as the other officers, with this unbiased Chance Globe. This magnificent device has been programmed with the identity of each and every one of you. In fact, there isn't a living soul on this earth it doesn't know.

"At random, it will approach an officer, state clearly who they are, and then it will pick one of you and do the same. Then that officer will join you where you are, so there's no need to move and cause a disturbance."

Whether Hane had exaggerated the Globe's ability or not, to know everyone by name, it didn't surprise me the Kingdom had developed such a tool. No one's life is personal anymore. Back home the first thing that happens when someone gives birth is horrendous. They take your baby away, right from the moment of delivery, and you don't see it again for weeks until they've confirmed it's a healthy child, with no genetic flaws. Disabled and incurably ill civilians were outlawed at the Great Reset, Year Zero. I was taught this was because they represented everything wrong with the Old Age, and opposed the values of the newly emerged Kingdom: power, health, and prosperity. Apparently, these people only served as a reminder of humanity's impurity, and for the world to rid itself of its past, 'it must also rid itself of impurity.' They didn't cover that topic much further in school, but for as long as I can remember I'd never seen a disabled person around the town, at least not someone 'born' dysfunctional. It was like they were a myth. I didn't accept that was a coincidence, nor did I believe when they came to my mother following her second pregnancy that the baby 'didn't make it.'

"Celadus Mardas," the Globe announced, hovering over the faces of one of the eight chiefs. He was enormous, the biggest of the chiefs there, but most impressive about his physique were his arms. They were twice as big as my thighs. Once the Globe stated his name, it went on to breeze amongst the crowd, not settling immediately on one person, as if it was trying to determine who was worthy. I prayed it wasn't me, it looked like he ate my kind for a staple diet. What horrors would await me then? I wouldn't last the first day.

Celadus' 'lucky lady' was someone I imagined to be a perfect canvas for him to work with. She was already double the build I was, and my own body was nothing to scoff at. Spear fishing had strengthened my arms, and my legs were toned. I was healthy, but this other girl looked like she worked for the Kingdom. 'Sophie Hartwell' was her name, and fortunately she was one of my own, from North America. The thought of opposing her in a fight gave me goosebumps, and my heart throbbed every time I pictured it. As far as I could make out from the girls around me, she was the most intimidating by far.

"Tobi Malone," the Globe continued, its voice feminine. Strangely, it sounded realistic, as if a woman was standing beside me, calmly reassuring me with a motherly presence everything was going to be fine. The lips of the girl who had held me so dearly – regardless that we'd never met – quivered, and her body went limp. Now I was the one holding her up, but it was ok, she was as light as a feather. She looked as delicate as one, too.

"Hey, *shhh*. It'll be okay," I hushed, with the smallest voice I could manage. She may not have known my name, but now I knew hers. She had been paired with a towering yet lean man, who was already marching toward her. He wasn't a chief, but I had no clue why. Frankly, all the officers appeared like they were bred to kill. There wasn't one I would've been happy to have.

Gingerly I released her from my grasp, and the guard stood beside her. I hadn't been this close to an official since confronting the chief, who occasionally met my eyes like it was a coincidence, but I made sure never to look away when he did.

"Commodus Stratis," stated the Globe, settled by his face. I'm not religious; I take one look at the world and I wonder how anyone is. Now though, I found myself praying, and begging to a God I didn't even believe was real. Every cell in my body was desperate. Anyone was better than him.

Don't pick me. Don't pick me. I wished I could've taken Tobi's hand again, but thick armor blotted her from sight, and I didn't want to startle the girl on my other side. She had enough to worry about herself, occasionally glancing at my cheek as the Globe hovered over our heads. I don't think she wanted Commodus either.

It was a good minute before the Globe settled, and it dragged like several hours. My past life, the life I would never return to, flashed before my eyes. The days I ate breadsticks with Jedidiah, and played darts with him and my dad; my first day at school when my mother was called up, because I was a screaming nervous wreck. Most of all though, most poignant in my mind was the oath I swore by Hamza and Olivia's graves: that I would find their son, and bring him back.

"I'm sorry," I muttered, for guilt had struck me harder than the baton had my cheek. I would never see his sweet, heartwarming smile again. I had failed.

"Aletheia Mirabel."

I dropped to my knees. No one dared catch me. There were

still hundreds left, hundreds of potential takers. But the drone lowered itself on me.

Scanned *my* face.

This…couldn't be happening. Soon I would wake up, and I'd see Jedidiah laughing over me. He'd tell me I hit my head on a branch as we chased each other through the forest like we always did, and that I'd been knocked out. I'd be a child again. A young, free, twelve-year-old girl who would appreciate life and my mother would be stunned by my change.

For a moment, I felt the weight ease from my shoulders, blinded by a trance that everything was so tragic it couldn't be real. Soon I'd explain it to Jedidiah, and he'd just call me a nutcase for the rest of my life. That would be the worst of it, simply labelled a 'nutcase' by a friend who was never taken. I braced myself. *Ok, now's the time to wake up. Now's the time.* But there was no time. No glorious moment of the sunlight stroking my eyes as they opened. No one waiting for me to snap into consciousness. I was, as ever, wide awake.

Commodus' hand dug deep into my shoulder, his cracked nails piercing my skin. I didn't dare look at him, but kept my eyes straight as he yanked me onto my feet. The vibrations of his laugh pulsed through me like a current, and a tremor spread from my shoulders to my toes, as if his touch was electrified.

'We're going to have a lot of fun with you.' Tirelessly I thought back to that day. The beating. His taunting. His gruff voice was all I could hear, throbbing in my head and reminding me death was close, and it wouldn't be fast. I didn't count on making it to the arena.

"Wait!"

As if someone had broken me from hypnosis, my thoughts came back to reality. Far, far away from me at the front rose the voice of a woman – the only adult woman in the court. The same woman I locked eyes with in the city center, the godly warrioress that stood silently by Hane's side, gazing at our doomed faces. Again, she cried out.

"Wait! You will not take her!"

Maybe I was dreaming after all, I couldn't believe what I was seeing. This woman, who was draped in a holy wine robe and whose rainbow range of jewels glittered like a starry night, had left Hane's side and was halfway down the aisle to reach me. Quickly at that. Hane, who appeared as racked with confusion as I was, just let her do it. Utterly lost for words. She came beside me and Commodus, but I still refused to look at either of them. My heart was about to leap from my mouth, so I kept swallowing, trying to keep it in.

"Don't say a word," she ordered, but very quietly. Her breath was moist in my ear. I wanted to answer her, but I couldn't shift my eyes from Hane.

He was looking in my direction.

"*Excuse me?*" he erupted, his voice wrestled by an equal share of rage and bewilderment. *Don't worry,* I thought, entranced by Hane's fury. *I'm not saying a thing.*

"My Lord-" suddenly Commodus tried to have his say, but he was promptly silenced.

"I did not address you!" Hane pointed his finger sternly, as if he had the divine authority to blot him out in a twitch. Commodus acknowledged this very quickly. "Explain this."

"I wish to train the girl."

Hane was taken aback. So was I. He scowled, as if wrestling for a response. Even still the woman held her ground, confident, no quiver or remote signs of fear, for I had finally mustered the courage to observe her.

After what felt like a millennium of nothingness – no voices, no movements, just anticipation – Hane spoke.

"And why is this?"

Good question.

"*Well?*" He was growing worryingly impatient.

She looked down at me, her eyes calm and reassuring. Somehow, I believed she knew what she was doing, however that comfort was shortly overshadowed by her response, or rather lack of response, as all she could manage was a belated sigh.

"I'll ask you one more time."

"I believe she needs me," she countered, just as I'd braced myself for the end. I was so deeply relieved Hane hadn't demanded for our deaths that I'd failed to process her response. Suddenly the reality of what she said hit me without warning, hitting me almost as brutally as a sword could have, if Hane had summoned it. A sharp blow right in the gut.

"Wait, what-?" I tried to speak out, but her hand came down on my mouth. Her eyes were no longer calm, but instead glared at me the same way my mother did if I'd come home too late. They told me if I didn't keep silent, she might silence me for good. But I pushed her hand away.

"No, tell me! What do you mean?"

The woman, glancing at Hane, tried to cover my mouth again, but I jerked to the side.

"*Don't touch me!*" I screamed.

In an instant, my arms were grasped from behind, locked to my sides by Commodus. To my astonishment however, the woman hit his arms away.

"Look at me!" She grabbed me like a naughty child. "Now's not the time for this!"

"You realize that by agreeing to train this girl you forfeit your position as my deputy?" Hane's voice drowned the chaos, bringing everyone's attention back to the front. I swear before he'd spoken, every single eye was on me, I'd never known such self-consciousness. My palms were drenched.

"I do." The woman recovered her poise, head held high to Hane's direction. She appeared to be in her mid-thirties, but her skin glowed. Her features were sharp, not round and squishy like mine, and the contours of her body formed the perfect hourglass figure I thought only existed in fiction. Her short brown hair boasted a salon-fresh sheen, and it had only just sunk in just how tall she was. Sure, she was taller than me, that's never a surprise, but now I realized she was even edging Commodus. With limbs so slender yet taut, she could've been a runway model and Olympian at the same time. As her emerald eyes braved Hane's scrutiny, I wondered whose stare was more piercing.

"And that for however long you stay with this girl you are no longer entitled access to the Holy Land?" Hane reiterated.

By the perplexed tone of his voice, this had to be a big deal.

"I understand." There wasn't a hint of regret to her tone, or even in her body language. She was set on her decision.

"Then I decree you are banished from the council, the Holy Land, and demoted to the position of advisor. Thus shall be your title until the girl dies, and *you perish with her.*" Hane's face was crimson, he was giving me the same sharp point of the finger he'd given Commodus.

Apparently, I'm destined to die.

"Commodus. Return to your line, and I will reinstate you with a student."

Without uttering a word, Commodus slipped back to the front. This was the first time I'd seen someone of his caliber genuinely fear for their own life. The evidence was plain on his face, undeniable terror, which he attempted to mask by keeping his head down all the way up the aisle.

I watched, head still pounding, as the Globe floated gracefully over an anxious girl in a group close to my own. Judging by the ethnicity of the group, a large majority of them white, I assumed she must've been British. Or Australian. An English native of some kind.

"Elena Rose," the Chance Globe called, at which Commodus gave another one of his sickening grins and marched over to her.

Once the process was complete and each girl had her own advisor, Hane repeated a few comments about what a high honor this was to be a part of, and then we were disbanded. Each group was led out of the court by their nearest exit either to the left, right, or rear, and because we were closest to the back our group was instructed to leave first, with the guards that brought us in. Now the advisors knew who they would be working with they were also free to leave. As I began to follow the rest of my group however, my own advisor's hand pressed against my shoulder, preventing me.

"Come with me."

This wasn't a question, nor was there a hint of uncertainty to her command, as if she knew she was breaking the rules. Silencing the two guards leading my line, who also thought her actions were outrageous, she took me by the scruff of my neck and led me on ahead of them, to a closed door, which opened like magic. She merely flicked her wrist.

CHAPTER VIII

THE JUNE ROSE

IT WAS DARK inside, impossible to see, but as the door slid closed behind us the light flared on, forcing me to squint. It was a storage room, though what it contained was beyond me. It wasn't a big place, but it was chocked full of dusty crates, not leaving much room for the two of us to stand.

"What the hell were you doing out there?"

The woman's deathly stare, which was scarcely different to my mother's, was back. It was like reliving every single moment I'd angered my mother at once, the fury from each collectively building in her eyes, like a wall of fire growing increasingly tall and wide, offering no room to breathe. Despite my terror, I managed to glare back.

"What were *you* doing?" I snapped, hardly sounding like myself. "Why didn't you just let Commodus kill me, instead of showing me up in front of *everyone*? In front of Hane…" I trailed off, losing my train of thought. I knew what I wanted to say, but the more I clawed for it the further it left me.

Sighing, she sat me down on one of the crates. Once the words left my mouth, I wished there was some way to retrieve them. All I could do was bite my lip again, half-expecting another beating. But empathy had rinsed away her anger.

"You're brave. I see that."

She crouched to my level, keeping perfectly still. The intensity in her eyes was off-putting, so I kept my head to the ground.

"But you're also reckless, and childish, and infuriatingly narrow-minded. What's your name?"

"A-Aletheia. Aletheia Mirabel."

"Aletheia, look at me."

It was still an order, but this one was in kindness. I didn't question raising my head.

"You're not going to die."

Did I just hear her correctly? Was she promising that? It sure sounded like a promise. I scanned over my possible choices of response, realizing I'd look stupid if I argued she couldn't save me if I'd only imagined it. Too many questions surfaced though – most not even relevant – causing me to grow fidgety and tense, so I kept quiet instead, afraid I'd hinder my hopes of survival with yet another foolish outburst.

"When you get back to your group-"

But I couldn't help myself.

"You've been demoted," I interrupted. "Why have you demoted yourself to my advisor?"

"Because I believe in you. You're going to pass the Trials."

So, she did promise.

"I can't fight. I've never fought bef-"

"The greatest warriors are not mere fighters, Aletheia. They're defenders," she rebuked, as if scolding a rebellious child. She drew in a long, exhausted breath. "When you get back to your group, you'll be in your own living quarters. Disobedience gets you beaten, or sent back to solitary, or both." Her face was stern. "Do as you are *told*. Do not question it, do not even contemplate it. When you are told to leave, you leave. When you are told to stay, you stay. And most importantly, when you are told to remain silent, you *listen*."

I just nodded.

"In your quarters, water is at your disposal, and you will be fed all the nutrition you need. In solitary, you will thirst, and starve. I can't stress how important it is to obey the officers. There's no guarantee for your life here, unless you do exactly as I tell you, understand?"

Perhaps already aware of my stubbornness, the woman covered these instructions slowly, checking every so often I was still following by pausing. Even the basics were reviewed, so it was difficult to not feel patronized: how I should always sleep when I'm tired, drink when I'm thirsty…befriend the other girls so I don't exclude myself as a target.

"What does it matter?" I spat. "I'm no good with people, and I'm not fighting those girls anyway. They're not my adversaries."

Clearly feeling sorry for me, like I was too naïve to participate in something so grueling, the woman's face softened.

"And what do you think happens to the surviving few, if they're from the same nation?"

The realization widened my eyes, my mouth half open but with no sound forthcoming. It chilled me to my core.

"Hane's been deceiving generations long before you were born, and he's good at it. Get those girls so dizzy for you they wouldn't dream of taking your life. That's the only way you can take theirs."

The woman was dead serious. I didn't have a choice, and we both knew it.

"I can't…kill them." I wanted to go home. Looking at my shaking hands was enough to assure me I was in the wrong place. This was not me.

Steadying my hands, the woman wiped a tear from my eye.

"You can't speak like that Aletheia, not here. Now, do you understand everything I have told you?"

"Help me."

I understood every last detail, but it was like I'd reverted to that timid child on the first day of school. Even the storage room frightened me. Everything my advisor said assured me more and more I was trapped in a nightmare. Nightmares let you go, though, and this one held on.

"Get some rest. Get your head straight. Soon the guards will call you for the Trials' second phase, which is a fitness assessment. Until then, keep low. You're not in the right mind to talk with people just yet."

With that, I was ushered out of the room, to my relief. It was cramped and suffocating in there. Being in the open hallways was better, but its emptiness reminded me of my farm house, my life at home. I yearned to hold my spear, the stench of raw fish plugging my nostrils once more. I missed the bitterness of the fire smoke wounding the flavor because Mom had cooked it too long, and the arguments we used to have about how long we should cook it for. Three years – three years had passed since Jedidiah showed me how to hunt and cook, and still my mother didn't believe me. If she wasn't careful, she burned everything, always concerned the bacteria hadn't been cooked away. I longed to catch fish again, and see the smiles of the old folk when I brought it to them in the square. Who would fish for them now? I wasn't making myself any better, thinking of my past life. Some things you have to let go, and I swallowed my longing.

Our living quarters were a whole lot better than I expected. It was still a trek from the court, but it was impossible to miss. No longer a stuffy basement hatch, this was a grand double door entrance, and arched over it was the same impressive carvings I saw by the court: winged lions, griffins, and other mythical creatures bowing before a portrait of Hane at the center, holding a cross. Again, my advisor gave another gesture for it to open, and it did, both doors slipping into the bricks like they never existed. Inside there were no cages or prison bars, and there wasn't the feel of captivity whatsoever. The rooms were naturally lit, but that's because there wasn't a ceiling, just an open skyway where the sun was free to shine.

Enough beds had been prepared for all of us: seventy-two in all, one for each girl. We weren't a large group, a lot of the others had hundreds of girls to one nation. Despite North America's sheer size however, we were few in comparison. Maybe at home they treated the people worse, and fewer girls survived it? That seemed a reasonable conclusion. If it wasn't for our farm and my skills with a spear, I doubt any of us – my family, or the town we provided for – could have survived the ever-increasing taxations.

The doors swashed shut behind me, blocking my advisor from sight. To my surprise, and utmost joy, there were no guards in our quarters, and most girls were already asleep. *Finally,* I sighed, slamming my head against the pillow.

"Aletheia, right?" murmured the unsure but familiar voice of a girl to my side. I'd heard that voice before, I could've sworn. Not Jenny's. No, not hers. I was so emotionally shattered I could merely twist my head, but upon seeing who it was I sat up.

"Olivia? Olivia, gosh you look better."

"Thank you, so do you. *Much* better," she smiled.

"You're just saying that," I sighed, trying to offer one back.

"No, your scar. It's a lot less inflamed now. In fact…"

Great, I thought. I only heard the word 'scar.'

"It looks very similar to something I've seen before," she continued, gently prodding her bottom lip. "Oh! Oh, what a coincidence. It's a lot like the June Rose."

"The June Rose?" I frowned, trying to entertain the idea the scar looked like anything other than a deep bloody gash.

"Yes, the symbol of Aletheia, who you were named after right?"

I gazed at her. I knew the story, but I couldn't recall a 'June Rose.'

"I'll show you. Come to the mirror."

Again, I said nothing.

"Come on." Olivia, seeing I was in no mood to leave the bed, offered her hand to help me up. The girls were still staring at me as we came to the bathroom.

Inside, a decent number of toilets were lined up alongside each other, but there were no cubicles or doors. No privacy at all. Along the wall were showers, which no one could afford back in my town. We had hot and cold water, but it was a faulty system, and more often than not, we had cold water in the winter and hot water in the summer. Promises were made by the Kingdom each year they would fix our boilers, and generators, but each year they demanded more money to do it. Look at this though; they could even provide showers for their slaves. And those mirrors. Mirrors those sizes could set you back a whole litter of piglets. No one dared to use something so valuable on items that indulgent. It was something of a fantasy, the Kingdom. I never knew such wealth existed.

"Look." Olivia guided me in front of the mirrored wall, a whole wall with mirrors that stretched twice as high as the both of us put together. It was unnecessary, but it exuded the Kingdom principles: power, health, and prosperity. And greed. I'd never seen my full body before, only slightly in the river's reflection, but it would ripple at the currents. The mirror I kept in my bedroom was very small, so I could only see my face or body depending on where I positioned it. This though was like meeting a whole new person, staring blankly at me. Lost for words. Amazed by the simplicity of its clarity, I raised my hand slowly, watching as the identical figure before me did the same, curious and oblivious to the scar until Olivia brought it to focus.

"See, the scar. It looks like a budding rose."

I gazed intently at myself, so close to the mirror I even saw the reflection in my amber eyes. I wasn't sure what she was talking about. It was a cruel combination of two lashings overlapping, except at the tip near my eye where it parted, giving way to a small pointed oval.

"If you saw the symbol you'd see it," she assured. "Those two stripes there are the stem, and where they split give way to the bud of the flower. It's uncanny."

"I guess so," I murmured, trying to cheer myself up. "Why's it called the June Rose?"

She shook her head. "I'm not sure. That's just how I remember it."

The following pause dragged for so long the tears pushed up, but she caught my hand before they fell.

"I'm sorry about before."

"No, I'm sorry." I rubbed my eyes as if they were tired, drying them as subtly as I could. "I shouldn't have pushed you away like that; you did nothing wrong."

Smiling, Olivia gazed into them, as if scavenging for a doorway to my mind.

"I watched you. You helped that girl in the desert. Carried her all the way to the city." Her bold blue eyes sparkled at me.

Why was this girl so fascinated with what I did for others? Wasn't she brought up with the same values I was, to put others before yourself? Realizing I was veering into the same mindset that ruined things before I scolded myself, and tried to think of an excuse.

"She was my friend's cousin."

"You knew her?" Olivia was stunned silent.

"Jenny Auburn," I grinned falsely. "The cousin of Jedidiah, my..." I stumbled over my words. Thinking about Jedidiah made my chest tight, and I wanted to cry again, alone without any of the girls here. "Good friend."

When I looked up again, Olivia was staring back, appearing eager for more details. But I couldn't carry on this conversation any longer. Abandoning all hopes of gaining the girl's trust again, I pulled away without excusing myself and collapsed onto my bed, sobbing into the covers so no one would notice.

CHAPTER IX

A GLIMPSE OF HELL

THOSE ARE PRETTY, I thought, as I gazed at the stars hovering above me, tempting me with their freedom. From here, they seemed within reach. I sat upright, expecting the night's chill as I removed the sheets, but there was nothing. Not even a light breeze. *That's unusual,* I pondered, but then a more pressing question took over. Where were the girls? A few were in their beds but over half of them were missing, nowhere to be seen. Carefully I got out, tiptoeing my way to the bathroom to see if any of them were in there, but there was no one. Nothing but an eerie silhouette of my figure in the mirrored wall, like I was a walking ghost.

Gently finding my way back to bed I sat down, hands to my head in an attempt to rouse any dormant knowledge. It was no use, though. Nothing was coming to mind. Just as I was about to give up the door to our quarters gave their familiar puff. I couldn't see who had entered, it was only light enough to see shadows, but I was convinced someone was approaching. Footsteps confirmed my dread, but I resisted the urge to hide in the covers. Why would they disturb us at this hour? With my eyes locked to the figure that had slipped from the darkness, I summoned every speck of willpower to stay where I was, upright on the bed. If this was the end, if Hane had changed his mind and no longer wanted us, I was going to die with dignity. My nails buried into my palms. There was no other explanation for the disappearances. This was it.

Biting back a scream, I got up – the guard had seen me, and was signaling me to leave. My hands trembled, and my head was a storm of emotions, but I didn't give in. I'd had enough of crying, panic, and desperation. Now, at least, was the time to stay composed.

I thought back to uncle Hamza's last moments, the day he fought with his life to protect his son. He wasn't timid or careful, he threw himself in, and so did Jedidiah. In honor of them, I would do the same. For the Cadman's.

Be brave. Be brave, I repeated, as I walked out from the archway where another guard stood. He cuffed me. *Be brave.* Silent I waited, not imagining what pain lay ahead as I wanted to, but focusing only on my breathing. Controlling my thoughts until the shivers ceased, and the only picture in my mind was my family, looking on at me proud, wishing me their farewells. It soothed me, in a way. I wasn't given the opportunity to say goodbye, yet inside it felt like I had. I had closure.

More girls rose from the quarters, around ten others, but I didn't give them a second glance. I knew if I did, I would only feel their hurt as well as my own, and that was a responsibility I could no longer bare. Chilling wind stroked the skin of my cheek, stinging my wound as we stood in the hallway. The corridors held a very different atmosphere at night: the statues seemed to move, and the tiles numbed your feet. Cold as ice. As we walked further into the ghastly darkness the temperature dropped, but so did my anxiety, not because I forced the fear away, but because it left me altogether.

Pausing for a second, I blinked, trying to take in what had happened to me. I had never felt a peace so real, as tangible as this, since the day I collapsed beside the river and dreamed of the life I had before, when my family was all together, even aunt Olivia. Warmth returned to my body, melting the sense back into my feet. Although nothing had changed, my perception of the situation had. It was as if I had escaped to a land of reminiscence, with each chilling step bringing more clarity to my memory.

Suddenly, it made sense.

When I was small, there was once a winter's day so cold the river froze over, and I sat beside it with Jedidiah, my feet caressing the ice. Gradually as the walk continued, I remembered more, as if I was reliving the moment. How I brushed the soles of my feet over its ice, smiling, relaxed from the breeze, and the company. It was Christmas day, the first day Jedidiah brought me to the river. His comfort…and the coolness of the ice on my feet felt so real, so present, I no longer had room to fear. It was like the cold floor had brought me back, back to that moment, and I could feel his arms behind me. Just as he held me at Christmas.

By the time we reached the next group of archways, I was so entangled in my fantasy I didn't notice where we'd arrived until the guards spoke. It was the court, where all the training equipment had been left to freeze in the midnight chill. *Of course!* Half-distressed, but also relieved there was no mechanism of murder in front of us, I recalled the conversation with my advisor when she told me they were going to assess us. I braced myself, glancing at each apparatus of torture that lay in waiting: weights, bars, and ropes. Everything I would have avoided for life. Then something unusual happened. We weren't ordered to take up the iron or start moving heavy objects, but commanded to keep in formation and follow the guards to the front.

Walking through the archway at the far end, where the chiefs stood earlier, I saw there was nothing inside but a blank stone wall and shiny floor. The floor was questionable, the first I'd seen of that material since we were offloaded from the ship – the same slick, smooth texture, just jet black instead of the darkish grey of the aircrafts – but other than that, it was a dead end. I turned back to the officers beside us.

"Keep walking," one of them demanded. He glared at me, his eyes like daggers.

What a joke, I grunted, being the first to walk forward, at which something happened I didn't think to be possible even in dreams, so instant and frightening I had to take several quick gasps. I was in a whole new room, brimming with technology, which had flashed into view in the space of a blink. The white coat workers were gathered in the center, eyeing us with eagerness, and we were each allocated one, our cuffs removed. I concentrated on the area we'd appeared from; it had the same shiny panels I saw from the court.

Warp panels.

I wasn't given the same soft-faced woman as before, but a strange, scrawny man with a beard growing in all directions. Other girls had already got started, doing whatever their white-coat instructed, and the two guards that brought us were no longer anywhere to be seen. My partner however, who embodied everything of a cartoon madman from his pointy chin to his fluffy hair simply stared at me, his beady eyes scanning me over as he paced around me.

"Yes, you appear well-built. Fit."

His accent was Italian. I couldn't believe it. I hadn't seen Mr. Milano for over a month but listening to this man was like being back in the square, carrying out my usual routine of selling fish to the townsfolk, and greeting him every morning. Could this day get worse? How many more times was the past going to creep up, taunting me with a future I'll never have? I longed to be back home, enduring the repetitive lifestyle of school and hunting.

Somewhere, however, in the midst of my sadness dwelled a sense of gratitude. The bitter chill of the floor, the Italian scientist I had been provided. I thought back to Jenny. The chance to meet a friend, as if reunited with Jedidiah himself. I cherished it. For a second at least, but then it all seemed too surreal, too familiar, like it had all been weaved together by a god trying to torment me.

Silently the man circled me, again, and again, until nausea forced me to focus on a singular point, desperate to block him out. I wasn't going to entertain my concerns of what he'd have me do, or if I'd be punctured by needles. Worrying wasn't going to make things better, *but whatever he does I can handle,* I assured myself. As if I wasn't confused enough, unsure whether I could yet pledge my trust to my advisor, I had another feeling to contend with. An urge rose, strangling the whirlwind of my grief and tranquility, driving me to a place I'd never known. My advisor's words thrusted into memory, aggressive and unwelcome, reminding me why she had stepped down from Hane. From authority. From power.

'Because I believe in you.'

Never had I relied on another person, or cared about their opinions of me. Yet now, hearing those words from a woman who could have left me for dead but didn't, that was something I couldn't ignore, and I had a responsibility to show her she wasn't wrong. Prove my life was worth fighting for. It was there, in the Gymnasium, that I first sought approval.

And I was going to get it.

The day's earlier drama affected me so badly I didn't even realize the girls were wearing new clothes until the scientist's cough snapped me alert. In fact, they weren't even in dresses anymore, but form-fitting, jet black jumpsuits with sturdy footwear to match.

Without revealing a hint of intent, the scientist unclipped a small device from his buckle and pointed it at me. It was like a pen, with a bright blue laser at one end, but unlike real lasers it was easy to look at. Slowly the light fell from my eyes and down to my neck, and my chest. It flowed gracefully to my hips, and over my groin, down my thighs and calves to the bottom of my feet. As it did, the tattered fabric of my school uniform fell away, transforming into the comfortable, porous fabric of the jumpsuit. I didn't have to gaze at my bloodied feet anymore, either – they were set firmly in boots, strong and supportive. I'd never known technology like it.

"Stand here."

At last, the tension ceased as the white coat gave his first instruction. I hoped to converse with the man, so I could draw more comfort from his accent, but he didn't seem very talkative. He had me step over a white platform, oval in shape. It glowed like candlelight. Taking care to push down any rising paranoia I watched as he stood back from where I was, where a holographic screen suddenly projected in front of him. The clarity of its visuals was astonishing, not blue and faded like in the sci-fi movies, but perfect resolution that made it appear the screen was really there. I could even make out what settings he selected.

Suddenly the soft glow of the platform shifted into a rough pulsation, growing brighter with each second. Racked with dread, I watched as sharp rays emerged from the light, enwrapping me like a cage, surging as high as the ceiling. I was certain the scientist was dropping below my line of sight, but the rays were too blinding to be sure. There was an unmistakable lightness to my feet, and as the light faded, I realized why.

I was levitating.

Gasping, and in a desperate bid to free myself from the vortex I thrust forward, but it was useless. No matter how frantically I moved my limbs, my torso stayed planted where it was. All I could do was gaze desperately into the man's eyes, pleading to be freed.

"Run," he ordered, unshaken by my anxiety. There wasn't a hint of sympathy to his voice.

Realizing my arms and legs were mobile, I jolted them back

and forth, in the desired motion. Although I was confined in the airspace, my feet braced the light as if it were solid, propelling my legs forward with the same drive I'd expect from a physical surface. I had a good rhythm going, my arms pumping vigorously as I pulled my legs one in front of the other, building momentum.

"Very good. Prepare for resistance one."

It was only when my limbs stiffened I realized what I was operating. I was trapped in some weird current of energy, and it was resisting my force, making it increasingly difficult to continue running. I could feel my lungs compressing; my chest weighing me down. Each minute, he would raise the resistance level, and then smile observantly as the gelatin-like consistency around me thickened, compelling my limbs back to center. Eventually the act of lifting my legs became an impossibility, like dragging lumps of iron, and the pressure on my arms was like continually pushing a wall. I couldn't even lunge my body forward to assist the motion. Every muscle locked itself tight. I couldn't go any further.

As I floated there, puffing violently and immobile, I thought back to the court, and my advisor. Strangely, she reminded me of my mother, serious but well-meaning, and I couldn't help but compare them. For a brief moment, I managed to close my eyes, reminding myself that there was still hope. I wasn't going to die at the hand of Commodus, and there was a possibility I wouldn't die at all.

You've just got to prove it.

Choking back a scream, my eyes shot open – the fear flooded back, shaking me from my peaceful vision. Every nightmare I'd ever had, *every one* of them had been the same. Never of Jedidiah's kidnapping, or his father's death, or the public executions of those who couldn't afford their taxes on New Year's. Had those still haunted me while I was asleep, I'm sure I wouldn't have lasted a week. It wasn't even about childish things like ghosts and demons, but in every nightmare without fail...I'd be falling.

They started after I'd turned eight. At first, it was a light-headed sensation, and I didn't think much of it. Very soon though, it escalated, as if I was dropping from a great height, which would throw me awake before I hit the bottom. I would try to get back to sleep, but if I did, I'd only fall again, and the ordeal would continue the whole night. My mother didn't understand me when I tried to explain it to her, she just thought I had insomnia. That I farmed too often and it was wearing me out, and I needed rest from school, which is what she gave me. It never helped though, and whenever a night came that I imagined myself falling, I never had a good sleep. I even asked my teacher about it one time in class. Another student called out saying they heard if someone dreams of falling and hits the ground before they wake up, they'd die. That was enough to give me a solid month of restless nights. Here, in the Gymnasium, it was no different. Fear clutched my heart. I was dropping down again, on my back, like living a nightmare I couldn't escape.

"Don't touch me!" I shivered, spread out on the oval platform which glowed smoothly again like nothing had happened. The white-coat was hovering over me, trying to help me up, but my outcry startled him, sending him several paces backward. Still, he said nothing.

This isn't happening.

Now I had a reason to panic. Realizing what I had just let slip from my suicidal trap, I shot up and ran to him. Despite my reaction, he appeared enamored by me, a thought I was quick to dismiss however. Fearful of punishment, I apologized over and over, showering him with eagerness to make up for it. Trying to explain my nightmares and why I acted the way I did, but it all came out a thousand miles per hour. My thoughts were chaos, I couldn't organize a single sentence.

Frantically, I scanned the room, jerking my head in all directions. Surely those guards would return to beat me – kill me even

– but there was no one. I hesitated. I at least expected the white coat's reproach, but still nothing came. Instead, the freakish man smiled and gestured me to return to the platform. I didn't waste time getting back in position, but I dreaded what would proceed. *Will fire shoot from the floor?*

My eyes were locked to him as he reactivated the screen, prodding in the settings for the second challenge, or floor of fire as I'd so convinced myself by this point. I wasn't wrong. I was about the fire, but not about the look he gave me. As our eyes met, I saw a glimmer of admiration, like he was trying to tell me I was doing well, *really* well.

Now the rays were back, encircling me round and round like an endless spiral which repeated whenever it reached the ceiling. Slightly different from the jagged, flashing-style rays previously, but still very bright. The white-coat told me to hold my hands up, and 'push.' Nothing dropped from the ceiling, but there was a definite heaviness on my hands. I was holding something up, but I couldn't see what.

"Very good. Moving to resistance two."

It was the same pressure as before, only this time it was above me. I'd never been strong, but here I had no choice, the force crushed me. I half expected I'd snap if I dropped my arms.

The horrific exhaustion I couldn't shake from my chest was back after a minute. I'm not sure how many resistance levels I exceeded. He shouted them out, but I was too preoccupied with not collapsing. I was down on one knee, and my arms had fallen to ninety degrees, shaking terribly. Sweat seeped from everywhere, there wasn't a dry patch on my body. I wanted to cry out for it to end, but the compressive force was even more unbearable than the last exercise. My lungs couldn't manage a word. As the rays died down and the pressure released, I flopped lifeless to the ground, crumpled on the cold surface.

"Very good." He extended his bony hand to me. "Follow me, will you?"

That was the first time he hadn't commanded me. I knew I didn't have an option, but it was enough. I felt human again. The white-coat had a definite grin on his face by the end of the session. He didn't give me any more clues, but I knew I'd given it a good run. Endorphins blazed through my bloodstream, rushing to every corner of my body and making me feel fantastic. Did I feel guilty I had discovered a good feeling while other girls may be crying themselves to sleep? No. For once I wasn't worried about those problems. I had taken the first step in accepting my circumstances, and working with them, not hiding from them. I felt ready, or at least I did, until I met the eyes of a dark-haired girl who wasn't from my group. An adversary, who was being dragged in amongst others as the guards prepared us to leave.

Someone I might have to kill.

CHAPTER X

CATCHING FISH

MY EYES WERE sore by sunrise. Over three quarters of the group were missing by the time I got back, and during the course of the night none of them returned. Jenny, Olivia, and even that girl who comforted me in the court, Tobi, were nowhere to be seen. I dropped to my mattress, shattered, longing for a good rest, but even though my body begged me to, I couldn't sleep the whole night. My mind wouldn't settle, taunted by the visions of their suffering, and ever so often remembering the cold glare of the adversary, her eyes trained on me like a predator. Instead, I waited, and watched above me as dawn rubbed out the stars.

The quarters were humid and hot. Not as hot as in the cells, but still impossible to relax in. I was still confined in the jumpsuit from last night's trial, which only made the heat worse, and I didn't know how to remove it. As the sun ascended higher bringing more heat into the quarters, I found I could kick off the boots to free my feet, but even that was a mission. They were secured so tight it was like an extra layer of skin: thick, sturdy skin which could flex, but appeared impossible to break.

Wishing I had something sharp so I could cut the jumpsuit I fell back against the bed above the sheets, still hoping I'd see the girls soon. I'd learned it was best to accept the unfamiliarities rather than dwell on them, so I tried to shift my focus onto the girls who were here. Whenever a bad thought crept in, I would stare at the people safe in their beds. I figured I'd be a whole lot calmer if I had someone to talk to, so I was anxious for them to wake up. They only woke, however, when the doors to our living grounds opened. Not to welcome the people I'd stressed over, but our advisors.

None of us uttered a sound. A niggling voice in my head warned me speaking was forbidden, so I didn't. As I walked up to my advisor and the others went to theirs, a thousand questions choked my throat, but I managed to swallow them down. Without being cuffed, we were led from our quarters, and a short walk led us to a room full of many varieties of fresh bread, dairy, grains, pulses, fruit, vegetables, fish, poultry, and meats all prepared on a table large enough for us all to sit. So much choice, and all of it better than what we had at home. Cooked and baked only this morning, I could tell. Warm savory aromas intertwined with the sweeter, fruity ones, intensifying the feast's fragrance and inviting me to try everything. I had to stop myself drooling as I reached for the walnut bread, hot and steamy as I ripped a chunk off the loaf. My advisor, who sat next to me, observed everything I ate. There was cottage cheese to spread on the bread and crackers, and the grains had been baked into delicious fingers of nuts and dried fruit. There was even cereal available in bowls, waiting to be poured over with velvety milk. However we chose to eat it, it appeared the grains were a very substantial part of the selection.

I was just about to stuff myself on one last bowlful of apple and oats when my advisor whispered to eat some chicken. Though it lacked sauce and seasoning, I wasn't going to argue. It was moist, cooked perfectly even, so I helped myself to more before the meal was up.

⊰

"How did I do then, last night?" I pressed, as we reached the Ludus. The other girls split off for training. It was just me and her.

"The examiner was very impressed with you, exceptional fitness for your age, but there's still plenty of room for improvement. How are you with weights?" She gazed down at me intently.

"I don't know. I've never used them."

"Would you consider yourself strong?"

Her tone was difficult to fathom, whether she was analyzing me physically or digging for arrogance.

"I've got good stamina, but I'm not strong." I stared at the other girls. They were already lifting. I dreaded it.

"And do you think you'll pass the Trials if you aren't?" She became more insistent, like she wanted me to circle to an answer I already knew, but was afraid of accepting.

Of course not.

"I've never done this before," I muttered, knowing full well I already sounded defeated. "Please tell me, how do I stand a chance?"

"*Will*, not strength. If you want something enough nothing will stop you from attaining it." She looked at me deeply. "You should know that."

What did she mean by that? Where had I shown will? This woman was making out I had it, yet the only times she'd seen me was in the Ludus and the city cent...

Of course!

"You saw me, didn't you, when I entered the city with Jenny? You looked right at me."

The penny plummeted. Only Jenny and I stood aside the line that day, the rest were chained. We must've stood out. That's why my advisor spotted us, and that's what she must've seen in me – the will to keep Jenny alive.

She nodded. "I could train you for decades, but nothing I can do will better what's in here." She prodded at my chest. "That's a gift, which no one else has."

At the far end of the court, I could make out adversaries training with their advisors. Whether it was due to my lens of negativity, or if the other nations really were exceptional, all of them looked determined and capable. Grunting the girls hurled their weights, some chucking the iron as if they were rice sacks. If I had gazed any longer my heart would've sunk, but fortunately my advisor caught me watching them.

"Aletheia!" she snapped. "Stop focusing on what the others are doing! This is *your* situation, not just theirs!"

Her outburst was enough to grab my full attention, and it expelled my woeful spirit. Immediately, I strolled up to a squat cage and loaded the weight. I didn't have a clue what I was doing, the plates were an effort to slide onto the barbell, and I could only manage one at a time, but I kept piling them on.

Once I'd decided the bar looked impressive enough, I braced my position, and my advisor came behind me as I lifted it from the rack. I was already dripping from the unholy humidity, so trying to keep hold of the bar was a whole lot tougher than I anticipated. My palms slipped on the steel causing my grip to go askew, re-correcting it put immense strain on my wrists. My advisor glared at me like she knew I was being foolish, yet remained quiet as I prepared myself for the squat. This was it, a make-or-break moment. Either prove I'm as good as the other girls, or forfeit my advisor's trust, and therefore my chances, altogether. After a few deep gulps of the clammy air, I gritted my teeth, and lowered my torso.

The pain was immediate.

My legs trembled dangerously, but I was so fixated on blocking out the agony, I couldn't even look down to check them. Keeping my neck stiff and head toward the sky I screamed, so loud I'm sure half the Ludus heard me. I had reached the pausing point, my muscles were crying, and now all I had to do was get it up again. Twice the task as before, and twice as important. I had to do this, not just for the advisor but for my own peace of mind. If I could do this, maybe I could beat the adversaries. Tears rushed uncontrollably down my cheeks as I tried to make the lift, forcing every fiber in my legs to contract and raise the weight. But I halted, a third of the way up. I willed and willed to force the last few inches, but nothing helped. I couldn't make the last push. My energy was finished.

"Aletheia!" my advisor roared. She caught the bar from behind me and pulled it back onto the rack as I fell. I collapsed a heap of bones, ashamed, embarrassed, and sapped of all hope.

"That was far too heavy for you! What were you trying to prove, how you can injure yourself?"

I was proving myself to you, I thought, swallowing back my anger so the words wouldn't bleed out.

"Pride gets you nowhere," she frowned, offering her hand. I didn't indulge in making myself look weaker, but I still took it. "It hasn't gotten anybody anywhere, and you'll be no different. Look at me." She took hold of my shoulders, but no matter how much I resisted I couldn't shake her off. "Do you know why the other people are going to fail and you're not? It's because they're relying on their abilities, but you aren't. You have something far stronger."

Affection had flushed all anger from her eyes, but it was only momentary. She withdrew the second I recognized it.

"This is the Trials' third phase. I suggest you take it seriously."

"The Gymnasium was designed to identify your abilities with a weapon, and then hone it," my advisor stated, once we'd crossed the warp there. "Are you skilled with any particular weapon?"

"No." It was amusing she thought she should ask me.

"Very well. What skill would you like to try first?" She was aware I disliked her for sure, but she carried on as if it were nothing. I looked around me. Not many people were operating the resistance beams and most were huddled around the sword zone. Many of the girls were adversaries, though I recognized a few as my own. I wasn't going to go anywhere near there. At the far end of the room, however, stood a lone ally with her advisor.

"Over there," I requested, pointing to the empty zone. As we got closer, I noticed the girl was learning how to handle an axe, which appeared awfully heavy, she could barely keep her arms straight. Silently I joined her, and she gave me a hint of a smile. I was in no mood to smile back, however.

"Do you wish to try wielding one or two?"

"Whatever you want."

I'm amazed my attitude didn't crack my advisor's tolerance, but she remained stable, and handed me one axe without saying anything else. It wasn't just heavy; it was pure iron, the blade spanning the length of my torso. I didn't know how anyone's wrists could bear such pressure; my first strike hit the dummy way off target. Instead of the middle of the chest where the bullseye was, I hit the groin, inflicting a shallow dent as I dropped the axe. It landed with a loud thud and many people looked my way, but I turned my back to them as I picked it up.

As soon as it was back in my grasp it was out again, my advisor promptly snatched it from me. It wasn't difficult to. My grip the second time was worse than before, and if my advisor hadn't taken it, I'm sure I would've dropped it.

"This isn't for you. We're trying another skill," she ordered, as she put the axe back. I didn't argue with her.

As the day passed by, I was offered more nuts and oats baked into an energy bar. I had several bars through the session, which was shortly followed by dinner: whole chickens, joints of beef and a large platter of colorful fruits, including one an ally told me was 'papaya.' I'd failed to find a weapon I was comfortable with the whole day, yet most girls had. And they looked confident.

I glared at my advisor. She had watched me for the entire meal.

"How much longer do we have in here?"

"Eat the chicken. You need more protein." She hit the bread from my hand. I almost threw the plate, sick of her voice and sick of the bland chicken, but one glance at her was enough of a deterrent. I froze.

"I still haven't found a weapon."

"Then we best prolong the session. We can start after you've finished."

"Let's start now," I demanded, removing myself from the table.

We covered everything. The swords were finally free but felt alien in my hand, more so than the other weapons. Realizing I held them like a wet fish my advisor moved me onto archery, which I expected to be good at due to my darts background. Nocking an arrow to the bow was difficult enough however, let alone pulling it back with the right tension. None of my arrows hit the dummies, all falling short but one, which dug into the post holding the dummy up. My advisor's sighs were enough to justify my growing self-doubt. There were only a couple of zones left. Most of the advisors were so proud of their students' first day, they were taken back to the quarters early, but a handful stayed for additional practice. I was certain every girl was comfortable with their choice by now. Everyone but me. I hadn't even made a choice.

"This is the spear zone-"

I didn't let my advisor finish; she was easy to interrupt. It seemed she'd lost her will more and more as the day dawdled on.

"I'm a spear fisher. I caught fish for the townsfolk where I'm from. If that helps."

I knew it didn't; I was idealizing if anything, but oddly, she came to a complete halt and stared me over.

"You fish?" There was evident disbelief in her voice.

I nodded.

"Are you any good?"

"Good enough. I fed the townsfolk every morning."

"Here, use mine."

Her energy had returned – she withdrew her spear from her backstrap, disregarding those from the rack on the wall. This one was nothing like what I used back home. It didn't stink of the river for one thing, and it was constructed of an extremely stiff material which resembled steel, but was much lighter. The blade head was a combination of two blades fused into a ghastly point, each sprouting from either side of the pole like wings, with a décor resembling feathers. If I had used this for catching fish, I'd have split them on impact.

"It's not like the others? Why's it so light and-?"

"Designed for mobility," my advisor cut in. "Heronium composition, which is an element found to be the strongest and lightest material for weapons."

"Well, it's nothing like my spear back home, and I've never heard of 'Heronium,'" I snapped.

"You're not trying to catch fish here, *are you?*"

Her eyes were violent.

"This is the absolute best we have to offer. If you can't take that, then maybe you'd fair better with your hands. Well?"

I was in no mood for another lecture. With a groan, I snatched the spear and looked at my targets: all dummies.

"So, you want me to strike these targets here?"

"Yes. But instead of treating them like dummies, I want you to imagine they're fish."

Her words were so unexpected I had to turn around to make sure what I heard was right.

"Fish don't have torsos. Or big score charts painted on them."

"Then this should be a breeze."

Sighing I composed myself, first picturing my river...and at once the figures around me melted into shiny scales. Carefully I crept behind one, sandals off and spearhead ready, honed in on the small target that was its gill. It stopped; it must've realized I was there, but it didn't move so I struck – thrusting the blade deep into its flesh, tearing through its ribcage as it exited the other fin. It was mine; I had it, but more were still swimming, frantic, terrified of the disturbance and keen to escape upstream. I didn't let them. My blade found the center of another, and then a third. I removed their flapping bodies and hurled them to the bankside, eyeing the next before I'd even detached the last. Once satisfied, I lowered my spear, at which the waters stilled, and the river fell silent.

When I came to, excusing myself from the wishful fantasy, only one dummy was left standing, the rest had been forced down. All of them were punctured, all in the bullseye, and where I'd turned so vigorously, I had swiped some with my pole, denting the ribs and heads. A couple had even suffered wounds by the blades stretched outward. One of the dummies had a deep gash from his nose to lower back where I crossed it. I gazed back to my advisor. Her expression reflected my feelings.

"You-what did you do?"

She could barely voice the words.

"...I caught fish."

As I followed my advisor to the next spear exercise, I realized those who had stayed to practice were no longer practicing. They and their advisors had turned to stone, incapable of withdrawing their awestruck gaze.

CHAPTER XI

A WISH FULFILLED

"THAT'S ENOUGH FOR tonight, get some rest. I'll send you some cheese and crackers before bed," my advisor uttered, her eyes rapt to our audience. I reached the quarters with a pounding head. *What just happened?* First, I was useless, and suddenly what my advisor said was making sense. I had a chance of passing the Trials after all – the adversaries' faces sure told me so. I wanted to hug someone, or scream into my pillow, but as the door opened, I remembered where I was. Sat nestled in their covers, still conscious but distanced from the world were Jenny, Olivia, and a few beds up, Tobi. Some of my other allies had returned, too, and they were all in a terrible state. Jenny had bruises across her face and arms, her forehead displayed a violent burn, and her eyes were red from crying. Tiny veins infested her eyeballs, engulfing the sincere white pigment of Jedidiah's gaze. I'd decided. She had his eyes.

I locked my arms around her, pulling myself forcefully onto her bed.

"Jenny! Oh God, what happened to you? What did they do!"

"Nothing you can change."

Her tone was apathetic, but as her dainty pupils found mine, she attempted a smile.

"You look beautiful now, Aletheia. Your scar's healed really well."

"*Shhh.*" I rocked her tenderly. "It's okay, I'm here now. I'm not letting you go."

"We failed the assessment, Aletheia. All of us here. Our advisors had to choose if we were worth saving…"

She grimaced, as if recalling a memory more painful than her wounds. The silence lingered, but I wasn't the one to break it.

"They killed them. Right in front of us. And made us watch as they beat us…until they died. They're dead."

Rage boiled within my soul, impossible to contain. I wanted to stay strong, to comfort Jenny, but nothing could keep the burning in, it was eating me from the inside. Remembering the death of uncle Hamza and the girls in the desert, I released Jenny and slammed my fists into the matrass over and over. Cursing the Kingdom and cursing Hane – loud enough for all to hear – hitting the bed until my hands ached. It wasn't a soft bed, and the more I pounded, the more I crushed my fingers. Tears gushed down my nose and cheeks, to the bottom of my chin as I cried in hysteria. Someone should've taken me away, they had every right to. Put me to death for my blasphemy alone regardless of the fact I'd woken several girls from their recovery time, which their advisors would not take lightly. But all that followed was a small, tentative voice.

"We're okay, though, Aletheia. They gave us another chance."

"No. You're not," I sniffed. "You're beat up. You're hurting."

"Please, there was nothing you could do." She pulled closer to me and rubbed my shoulders. Something about this felt too familiar, and it stung my eyes. I repeated her words trying to calm myself, but it did the opposite.

"There should have been! I can't cope seeing you this way. You." I looked back into her eyes. "You remind-"

"I remind you of Jedidiah?"

I gave a solemn nod and sucked my knuckles. I was a child again all of a sudden.

"You couldn't save him either.'

A final tear trickled down my face, but she caught it with her thumb and rubbed it away.

"I distracted him. I could've saved him, and those girls in the desert. Stopped what happened to you."

"But you did stop what happened to me. You saved me." Her voice was soft. "And I see every bit of him in you."

Those words soothed me, and burned me all at once, and nothing could keep me from staring into her eyes. Those gentle, familiar eyes. Her very presence…it was like I was back at the river, waiting for him to tell us when to head home.

"Everything he told me, it just made me want to meet you more. I knew I couldn't, you were too far away, but I hoped to meet you every day," she continued, stroking my face. "Every day I wished to meet the girl he told me was courageous and strong. There were no girls like that near me. No one I could trust. But you. He couldn't speak higher of you."

I couldn't process what she was saying, but I didn't need to. I focused on her voice, that faint whisper of kindness that had long left my ears, immediately inviting itself back. Knocking on the walls of my heart, waiting to be let back in. She pressed my scar lightly.

"You take pain you don't deserve, for the sake of your goodness. That's who you are. Aletheia, whatever happens to me please know, it was an honor to finally meet you."

I had no words to offer. Her voice had reached my very core, resonant in my bones until I could think of nothing else. No tears, no smile, nothing to give. She had possessed my being, and there I sat, clutching her tight.

We slept that night, huddled together amongst the covers, family. I'd never got as close to someone as I had with Jedidiah, but Jenny was more than an ally. She wasn't just someone I'd be forced to tolerate. No, if there was one thing the Trials could never take away from me, it was the day I saved her. The day we became friends.

∾

The next day ran different from before. My advisor, who I decided to dub 'Happy' in my mind, took me to a new part of the spear zone which contained a very large wooden post. It was like an enormous tree trunk, but instead of branches it had thick straight arms spread out from several places: at its base, near the peak, and various areas of its middle. Some of the arms had nothing attached to them, but others had chunky score pads which were heavily padded. I couldn't work out for the life of me what it was. Happy retrieved a blunt spear.

"Gladiators used these to enhance their awareness, agility, and speed. When you hit one of the pads it will trigger a sensor which will spin that section. You must continue to hit every pad you see while avoiding the arms."

"That sounds impossible."

The arms weren't far from each other. It certainly looked impossible.

"It's only impossible if you think it is."

With my weapon in hand, I brought myself to the post. I knew when I struck the pad the trunk would spin, but I had no clue what speed. The arms looked solid, and I was sure if one hit my head fast enough it would put me out. All the more reason not to fail, I suppose.

Thump.

It started, me and the training post, and a spear to get me through it. As my spearhead met the pad the arm behind me hurtled forward. I turned swiftly to avoid it, and ducked, and as I did, I saw another pad and struck. I continued to hit the pads, immediately turning to avoid the arms. They did move fast after all. Too fast. One swiped me from under my legs hitting my shin. It brought me down straight away, where I fell in the course of another moving arm. It slammed into my nose before coming to a halt.

I lay on the floor clutching my leg, and as I reached for my face, I felt wetness. It painted my fingers a vibrant red.

"Get used to one section moving first before you start on the others," commented Happy, as she handed me a tissue.

After dinner we had time to talk again, Jenny and I, alone in our quarters about life, and Jedidiah. First though, I helped clean her up in the bathroom, soothing her bruises with a cloth dipped in cool water. I told her everything: the details of Jedidiah's kidnapping, how I provoked it, and his father's death. I told her about my promise by his parents' gravesides, the spear fishing, and my other promise to be the best spearfisher yet. I clarified my plan had been to use my fish earnings to fly to the Kingdom, and then trying to keep the mood light I joked how I was lucky enough to get a free ticket. Jenny found this amusing, which was good, because if we didn't laugh, we'd cry. The stars shimmered once my story was up, and there Jenny sat, amazed.

"You truly miss him," she uttered.

"I do. I at least owe it to him to try."

I caught myself before the sadness crept in. I was only strong enough to think of him for so long.

"How did you do in the Gymnasium by the way? Did you decide what to take forward?"

"I realized I have a pretty good aim with the knives."

"Yes, I saw you," I smiled. "How did that come about?"

"I don't know, I've never touched a knife before. At least not when I'm not cooking. I guess I've just got a good aim."

She was too modest. Watching her performance in the Gymnasium was breath-taking, and I knew there were adversaries giving her the eye. She's the one Happy should've been training, at least that's how I saw it.

"So you're taking up the knives? But what about the axes? How did that go?"

"Very well, actually. I think my advisor wants me to take up that skill as well."

"What, as well as knife throwing? That would be too much work, wouldn't it?"

"Apparently he sees a lot of potential in me…with weapons at least."

I smiled at her again, drawing closer to her so she could see me through the night's veil.

"He would be stupid not to."

Jenny was the first to drift off of the two of us, but we were the last ones talking that night. Everyone else fell asleep long ago – a very long time ago, I guessed, because the paleness to the sky told me it was dawn. Yet I wasn't tired, and neither of us were fighting sleep all through our conversation. It was the first time in forever I chatted with someone like that.

Silently she slumbered, breathing ever so gently. I really needed to get some sleep. I didn't get any the night before, but I couldn't miss this moment. Nibbling on the crackers Happy delivered, I stroked her hair and sat back, losing myself in the serenity of her breath. That small and harmless puff, warming both the cold air and my hurting heart.

CHAPTER XII

THE PURGE

IT WAS NEARING summer from what I could tell, peering into the hazy clouds of morning, when the door opened, and our advisors entered. Normally only a couple would come to collect us. This was the first I'd seen every girl's advisor in four years. *Something's wrong*, I thought, as I got up to search for Happy. As our eyes met my pulse palpitated. In her eyes was genuine fear, not shadowed by her usual indifference, but undeniable fear.

No one made a sound, not even daring to whisper as we were gathered. By this time, I'd grown capable of reading her wordless gaze, and I knew she didn't want me to ask. What began as curiosity, or an incline to something dangerous became immediate terror however, as I was forced to stretch out my wrists to be cuffed. They were tighter than I remembered; they cut into my skin, forming red marks.

In strict formation, we were led down the hallway with our advisors, all walking in pairs, at which we turned into the opposite corridor of the one we usually took. We were going somewhere new, and from Happy's expression, somewhere she didn't want to go. I was aware we'd been schooled for a long time, considerably longer than I expected, but was this how it would happen? Not even so much as a warning as to when we'd be shoved in the arena? Or was this something else? Had Hane given up on the Trials altogether, and now we were on our way to disposal? No. Surely, no. He needed us for something. *What did he say again?* I scavenged through all my existing memories, every word I could remember from Hane's speech. *The Kingdom's Daughter. Mother of his army.* What did that mean? Was the survivor to lead his army? Why would he go to so much trouble for a new leader? He had plenty of options on his doorstep…and why girls? The more I rinsed my head for logic the less I could find. Nothing made sense. We had no purpose.

Oh!

The girl and her advisor in front had vanished before my eyes, I was so preoccupied with my thoughts I'd failed to notice where we were. Ahead of us was a wall, the same shiny warp panels at its base, and it was my turn to step on.

Hesitantly I approached its gleaming surface, Happy didn't rush me, so I took slow and steady steps. I stopped one inch from it, immobilized, but taking a long, large breath I managed to urge myself forward. The transition was no different, but the dim, entirely black room was very different from the Gymnasium. The synthetic lights gave the whole room an eerie fictitiousness to it, like I'd stepped into a dream, and it appeared the walls and floors were constructed of warp panels. They had the same glossy finish. Carefully I turned to Happy who was still close to my side, and I could just make out her face. The light was so faint it was impossible to see further than a few feet of us. She scanned our surroundings, her eyebrows knitted. It appeared this was new to her as well.

"Ruby Adams," called one of the officials. None of us could see him, but his voice drew our attention to the distance. Silently the girl, Ruby, was issued forward by her advisor. Swallowed by the thick shadows. The only time we'd had our names called in this manner was at the pairing. Something was seriously wrong.

"Aletheia!"

A tiny voice grabbed my attention from the disappearing girl. It was Happy, who had leaned right to my level. Why was she being so secretive? My head hurt with questions.

"What?" I kept my volume to the bare minimum.

"You need to listen to me very carefully now, understood?"

I nodded.

"This is the Trials' fourth phase, the preliminary to the main event-"

"But I thought the fourth phase *was* the main-?"

"*Shhh!*" She was stricter now. "Don't talk. Let me explain!"

I nodded again, biting my tongue.

"I've been watching Hane, he doesn't know what I know, so listen carefully. He has decided to host a televised showcase of every girl in the Trials. Several nations have been processed, and now it's North America's turn."

I was desperate to cut off Happy again, but by the franticness of her speech I knew there was little time.

"It's called 'The Purge,' and it's designed to narrow down the competition. There's too many of you, and he wants a grand, exciting showcase to get the public interested in the Trials. Eliminating most of you this way does both jobs for him."

That was something I hadn't considered at all, but upon hearing it, it made so much sense. Hane had kidnapped people from all over, not just my nation. Some groups were very large, and others considerably smaller, but altogether there were enough of us to fight for years. I gasped. What were we in for, if this was a way to thin the numbers?

"Please tell me. What do I do?" My tongue hurt – I'd kept my teeth clamped to it the whole time – I could hold in the anxiety no longer.

"You go in. There will be challenges to test your speed, strength, agility, and stamina. All lethal, but that's all I know."

Without warning, she took me in close like a mother would. She'd never been so intimate with me before.

"You can do this. Believe in yourself."

I trembled violently, as violent as the day I met Happy, when she rescued me. It's ok, I urged, battling the desire to scream for my family. *Happy believes in me. I need to believe in me.* I closed my eyes, took several slow breaths and gradually eased my shoulders. If anything, worrying would only make it worse. That's what it did for Jenny when she failed her assessment, and I had a responsibility to pass this trial. If not for Happy then always for her. Always for Jenny.

Time didn't just pass in that environment. I waited, for what felt like days until the next name was called, not knowing if the previous name had made it through. I could only listen, only anticipate the moment my name would be called, nothing more. It was like in the four years I endured the harsh training and discipline of the Kingdom, nothing had changed at all. Though my adult body told otherwise, inside I had always been the same nervous girl I thought I'd left at the pairings. All it took to revert was uncertainty, however brief, and suddenly my confidence was gone. *Stay strong,* I ordered myself. My doubts were just feelings, I could overcome them. I had found a sense of stillness, and my restless mind wasn't about to steal that from me.

I found it better to shut my eyes, at least then I could shut the world out, but occasionally I'd let them open to glimpse Happy. I didn't know how to feel about her, but her presence alone was enough to give me some ease. Some form of security.

"Aletheia Mirabel."

Already weakened by anxiety, the trial began before I'd even set foot in the room, which once I'd crept down the hallway, I found to be a large cube coated in the black tiles. I was helped onto a small circular pad which instantly descended once my feet were on, and I nearly lost my balance from the speed of its drop. I looked up, but from where I fell there was a tile in its place. These tiles were different from the others however, because the fixings glowed bright. Light flooded the whole cube despite the blackness of its walls. The room was both bright like the sun, and gloomy as the night.

Seconds passed, and the white light deteriorated to a gory red: an omen of my fate. My head shot behind me, expecting the worse, but it was all the same. From every angle the room cried blood, death. Yet I saw nothing to impose it.

A flash! The red light suddenly flashed, and in doing so it snapped to white again. I panted, jolting my head for answers. It came...

In the form of an arrow.

First one, which I avoided by sidestepping from the platform, and then a flurry of arrows spurting from the wall, all of them trained on me no matter where I threw myself. It's like they knew where I was about to jump. I tried to vary my motion and become less predictable, but they still bore down on me. I was like a hapless fly, trapped and darting around in a jar with no exit or means of breaking out. As the arrows shot out the tiles rippled. I couldn't see where they were being fired from, the walls themselves became water-like, ebbing and flowing. I couldn't focus.

Launching myself to the opposite side of the room I felt the body of an arrow breeze through my locks, but I couldn't pause for breath. Another flew a pin's length from my foot. There was nowhere to run, and my breaths were growing short. One of the arrows scraped violently across my arm, tearing away the black fabric to expose raw flesh before oozing blood, but something distracted me from it. Ahead of me and just within reach the panels formed an exit. At first, it was hard to make out from the other lively movements of the cube, but it quickly registered with me.

I threw myself at its crevice, breaking free from the arrows' range, but it granted me no security. No time to catch my breath, or gather my thoughts. There were monkey bars set above a bed of blades all gleaming and sharpened. It would only take one to cut me to ribbons, here there were countless. The wispy sound of flames pulled my attention to the ceiling – several flamethrowers had ignited. Knowing my only option was to leap for the bars, I did. As my hand braced the steel I heard the flames crash to the ground, heating my back to an uncomfortable degree. My other hand swayed aimlessly in the air, struggling to find the next bar, but getting a glimpse of the spikes below was enough to keep my gripping hand glued. My heart pushed to my throat, stomping on my vocal cords and rendering me incapable of a scream. Both the heat and stress of the narrow misses left me soaked, making it increasingly relentless to keep hold of the bars. I hauled myself down the bar frame, the platform within my grasp.

What?

It occurred to me suddenly – seizing my mobility – that the spikes were no longer far below. They were a few feet away. Almost vomiting from panic, I pulled my knees up. It was harder to move this way, however, which slowed my pace considerably. *This must be it. This is how it ends.* The ceiling, with me clung to it, was descending into the barbed floor. I had maybe twenty seconds to pass through, and with my legs forced higher and higher, until I was kissing my kneecaps, that was too much to ask.

Urging myself on, and slipping just before I reached the platform, I knew I had one shot to jump. The blades were almost brushing my back, but I had a new concern. In front of me burning on and off in sequence were another set of flamethrowers. There were no two ways about it, my life depended on timing, and reaching the platform. Two factors, one opportunity, and no time to think. As soon as the fire stopped, and the blades clawed my back, I leaped. The fabric of my jumpsuit tore as I made the jump, but instead of clutching myself, I scrambled forward. The wall of fire exploded as I did, singeing my back.

I cried out.

As I lay on my front, shots of unholy pain screamed through my nerves, constantly prodding me like jagged fingers of steel. My whole body thrashed, tormented by the agony. I wasn't fast enough.

With all my senses attacked by pain, I could barely focus ahead of me. If there was something else to contend with, like a raging bear or swinging axe, I would've been done for. For now, at least, everything was silent, but this gave me no peace, no assurance the worst was done. Happy was clear. Somewhere the Kingdom public were laughing at me, viewing my torture from some livestream. They'd want a show, much more than this. No, it couldn't be over.

My fears were shortly confirmed. A thick wall crashed down behind me, shaking the ground where my broken body lay. I was helpless, my only salvation being my desire to stay alive – it was all that empowered me to heave myself along my belly as the wall pushed my flailing feet. There was a wall ahead, and a wall behind, but it was closing in on me.

Startled and pushing down my pain – which was too crippling to concentrate on – I struggled toward the far wall, where there hung a thick chain. There was nowhere else to go, and the rear wall, though slow, wasn't stopping. Feeling a horrendous tightness in my lungs, I tugged at the chain, but it was hard to handle and slipped from my grip. Grunting I tried again, this time wrapping it around my wrist. The wall in front was gradually rising, so I kept tugging, summoning all my strength. My shoulders burned, but the real burn on my back was worse and fogged the pain. My hands were still dripping, forcing me to circle the chain further up my arm. The wall was almost halfway up, and I couldn't tell where the other wall was. I could only pull, and hope and cry to be rescued.

Occasionally the chain slipped, pulling my whole body with it as it shot back into the ceiling. On the fourth time, though, I lost my grip and the wall dropped, something crunched in my shoulder, and a sharp pain followed. It was torture, but sheer grit kept me pulling, wrists strained and hands bleeding, until I was satisfied with the height of the wall.

I was so fixated on getting the wall up I'd disregarded the rear wall, so naturally my heart jerked as it pressed my ruined back. That was after the sudden agony however, which triggered a flow of tears. Trying to keep my focus, I untangled the chain from my arm and shuffled as close to the wall as possible, but as I pulled from the wall behind me something made a sticky ripping sound, like Velcro. I didn't look back, but I was convinced it had removed a deeper layer of skin. Aware I might die from the pain alone if the wall pushed me again I wasted no more time – the chain was slipping from my grip quickly. I clenched my eyes, released the chain and dive rolled, screaming in untold grief as the floor grazed my back.

The wall collapsed.

CHAPTER XIII
MYSTERIOUS MERCY

WHEN I WOKE up, my limbs, my thoughts, and my pain had paused. I was trapped by a weightless sensation that flowed soothingly over my body, not carrying with it the same heart dropping feeling like in my nightmares. Instead it whispered to me reassuringly, the sensation, in a soft woman's voice which sounded familiar, but I was too sedated to pair a face to it. It didn't fade however, but increased in volume until I was forced to open my eyes, overwhelmed by the sunlight that had long escaped them. It made them water.

I squinted, trying to read it: the majestic star in the sky that can be seen even by day. It appeared to be watching me, looking down at me and expecting me to get up, willing me on. Everything changes in the Kingdom, but its light remains the same. It has always been, and will always be, right there in the sky.

The hope of a new day.

"Aletheia? Aletheia sweetie, how do you feel?"

The voice grew clearer, and even though I couldn't see her, I knew she was there. I knew where I was.

"That. Light."

Although my head was clear and my thoughts fluid, I could only spit those words. Something heavy rested on my throat, and coughing didn't ease it. I turned my head to the side, where I knew the voice had come from. My sight was so obscured I couldn't even make out the lady's features, she was an overhanging shadow. I let out another unhealthy cough, followed by a series of smaller ones.

"Lois, close off the stream, it's affecting her eyes!" ordered the voice. Incredibly, the moment she spoke the sun vanished, leaving us in darkness until smaller lights came on. Their light was soft and dim, so my vision soon adjusted.

Overhead stood the beautiful, crimson haired scientist who gave me the hydration capsule, and nurtured me through the withdrawal. Further from her was Happy, who appeared like she had been waiting for me too, but she didn't want me to know. There was a definite relax to her frown, which was abnormal, but nothing to tell me she'd been worrying. I didn't concentrate on her for long, suddenly I was aware of why I felt so light, so relaxed. I was suspended mid-air, engulfed by a strange bluish current similar to the resistance fields, only this one was air-like. A cooling wind, massaging my skin and filling my body with a tranquility I couldn't fight. I was nervous, not sure what had happened since The Purge or who had survived, but there was something about the current that wouldn't let me struggle.

I looked back at what was once the sky in an attempt to figure out where they hid the sun. I'm sure it was the sky before, but now it was a plain ceiling.

"What happened?" I was still weary, but as the time passed, I grew more assured of myself. The scientist, who had wandered over to some hologram of a graph, came back to me and lightly brushed my forehead.

"You sustained third degree burns to your back-"

"You were close. Lucky you got away with just that," interrupted Happy.

"The injury on your forearm was just a flesh wound. Fairly deep, but nothing serious-" continued the scientist, but I didn't let her finish either.

"Is my back ok?" I stiffened; dread had punched down my peace. If I wasn't in a fit enough state to compete in the Trials, I couldn't imagine what Hane would do with me.

"You're better. We had to keep you in this Revival Field though, which keeps your brain activity down until you reach a state of physical stability. That's why you haven't been conscious for three months."

"What? *Three months?*" I tried to sit up, but my back hadn't awoken with me. "How's that even possible?"

The more I thought about it, the more I convinced myself Hane had it in for me. That surviving The Purge hadn't done me any favors at all. I wondered if I was the only one. If the other girls either lived or died, and weren't stuck in the miserable in-between like I was, pumped with God-knows what through their arms. There were numerous drips prodded in my skin, thick with a purple substance.

Panicking, I extended my hand to the scientist, which she cupped in her own.

"Calm down. The Revival Field regenerates broken body tissue much faster than it could naturally. We call this process accelerated cellular reconstruction, understand?"

I nodded as if I did, but my head circled. It felt like I might've gone back under the field's neutralization effect at any moment.

"We've been monitoring your progress daily, and feeding you with an energy serum so you don't physically weaken. Don't worry if you don't understand everything I'm saying, it's the effect of your brain's recent inactivity. You'll get your focus back soon."

"You're a lucky girl," stated Happy, who watched briefly as the scientist crept back to the graphs. "How are you feeling?"

"Tired," I muttered.

"Hane has agreed to start the Trials only once you've recovered. He wants full participation…and no one can argue you don't deserve to take part."

"Hane is sparing me? He's waiting for me?"

Again I tried to sit up, but I was locked down and it was making me frustrated.

"Calm down. You survived the trial, it was only right he let you recover. You're not much of a delay anyway. We have good science to deal with you quickly."

"Where's the roof gone?" I blurted. It wasn't relevant or important, but not knowing was eating at me.

"It's still there, that's just how it appears," answered the scientist, who returned to my side. "It's called the Stream. An invisible barrier to the human eye, which is semipermeable, so it keeps out the weather conditions and filters natural light. Your living quarters has the same technology."

So *that's* why it appeared our quarters was in the open. I would've worked it out myself had it rained and our quarters remained dry, but this was no place for wet weather, not like home. I missed it in a way. I missed everything that reminded me of the free days, even if they went unappreciated while I had them. It's a funny thing, perspective. Never knowing what you have until it's gone.

I only spent a couple more days in the lab until the scientist – whose name I learned was 'Rose Nightingale' – cleared me to return to my group. I went back expecting the worst, haunted by a voice that told me my friends would be gone. I thought back to The Purge. I knew how grueling it had been, surely my group couldn't have fared much better. The doors to our quarters were always swift to open, but that's because I'd always known what I would see behind them. This time it was different, like I was watching them in slow motion: a lengthy and gradual movement that burned my heart to watch. All in my mind, a byproduct of my mental dormancy, but tormenting all the same. I had to catch myself when the waiting was over, as I stared into a place long forgotten in my dreams. I was taken aback, but my feet stayed planted. Only for a moment however, until I rushed into Jenny's arms, then Olivia's, and Tobi's. I told myself I'd stay strong, that there'd be no more crying, but the sight of them together sent tears streaming down my face. I craved their warmth, and now I had it. I wouldn't let them go. Clutching them as if my life depended on it, I embraced them all at once, shaking from nerves and joy.

I found out nothing had changed. They survived The Purge and had been training since, counting the days for me to return. Apparently they were aware I was alive as one of their advisors passed on the information, but I couldn't understand it. No one was allowed to know anything, other than when training would start and when we'd be fed. We had no rights, so why would they tell them? Sometimes I had to remind myself where I was, when it started to get familiar, because I couldn't bear getting too close to friends I would only have to leave behind. I told myself again and again we *didn't* have rights and we *were* slaves, nothing more. It was easy to forget though. None of us had even seen the arena for as long as we'd been there, and being with the girls made life easier, even fun sometimes. That was the worst part. I had no problems with our quarters or the people inside, or even how it was run, but whenever I felt myself relax, I'd want to cry again. The worst form of prison isn't a prison as such, like the dungeon we were kept in before. No. What's unbearable is when you know your future, and that you can't escape it.

After I'd released my tears and settled into the reality that for now, everything was ok, I realized one of my friends, Cindy, hadn't come to welcome me, which was strange. I wasn't as close to her as the other three, but I was still keen to listen to her stories.

She was hunched up in the corner, her face turned away from us. Jenny must've noticed me watching her, as I tried to greet her she pulled me back, firmly, at which the veil of ignorance fell from my eyes. Cindy was never alone. This was the first I'd seen her like this. Where was her best friend, Mia? Sometimes, even though I thought I couldn't live without the truth, I often convinced myself that I couldn't live with it either. Despite my best efforts, my head always battled me on how much easier it would be to never know. I knew I would have to ask, have to console Cindy, but right then…

I didn't want to know.

✄

"Aletheia? Aletheia? *Aletheia!*"

"*What?*" I grunted, still engaged with the task at hand. Trying not to get smacked in the face again.

"You're needed in the court. They're calling your group for a meeting." Happy frowned.

"Can't you tell them…I'm preoccupied at the moment?"

She halted the arm with her palm.

"It's mandatory."

"Fine," I sighed, throwing my spear down. I worked up a sweat on the rotary trunk, so it was annoying I had to leave. After my long absence from the sessions, it was only a few days ago I'd found my rhythm again.

"You'll need that," she snapped, as I made my way to the warp. We glared at each other first, but I still picked the spear up again. Eventually.

When I reached the court a ring of girls were already swarming a Kingdom official, each of them armed like I was, so it was an effort to get within earshot. I've never been good with crowds. I've always found myself slip to the back whenever one forms, but this was different. They never called meetings like this. I needed to get to the front.

"...in pairs you will fight one another, then when I call your name, you will fall defeated. Each of you will take turns to learn the honorable code. The code of surrender, and acceptance of your death," finished the officer, as I'd made it close enough to hear him. That was what I heard, but there was no time to ask anyone to fill me in.

"Aletheia Mirabel."

One of the crowd members pushed me forward, and I stumbled into the center. I tried to pull back again, but the official caught me on the shoulder.

"And Sophie Hartwell," he continued, at which he issued her to join me in what had become a miniature arena: a ring of people, and all of them huddled close, eager to spectate. Sophie was one of the few people who didn't commune with the group like the rest of us. She was reclusive, like Cindy had become, and the tallest girl in our quarters with mass to match. Not fat, but dense layers of muscle. She even bulged from her armor, which was the heaviest available. She looked down on me, as if deciding whether she would end me straight away, or let me throw a strike first. Either way, she had the duel in her hands.

In her right hand stretched a long, thick poll mounted with a mace head, similar to a club, only it resembled a drill bit. It was an unusual weapon, but what was even more interesting, because no one else had one, was her full body shield. I'd once tried to hold one up myself, but it took both hands, and I could barely heave it above waist height. Every fiber in Sophie's forearm tautened under its weight, but as she approached me and raised it, she held it there without complaint, her already-impenetrable body hidden by its huge width. I knew the only chance I had, the only factor on my side was speed, which relied on timing. It wasn't essential to win, this was only an exercise. Opposed to someone as frightful as Sophie, however, I soon forgot it wasn't a real fight. I felt sick.

"Now remember, light strikes, and keep your distance. Fight

as you would, but remember this is only a demonstration! Neither of you are adversaries, understood?"

The official yelled over my thoughts, enough for me to snap awake again. I nodded at him, but Sophie's eyes refused to deter from mine. I shuddered and assumed my stance, glaring at Sophie whose shield hid all but her face and feet, waiting for the official's cue. I had an idea on how to approach her. Her sheer power would be enough to trump my mobility, so I had to create an opening somehow.

She rushed me.

I'd contemplated my first move so intently my attention slipped from the official, who had ordered us to begin. In the same way I avoided the first arrow in The Purge, I found myself sidestepping to the right – a rapid, wide step that just got me out of Sophie's range unscathed. This would've been the perfect opportunity to counter; she'd dropped her guard. It was all so sudden, however, that instead I found myself stumbling backward and almost immediately she turned to follow-through. Without thinking, I drove my spear forward, which forced her to retract and absorb it into her shield. The impact sent a sharp vibration through my pole and wrists, and a loud clatter resounded. Everyone gasped, including the official who I realized was mesmerized. Every eye was pried to the duel like it was real. In response, Sophie pushed the shield towards me. I jumped backward, thrusting my weapon into its thick iron. This continued for strike after strike, yet still I resisted the urge to dash around her shield as I distanced her. *Just keep your distance. Keep your distance.* Any moment now, she would tire and swing her mace, and that would be my chance, possibly to disarm her if I hit right. But I forgot her mace wasn't her only weapon.

I tried to deflect it but she rammed her shield forward, wielding it with enough power to rip the spear from my hands, and before I had a chance to react, her shield found my nose. This is how she'd been trained, no nonsense, and no question. A killer.

As I raised my head and the fuzz cleared, I realized my spear was hovering above me, but that's not what worried me. Its blade was eclipsed by eyes even sharper.

"You! You there!" The guard pointed at her, marching up to her with aggression. She gazed back blankly. "I told you to hold back. You were not to-" He gawked at me; I imagine I wasn't pleasant to the eye. "Raise your finger!"

I was too concerned about the blood to question him. Keeping my nostrils held tight, I pointed to him, tilting my head back and forth in an attempt to stop the blood flow.

"The *left* hand!" he demanded, as if I was supposed to know already.

Switching hands forced me to release my nose, which spilled onto my breastplate, staining the Kingdom's lion crest.

"*This is called the plea!*" he bellowed, so loud it's possible the adversaries further down the court could hear him. "As traditional of the Roman games, it is your opportunity for mercy. Some of you will fight valiantly, yet fall to an opponent with even more valor. Should this be the case, and the public still consider you an asset to the Kingdom, you have but one chance to request a pardon for your loss so you may live to contend another day. Ultimately Hane shall be the judge of your fate, but he is sure to bend to public opinion, understand?"

The crowd murmured in agreement.

"The public are your lifeline – they stand between your life and death. Should you grow too weary or suffer a wound too severe, you may drop to your knees and request their mercy by your own resolve. If you or your opponent do this, you must both cease! To strike an enemy while they are vulnerable is to kill with dishonor, and those who do will share in their death. I suggest you drop your weapon the moment your opponent pleas."

After he'd extensively covered the importance of falling to our 'knees' and raising our 'left' hand he turned back to me, demanding I grab Sophie's thigh who still hadn't moved the spear from my face. It was like the guard had put the action on pause, and if permitted she would've more than happily resumed.

"If you wish to leave a lasting impression on the Kingdom, the motherland of all nations, you have a responsibility to represent your own nation with honor. Gladiators *died* with honor, as well as fought with it, and we expect no less of you.

"We will practice this for the remaining hours of the day, as it is critical, not only for you, but your nation's legacy. If the decision of your plea is death you must confirm you accept this, as shown here, by grabbing your adversary's thigh. Do this, and you will die with bravery and therefore respect, which reflects your homeland and lives on as the unwritten foundations of what makes it relevant, and admirable. If you do not, if you die in fear, you will bring shame upon your nation. This burden will be your family's to bear, and the generations to come. When you die, do so a warrior, not a slave."

⚜

I craved my bed once we were released but Happy, who returned upon arrival of dusk, had other plans for me. She took me to the Gymnasium.

"What are we doing here?" Thinking about death all afternoon had put me in an awful mood. In truth, I didn't care where we were, I just wanted to argue.

"I'm going to be straight with you."

She jerked her head back and forth. The Gymnasium was empty, the other girls had been escorted to our quarters. We were the only exception. Once confident we were alone, she gave me a jagged look, like she was in pain.

"We've got problems."

EPISODE II

TRIAL OF TRUTH
THE PRESENT

CHAPTER XIV

GENESIS

THE CLIMBING CLAMOR of the audience jolts me from my reverie, at which Happy extends her hand. It's moist like my own, glistening in the torchlight, except I'm wet all over, bound in a bitter odor. My throat is parched.

"What about you?" I accept it, and she helps me up. My tailbone throbs.

"This is as far as I can take you. I must take my place in the stands."

An urge overcomes me, all of a sudden, and I find myself in her arms again. I still cry, but her loving grasp seems to empower me.

"Go," she whispers finally, as I release her from my desperate clasp. I know what must be done, and I can't hold her forever. But I wish I could.

Reluctantly, I turn to the exit, refusing to watch her leave. Instead, her footsteps grow ever more distant until I know I'm alone. I stare blankly at a force field separating me from the passage, shimmering in an azure hue. Hesitantly, I prod it with my finger, which passes through. As does my hand, and my arm...

Whoa!

I wasn't wearing armor, which I didn't even realize, but as I walk through the force field it materializes on me like it had always been there. A spear too – the same one that belongs to Happy – immediately graces my hand as I continue to walk into the daylight, during which 'Star-Spangled Banner' booms from the Colosseum.

I gasp.

Here it is. Everything I've been training for. The very place I could only imagine until this day, hoping and praying it wouldn't be too dangerous, and that there wouldn't be as many traps as they showed in my textbook at school. There's nothing to be wary of, no signs of impending danger, but it's enormous. Five, maybe six times bigger than the Ludus: thousands upon thousands of spectators fill the stands, clapping and cheering with thunderous enthusiasm. It's ovular, and furthest from me is the stand where the authorities sit beside Hane, whose eyes dagger me as I take my entrance. There's no mistake about it. He wants me gone.

"What do you mean I didn't pass The Purge?" I cried, heedless to who might've heard me. "You said I had! You said-"

"I *thought* you had!" Happy urged, trying to steady me. "I thought Hane had given you a chance, but he's been planning to kill you from the very beginning! I heard him Aletheia! I heard him with the council!"

"What? How-"

"Just listen. You are not here so Hane can find a new leader – you're here because he needs a new army. The rebels outside are growing stronger. They have tried to overthrow him thirty-two times, and every attempt has brought them closer. The Kingdom public are losing faith in him, and they're already sympathizing with the rebels because they don't feel safe. The Trials are a tool to win back loyalty. Hane's army is full of strong males, but it lacks females, and he intends to cross the survivor's DNA with his soldiers to create a superhuman race. You're a science experiment. A promise of security."

"...He's going to breed us?"

"Not naturally, that would take too long." She reached out to guide my eyes back to hers. The room was whirling around me. "Genetic engineering. With our technology, it won't even take two years to clone an army, and once he's identified the genes to construct the perfect soldier there's no limit to what he'll produce. That's where you come in," she sighed. "I went about it the wrong way when I volunteered to train you. I showed Hane up in front of everyone, and he doesn't take those things lightly. I'm ashamed to think he'd forgotten it."

"What do you mean?"

"He doesn't care about you – it's *me*. He wants to kill me." She froze, on the verge of tears. "The advisors signed up at the prospect of becoming Hane's deputy, and gaining fame, but there's a condition: the failure of a student reflects the abilities of the teacher. If a trialist dies the advisor must die with them."

The noise is so overpowering I can barely hear the music anymore. Now that the audience realize who I am a majority are booing me. My stomach churns, and my knees wobble. It's unbearably hot out here. The sun is beating down on what appears to be miles of white sand, yet my teeth are chattering as if I've arrived in the artic. There's Happy, she's taken her seat. She has her own private stand, and opposite her on the other side of the arena is the second advisor. The advisor of the one I'll be fighting. My adversary.

"Aletheia Mirabel!" the announcer repeats again. He's Hane's deputy, the one who helped plan my demise. I gulp. Everyone's set on burying me.

"Hane decided the moment you were meant to die in The

Purge for you to be pulled out in front of everyone, so you look favored," Happy continued, after a lingering moment. "If he executes me for showing him up in the court, he'll lose more support, but if you die in the Trials, he can kill me no questions asked. He knew sparing you when you should have died would make the public furious, because then they'd think his motivation for keeping you alive is for personal reasons, not their welfare. The Trials were supposed to win their trust back, and if he displays you as his favorite while his people root for the strongest, it's only going to turn them against you. His deputy gave him the idea for the plea. If you use it the public will demand your death, and when Hane obliges he'll recover their loyalty. That's the only reason the plea exists." She couldn't say much else, I wouldn't respond to her. In the end, she left me standing there, alone. Deafened by my thumping heart.

I gaze at the overwhelming size and power of the audience surrounding me. *They're here to see me die.* I'm crying again, but I'm not afraid to show it. When I die it won't matter.

"Enter Lucy Robinson!" the announcer bellows, which rings my ears. He's mic'd up, but he still insists on screaming everything. An anthem I recognize resounds as the girl emerges from the gateway opposite me.

"Please welcome Aletheia Mirabel of North America, and Lucy Robinson of Britain," Hane's deputy repeats, taking his seat as Hane rises from his own. I swallow hard. Not only do I have to kill this person, we share a language. An innocent, one-of-a-kind adversary full of wants, needs, and dreams, whose every word I'll understand.

What if she begs me not to kill her? What then?

We halt, seven or so paces from each other. Lucy is far younger than me. From her face and soft complexion, I presume sixteen, but she may be younger. Her unsteady gaze and pupils' innocent twinkle exudes her lack of experience; she's fighting to keep her eyes from the floor. She must be one of the youngest. *Still,* I remind myself. *She survived The Purge.* I have to stay focused. Anyone who's made it this far will be no easy kill. Every fight could be my last.

"Settle down. Settle down," Hane orders over the crowd, at which they immediately silence. The atmosphere is so still I can hear my heart. It's trying to flee.

"Here I give you the first contenders. The first trialists to compete for the cause of our nation, and the world, so that mankind may finally rest in the assurance there will be nothing to stand against my leadership. Nothing to overthrow the Kingdom. Through these brave women who have devoted their lives to this new era, we will give rise to one champion who shall be honored with our wealth, our respect, and our gratitude, and they shall lead a new army. A new legacy of freedom. They will take back from the rebels – who have sown nothing but misery – everything they have stolen from us. They will enforce justice, so that all who dare question our desire for a better world will perish at their feet.

"Valued citizens of the Kingdom, I give you Genesis: the beginning of the end of the days where sorrow is rooted in the hearts and minds of man. Through the Trials we will find our savior, and through the trialists' deaths will arise new life. God's blessing be with them all, and to all, may you die in the confidence of a better tomorrow. Let the fifth phase of The Kingdom Trials… commence!"

A gong sounds, and the crowd rises in uproar, already cheering, jeering, hissing, and screaming at us as we both weigh up who's going to make the first move. I assume my stance, squeezing Happy's spear with heavy intensity. As long as I keep hold of it, I have a chance. My adversary has a sword, but even though she's not handling it confidently my head's still screaming for me to stay put. I'm frozen solid…but so is she.

"Move! Strike her!" a member of the crowd cries, who's near

to me and sat at the front. I can't be sure who it's directed at, but a good guess would be they're pushing Lucy to kill me.

I glance at the crowd, my spear refusing to release Lucy from its quivering tip. There's hatred in their faces. Their size and animosity is so unnerving, I can't even find Happy again. I'm giddy, no longer able to perceive the presence of someone behind me until they bellow in my ear.

"Move!"

I turn to face a Kingdom guard with a long glowing rod. Before I can grasp why I'm prodded in the back with it, which triggers a horrible pain identical to what I'd experienced in The Purge. I clutch my screaming skin, feeling a small gap where my suit has burnt away. Lucy too, has an official on her tail, but upon seeing my distress, she hits his prong away, taking many steps back as she does. Closer to me. Fearing another jab, I charge at her, but she knocks my spearhead aside, and doesn't attempt a counter. Anticipating one, I leap back, bracing myself for her sword, but she stays planted.

"*Fight!*" the guard's voice rumbles through the arena walls, exploding my nerves. Terror forces me to lunge at the helpless girl again and again, but she shrugs off each strike, backing further away with every deflection. Even as I lower my spear, straining to filter out the toxic concoction of ridicule and threats plaguing me, the girl makes no effort to strike.

"I don't want to fight you!" the girl wails, her eyes welling. She says it with such conviction I almost believe her, but I still manage to slash at her sword in a downwards trajectory, which forces her arm to lower, leaving her open for a clean impale. If she's trying to throw me off-guard, she's done it at her own cost.

The spearhead tears across her arm as it homes in for the kill, but before it finds its target she falls backward, breakfalling from harm. Her sword drops to the ground however, so I hit it away with the spearhead, hard. The crowd can't contain their excitement

– if I kill her now, I could prove myself worthy of their approval. *This is my chance,* I urge to myself, but my arms lock again. Lucy's crying, but those tears aren't false. They're too bitter. Her face is too screwed up. My own tears in the desert; the tears in the cells; the tears that flooded my blood-stained street when they struck my father and carried me to the ship; the tears that strangled my voice when I begged the officers to release Jedidiah – it all comes flooding back as I watch this girl, drowning me under their combined mass. I can't breathe. My hands lower until the spear is dragging by my side. I'd rather die, in the knowledge that I did so in grace, than live forever through the death of another. Especially one so sweet, so harmless. I can't do it.

There's immediate relief in her face as the spear falls to my waist, she looks on at me holding her bloody arm in an almost grateful way. I'm instantly drawn to the surrounding gates however, so there's little time to admire her starry gaze. A harsh sound of churning metal overpowers even the audience as the barred gates rise. They're not gates. They're cages. From them emerge three tigers, one from each cage. One of them attacks the guard that released it, and he is thrown to the ground, at which two men rush to bat the tiger away and carry him off-scene. However long these animals have been kept in those cages, it's too long.

By reflex, I sprint toward Lucy again, though not to strike her – to throw her to the side as the first tiger pounces. I grab her in time, but not fast enough to avoid the claws as they rake swiftly against my breastplate. It dents it beyond repair, its claws are diamond hard. The animal rises to its hind legs as it hurls itself for another scrape at me, but this is no human. No young girl. Without the slightest consideration for its wellbeing, I lunge in, where its stomach slips into my spear. Its blood drenches my hands. I gag at the sight but recover focus. From the corner of my eye, I see a new threat, this one in the form of a rhino, and it's rampaging in my direction. Lucy is being pursued by the tigers, but there's no time to think. I evade the beast's horn by a fraction, but I can't keep hold of my weapon. It falls near the rhino.

"Help!" Lucy shrieks, but the rhino has turned on me already. I can't even stop to see where she is – I have just enough time to scramble to my feet and avoid the second charge, landing hopelessly on my stomach again, winded.

I squirm on the burning sand, gasping, with only enough energy to roll from the rhino's hoofs as it goes for its third charge. *This isn't right,* I groan. *It was never meant to end this way.* I see the graveyard, how I knelt by the graves of Uncle Hamza and his wife. I did not come through all this, all these years of torture and misery, for this.

I grit my teeth and rise; the rhino's horn is trained to me, but I see Lucy's weapon a few feet away. I leap for it, as the rhino comes in full force, at which I throw the sword and roll, choking on the dust it throws over me. The blade buries into the rhino's skull, and it squeals and stampedes in all directions, crashing into a gate which partially shatters. A large group of officials hurry there, throwing chains in a bid to contain it.

My blood freezes.

Ahead of me, two tigers are tearing away at the remains of Lucy's body. Her head is detached and disfigured, lying near one of her arms with half its skin hanging loose from her skull. Below her corpse and around the large radius of her dismembered limbs the sand is a deep red, verging on black, like a gaping void to hell. An officer takes my arm from behind.

"Come with me."

As I'm pulled away, I gaze emptily at the body, the once living child whose eyes softened my heart, gone. Never to return. I can't hear what the crowd are shouting. It's too loud to ignore, but everything is muffled. I can't focus. I'm so. Cold.

CHAPTER XV

SOMEDAY

A GUARD ARRIVES at my door to find me holding my stomach. I haven't scratched marks in the wall like I did the last time I was in these cells to keep track of how many days could have passed. There's an old bottle cap lying at the far end of my cell I could use, but I'm too drained to move. I haven't been fed like before, and I wasn't given a drink. I know I couldn't have been here for many days, but in utter darkness and silence each day passes as slow as a year.

He opens my cell. I want to leap up and run out, possibly take my chance at running to freedom, or at least as far as my legs will carry me before I drop, but I submit to my reality and push the urge down. The guard hauls me to my feet and guides me through the entrance while supporting my weight, much like what I did for Jenny. We're slow to proceed up the steps that lead out from the basement. There are many to navigate. He instructs me to take them one step at a time, taking the full strain of my weight as I work my way up. I'm so stripped of energy I'm already bathed in sweat; it's dripping from my nose, ears, and eyebrows. The guard however is comfortable, holding me firm as we pass two thirds of the stairway. It doesn't surprise me. I'm sure he could even carry Sophie with ease, his triceps ripple in the orange torchlight, cut symmetrically on each arm. It's like the Kingdom officials are the picture of perfection, yet Hane still wants more? I think back to what Happy told me. Breed superior warriors using our DNA? What's wrong with what he has? Is he really that scared?

Keeping my eyes half-closed to filter in the light I allow the man to escort me down one of the many hallways. I know now, by experiencing the enormity of the arena, the sheer scale of this Colosseum. Considering it contains the Ludus, Gymnasium, The Purge zone, laboratory, the arena, and every nation's living quarters all under one roof, the work that went into it must've taken years. Perhaps decades. The incredible craftsmanship of the statues around me signifies this building's importance, and extreme care has gone into even the minute details. Within the pupil of one of the lions there's a small engraving of the Kingdom crest: another smaller lion, within the eye of this large one. Below me too, strange symbols forming a pattern on every tile I tread. Each tile is only one square inch, however as we continue, I notice they all contribute to a greater mosaic. It's a picture, within a picture, within a picture.

We progress further down the hallway, but it only leads to another. I'm fatigued, and every footstep triggers more sweat even with the assist of the guard. Each time I droop forward I want to vomit, but the guard catches me and pulls me back, supporting my lower back as he does. Around me the surroundings distort and spin, but I glimpse what looks like soldiers with a handful of girls. One of the guards is Celadus, Sophie's advisor, but I'm so drunk with exhaustion, it takes several seconds for me to remember. Near to him is Sophie herself, her eyes dark and fierce, glaring at me like the guard's dragged a lamb to the slaughter, soulless and apathetic to my agony. Beside her stands Commodus. I'm not sure if it's a mirage of the mind, but he too is staring straight at me, grinning openly. I scan the girls for my friends, who must have already experienced the arena. Bloodied and bruised: an attribute that unites them all.

"Trialists, you have been selected to compete in a contest of Parlay," Celadus announces, once I'm within earshot of the group. "Either all of you win your next round of fights today, or your entire group shall be forced to compete in two fights each day they compete."

I'm veering on delusional, but I still understand the situation. I can't keep it in.

"What? That's murder!"

I try to step forward, but I come over horribly sick and fall back into the guard's arms.

"Silence!" His finger locks onto me. "You do not speak until spoken to! *Understand?*"

I give the guard a look to check if he's on my side, thrown off by his caring embrace. He looks back knowingly, as if he's telling me to stay calm. I nod and clutch him tighter.

"If you win, however," Celadus continues. "Lord Hane has agreed to relieve your group from the Trials for three months. During that period, you will have all the time you need to rest and train."

I freeze, allowing the hope to bubble up. My mind floods with joyful visions, like relaxing in the quarters with Jenny, and eating a platter of cheese and crackers, but Happy's warning thrusts into my memory, popping the joy to nothing. It's a ruse. Hane's playing the advisors like puppets, having me starved in the cells so my shot at winning a fight is distant, practically undoable. He's selected *me* to compete in the Parlay for that reason, knowing it's an offer the advisors won't refuse.

"We need this, girls. You need it. We need to ensure you are ready for the challenges ahead," he stresses. "All of you have survived the Trials already, and that's all you need to do again, but you must *kill* your opponent. Those are the terms, are we clear?"

Each girl nods uncertainly, except for Sophie who continues to stare at me.

"Believe in yourselves. This is what you've been training for, and we know you all have the capability to achieve greatness."

His words leave a bitter taste, but I swallow it down. The advisors make out they want to help us, but they're as false as their sentiments.

"Do us and your nation proud," Celadus finalizes, and with that, he signals us to follow him.

We are led down more hallways, huddled together but free from physical restraints, no cuffs, chains, or bonds of any sort. I suppose this is the advisors' way of saying they trust us, or that to attempt an escape is futile. Probably the latter. I dare not talk to anyone, but inside I'm dying, desperate to ask someone if my friends are ok. I have every confidence in them, no doubt in their abilities. But what if they released the beasts on them? Could they really survive something that brutal? I'd only made it out by sheer luck, and even then that landed me in a cell. What if they're in trouble too, injured or worse, what if they're not with me... because these are all who are left? This train of negativity draws me further away from reality, but it isn't long before some unfamiliar voices tug me back. They're round the corner, talking and laughing with each other. Laughter. Something so alien to me that all of a sudden, I'm intrigued to know more.

Keeping close to the group, I peer down the passage as we pass it. There are two men with their backs to me, engaging in a light conversation and playfully hitting each other as they walk, which relaxes me. That was what we used to do, Jedidiah and I. We were always...

Something indescribable stops me in my tracks.

I've stopped, yet the rest of the girls are still walking. Celadus turns his head to me, but I ignore him. I can't breathe. Am I wrong? So…so familiar, the face of the man that I gaze at so mystically, like I'm staring out from the edge of space and time, looking into the universe from a heavenly perspective. It's like I'm not myself anymore. I'm not thinking as myself anymore. My mouth drops open at the sight – the overwhelming and powerful sensation of peering into something that seems so distant, so illusory, yet as real as the sweat on my cheek, or the blood that pulses through my veins at such amplified pace. Both men have turned toward each other. I can see their profiles as clear as crystal water, like the flowing river I used to study every day, waiting. Waiting. Waiting for that fish. A powerful shudder works from my spine to the tips of my toes, and now I know what it is to be in awe, true and divine awe. I'm staring at it. And it's within reach.

Dropping all sense of despair, pain, and fear, I hurl myself down the corridor toward the two men. They turn instantly, and as they do, I see his pupils dilate. I draw every last breath from my lungs.

"Jedidiah! *Jed!* Je-"

He catches me in his arms, his firm, masculine arms. He's a man, a solid man like the rest. But he hasn't changed. I'm holding him, I can't pair together a sentence. I'm holding him. I cry violently into his chest, holding him. My life, my everything. He's in my hands again. Locked around his broad back my fingers tremble, clutching him as tight and as desperately as I had my father the day I was taken from him. As if my whole life from the point of his absence has been a lie I'm taken back to a place I can embrace my father again, kiss my mother and tighten my sandals to meet Jedidiah by the river. The life I thought had escaped me, flooding back all in the few seconds of bracing his body, losing myself in his unforgettable warmth.

"A-Aletheia," he chokes. Tears stream down his cheeks, and yet he's beautiful. He hasn't changed. I reach for his neck to pull his head closer to mine. But I grow faint.

"Aletheia!" He catches me from dropping. Reality has come to take me away again, sudden and stealthy, like a thief in the night. It's back in the form of my sickness, and the bulky figure of Celadus marching in my direction. Even compared to Jedidiah's physique he's almost three times the size. He eyes me like a fish he's about to impale.

"Slave! How dare you run from me!"

I don't dare look him in the eye. I push closer to Jedidiah. I won't let him steal this joy.

"She is no slave, Celadus!" Jedidiah explodes, gripping me tighter in response, which takes him aback.

"She is not a slave? Boy, she is property of the Kingdom. I demand you hand her over!"

I watch him, frozen to the bone. Even with Jedidiah beside me, I'm afraid again. Jedidiah pauses before he responds, containing the rising rage that darkens his countenance.

"What is to become of her?"

Celadus, before considering a response rips me from Jedidiah's hands, and as he goes to retaliate several guards surround him, weapons aimed. I wince as Celadus breathes down my neck. His grip on my wrist sends a throb all the way up my arm.

"She is to be punished, as a slave should."

"Are you threatening me, Celadus?" Jedidiah glares at him sternly, undeterred by the men around him.

"Not you, Cadman. I wouldn't dare to challenge someone of your *superiority*. But this girl is to be punished."

Jedidiah speaks again, slow and authoritative.

"Then have your men lower their swords, and tell me what is to become of her."

Reluctantly Celadus signals his men to fall back, and Jedidiah walks closer to him. Closer to me. He's too close for Celadus' liking – his grip on me tightens.

"She is to be flogged. By my hand."

My heart sinks, and the memory of The Purge strikes me like a mental lash. The pain almost ended me when I was fit. A flogging. It will be too much.

"By your hand?"

Jedidiah freezes.

"You can't. You're an executioner!"

"She has already defiled the Kingdom as it is! An embarrassment to her nation, refusing to fight an adversary, and now this!" His eyes burn and fists clench. "This disobedience of my authority, I will not stand for it! Ladarius, fetch me the tools." He points fiercely at the guard who assisted me out of the cellar, who nods and runs from sight.

"You can't do this! You *have no* authority!" Jedidiah objects.

"Wrong, I *do* have authority! These slaves have been submitted to me under Lord Hane's command. I can do as I please with them!"

Celadus has become a raging lion, ready to strike down anyone who opposes him, yet Jedidiah edges closer. I fear the worst.

"I order you to stand down! Hand her to me!" Jedidiah scowls, reaching for me. I pull closer to him, but Celadus wrenches me back.

"This is an abomination! You think you can question the authority granted to me by the Lord?"

Ladarius returns with a whip, hammer, nails, and large rope netting. He hands the whip to Celadus.

"You better watch yourself, Cadman, or you'll be next!"

My eyes fix to the long, rough leather of the whip. It has marks of repeated use, and from a distance, it appears alive and nimble, slithering in Celadus' hand like a serpent. Hungry for blood. I swallow hard. Fixed to the leather are miniscule blades – as Celadus holds the whip closer I see the head of each blade clearer, stained red from previous use. The leather too, is tainted by gore.

This has been used to kill.

Once he's handed the whip to him, Ladarius heaves the rope to a wall, securing the net in place with the nails. It's heavy. He requires more guards to help him. I can't work out what it's for, my mind is racing at the sight of the whip. As the net is nailed up Celadus gives the command.

"You. Hold the rope!" he sneers, pushing me forward.

I turn in a desperate plea for Jedidiah, but he's stunned silent, bathed in sweat.

"No-Celadus, you can't do this! *Celadus!*" he bursts, as he tries to grab the whip, but he catches the leather, and it bleeds his hand. Celadus pushes him back.

"Do not interfere!"

He turns back to me.

"Slave, you are to hold this rope for every lash, and every time you let go you shall receive another!"

I grip the net tightly, already reliant on its support. I'm so weak, falling…my grip loosens and releases. Two guards drag me up again and push me to the wall, tearing my clothing clean from my back. I'm not wearing underclothes, so I push closer to the wall to conceal myself.

"Aletheia!"

I hear Jedidiah scream, and then an array of footsteps rushing. I hear him struggle, other men struggle, and then silence. Keeping my hands firmly around the rope I angle my head to him. His eyes are wide open. He's shaking and the guards have him pinned.

"How many lashes?" he cries out, trying to push free. There are too many guards. He's overpowered.

"Until I deem fit," Celadus replies, but without facing him. I watch as the whip rises. It's like waiting to be struck with the baton again, only I know the pain will be worse.

"*How many lashes?*" Jedidiah grunts, as he shoves at the guards. There are several of them, but he's determined.

"Hold him!" Celadus orders.

Jedidiah's breaking through – he's getting close again, forcing the guards forward with him. Each lunge pushes him closer to me, and I desire to reach him, but I know he's endangering himself.

"Stop! Jed you'll only hurt yourself! You can't stop him!" I beg, but he doesn't listen.

"You'll kill her! You'll *kill her,* Celadus, that's what you do! She doesn't deserve to die!"

Celadus raises his arm once more.

"She's just a girl!"

I see the impending lash and drive my head to the wall.

"*I'll do it!*"

There's a pause, and I look to see Celadus' reaction. He's lowered the whip altogether, mouth open at Jedidiah's proposal.

"I'll give the punishment," Jedidiah pants, looking at me with brokenness. With red, teary eyes and a quivering lip.

"You will do it?" Celadus confirms, turning to him. My heart is racing.

"Yes. Ten lashes, as standard. I'll do it."

I study him intently. My pain is nothing in comparison.

"Very well." He hands Jedidiah the whip. "Same rules apply, Cadman. She releases the net, and you give an additional lash, understand?"

He nods and approaches me slowly, pausing to stare at the men that have closed in on us. They cower back. It's just me and the friend I have been searching for. The boy who once gave me so much joy, now preparing to inflict the greatest pain. He's crying, but fighting hard to keep it together.

I look at Celadus one last time – he smiles, as the girls beside him watch in fevered silence. Holding tightly to the net, I turn away, head to the wall. I know Jed wouldn't want me to see him do this, and I have a duty to wait. Wait until it's over, until it's all through, and he's saved me. I owe this to him.

Crack!

I hear the whip slice the air as it imposes on my skin. It hits in an instant, but the anticipation lasts almost a lifetime. I cry out – it crashes against my back with such tremendous force, my whole body is rammed into the wall. I hit my forehead as the lash settles, I'd wavered in confidence and tried to look at Jedidiah again. It throbs, and I consider reaching for it, but then the sting comes and my limbs lock from shock. I gasp, refusing to let go of the rope, and plant my head to the wall again, which is damp with my sweat. I'm not going to let go, I'm going to take it. Each and every one.

The whip collides again, and I'm forced to bend my knees to prevent myself falling immediately. A great strain is forced upon my wrists, which are all that's keeping me from the cold ground below. Holding in a scream, I contract my back muscles and pull myself up. Again, I push my head to the wall, weeping and trembling on the net to such extremity I know the third strike could finish me. But then I'm gone, and I've lost Jedidiah, and I've failed, and I can't let go.

I won't let go.

Another lash follows, and another, and with each one I take a sharp breath to keep myself conscious, refusing to cry any longer. Holding onto the possibility of lasting through the pain, and being with Jedidiah again. Occasionally my palms slip but I keep them glued to the rope, until they bleed. The blades on the leather dig into me further, tearing up more flesh as they exit my ruined back. The floor is a pool of blood. It's gushing down my legs. Jedidiah is still sobbing, but I know to look at him will break me. Hearing him like this is mental flogging in itself, but to see him this grieved would drain me of all strength. For him, I must not look back.

Crack!

The eighth lash lands. It steals my breath. I struggle to hold myself up. I fall but keep my hands on the rope, hanging there. Gripping for life. It's as if someone has opened my back with an axe, ceaselessly digging for my spine. The power behind the leather has winded me, but in this position, I can't take in oxygen. My mouth is gaping, but my lungs have shut down.

I'm choking.

With one last surge of will, I tug myself upright, but my arms give out. Instead of hitting the floor, however, my body wilts midway, cradled by soft hands. They enclose my waist, guiding me to my feet. I turn around to see Jedidiah's face, but inches from mine. His hands are drenched in my blood, but I don't squirm. I don't panic. I just stare at him again, as he does, at which he brushes a lock of hair back behind my ear like he did when we were kids. He doesn't say a word, I can't say anything either, but his eyes tell me I'm ok. I'm going to be fine. We're going to get through it.

Returning to his position Jedidiah readies himself for the last lashes. I turn back to the wall. Before there's time to drift into a fantasy – being back home, playing as a kid and remembering the good moments – the ninth lash strikes me. I wail out, grunt and clutch the rope even tighter. *One more, one more. Just one,* I repeat, rerunning those words over and over as the fuel for my entire body. My physical strength has escaped me. I'm holding on only to the hope of a better future, a future with Jedidiah again, and the image of his face. His wonderful, reassuring presence that locks me in a trance of composure, of spiritual tranquility. He's my strength. He's what's pulling me forward, and he's the source of my will. I'm doing this for him.

As the final lash tears at me, and I hear that sinister crack for the last time, I see my life's suffering flash before me: the struggle in the desert, over, and facing the loss of Jedidiah and my family, in the past. The moment I wailed over the body of the girl who fell, and how I endured such overwhelming pressure carrying

Jenny. Then my adversary who was brutalized and murdered in the arena, Lucy, I see her too, but before her last moments, her face as pure as moonlight. Everything hits me at the speed and force of the final lash, like that lash was the end of it all. The last time I have to experience those things. And then comes the footsteps. The sound of my approaching savior. His hands slip over my own encouraging me to release them. As I do, he sweeps me from my feet, pressing me close to him. He drops the whip where he stands. It's dripping with gore.

"I'm taking her with me."

Celadus attempts to object but the other guards simply withdraw from our path, and we proceed up the hallway, leaving the hurt behind us. Leaving everything behind us, and moving on to a new future. As he takes me assuredly in his arms, cradling me against his chest, he whispers something to me. The words alone numb my burning.

"I knew I would find you. Someday."

CHAPTER XVI

TOXIC IDEALS

I'M LAID OUT on my stomach as Jedidiah lifts me onto a table. My body is going into shock. I'm convulsing and scratching deep into the table, but the pain won't go. I can't shut it out. The cutting agony is shearing me to nothing, and no matter how many times Jedidiah rushes back to comfort me, his words ricochet. It's like I'm being strangled by countless layers of cellophane, and it's stifling his voice. A barrier that obscures his face, where I'm forced to suffer in isolation. I scream, crying desperately for someone to help me. The pain has consumed my ability to see anything past the torment. He runs aside to hold my hand, but I can't hear him, and in frantic terror I pull my hand away. There's demons here, they're grinning at me, so I slam my head down to block them out. Jedidiah rummages urgently around the room, which retrieves my attention. He's already gathered some towels, and next to them is a needle. As he rampages through his cabinets and drawers he tosses bottles, which smash on the floor. He shouts, frustrated, but

I can't hear him over my own cries as I writhe helplessly on the marble. I know this isn't helping him, my tears are only fueling his stress, but I'm falling further to hell by the second, a place of hurt I simply cannot bear. I'm slipping away. Darkness is trying to take me.

His kind face pushes back into view – he's holding a small pot and the towels which are dripping wet. He says something else to me, and proceeds to spread the towels over my back. It's horrible. The water seeps deep into the wounds and a sharp sting amplifies the burn. It's like I've been bound to an open flame, and emerging from the blistering heat are knifes that jab ruthlessly, puncturing me as deep as the blades allow.

"Stop! *Please stop!*" I wail, but Jedidiah firmly works the towels into my wounds, showing no acknowledgment to my distress. *I trust him. I trust him,* I repeat, pulling at my hair and pounding the table as he continues. He tosses the towels down, which are so thick with blood they're black.

"Aletheia. Aletheia, you're doing well."

I make out his voice; my head pairs together some words. He looks at me intensely, as if into my soul.

"I have to apply this cream now, ok? It's all I've got."

He holds out the pot to show me its contents, which is syrupy.

"It will regenerate your skin, but it's going to hurt. It will hurt a lot." With the other hand, he reaches to run his fingers through my hair, stroking the top of my head. I panic.

"No! No, no, no! You can't!"

He tries to hush me, but I speak over him.

"What about the medical center? What about…" I'm fading. "There's that-the revival field Rose put me in. Please take me there!"

My head drops, like it weighs a hundred pounds all of a sudden, but Jedidiah catches me by my cheeks.

"I can't. The recovery takes too long – this is our only option. Aletheia, stay with me!"

His desire to keep me conscious snaps me back, and I grab both of his hands. I try to breathe.

"Ok. Ok. I trust you."

He takes the pot and rushes to the side of me, but not before kissing my forehead. I'm bathed in sweat, but that doesn't deter him from kissing me.

"Argh!"

He rubs the cream into my back, and I'm so overtaken by pain, I can't even spit out the words I'm dying to: to urge him, *beg* him to stop.

"St-stop!" I finally cough it up, but he tries to calm me and continues to rub the cream deeper. There's no other option, he has to ignore me, but the burn is indescribable – more intense than the lashes put together. Again, he assures I'm doing well, that it will soon be over, but I'm incapable of speech. My body has never shaken so violently. Jedidiah is hard-pressed to steady me and apply the cream, but as he rubs in the last handful as if miraculously the stinging ceases, and the pain dulls.

"You did it. It's over," he sighs, with a gentle smile.

"Barely," I utter, lost in the depths of his ocean-tinted irises. Jedidiah's family were some of the few who managed to escape their homeland. They never went into too much detail about it, but apparently Britain had it worse than any other nation. There's unrest everywhere, but in comparison to the wars in Britain where I'm from is a sleepy town with not much to it. It's a tragedy he had to leave his home, but if I ever saw him dwelling on it, I'd try to cheer him up by telling him he had the best voice in the area. Whenever I had the opportunity, I would simply marvel at it. Even now, I find I'm doing the very same thing.

"Drink some water; you need it." He picks up a small cup and presses it to my lips. They are dry; my tongue brushes the cracked skin as I sip, which is all I'm given before he takes it away from me.

"Just small sips for now. The cream's repairing you, but as it does your body enters a delicate state. Too much and you'll vomit." Pulling a chair from under one of his units, he sits by me, slowly massaging my head again. "You're going to be fine."

"I know." I reach for his other hand, and he cups it.

I've reached a place of peace again. No one is about to take me away or do me more harm. It's just me and him. Now is the right time.

"What happened to you? When you were taken?"

Jedidiah looks down for a second, trying to muster a response, but all that follows is a brief sigh.

"Jed?"

"I was taken here. I was an asset to them."

His eyes meet mine again. He wants to tell me, but it's clear no one has confronted him about this before. Too clear. I squeeze his hand tighter. His breaths have grown erratic.

"I'm sorry. I shouldn't have-"

"No," he interrupts. "Don't be. I need to deal with it. I want to share it with you."

My heart sinks at the sight of his grief, but trying to stay strong for him I nod, waiting.

"Turns out my father and I weren't alone when we trained in the forest. We were being watched. Kingdom spies were following us." Jedidiah chokes, pulling his hand from my hair to wipe the tears. "They recognized potential in me, so I was taken here and put through training. It took years, but they gave me no choice."

"Why? The Kingdom kill people who train?"

He nods. "And they would have, had I not complied with their demands to use me as a soldier, but they saw something in me. They were reluctant to lose it."

He falters, but shakes his head and breathes deeply.

"I had to. It was an opportunity, and I knew that someday we'd find a way to overthrow Hane. And I wanted to stay alive, for you, so that when our paths crossed again, I'd enjoy a future with you. We'd have nothing to worry about anymore."

We'd find a way to overthrow Hane. Why do those words enrage me? I bow my head, fearful of what might spew out of me if I look at him any longer. The more I think it over, the deeper the poison seeps, until it's pumping through me, corrupting my blood. A toxic ideal. And it came from him. From *him*.

"We'll never escape the Kingdom, Jed. They're always here. Everywhere I look. We just can't do that."

"I wanted to live for you, because I knew you'd be the one to bring the Kingdom down. I always knew it, and I wanted to help you," he replies, which takes me aback. "It was never about me standing up to Hane by myself."

I'm silent.

"Even your grandma saw it, remember? You told me everything she said. You haven't forgotten, have you?"

No, I haven't, I think, but I shrug it off. Grandma wasn't a realist; she was just trying to cheer me up. I was always upset, always venting my frustrations about how poor we all were, and how we could only afford to see them at Christmas, and every year she'd sit me down and tell me I was special. That she was certain I could change the world if I'm willing to stand by what I believe. 'History is forever writing itself' she'd say. 'We just supply the ink.'

"You haven't," he continues. "And she was convinced. This generation's going to be different Aletheia, and you know why that is. You know exactly."

He pauses briefly.

"With the help of the nations, we're going to do it, I promise, and I will take it upon myself to ensure you survive the Trials. You *will* survive, understand?"

I offer a faint smile, but I can't digest what he's saying. The thought of swallowing it makes me queasy.

"I'm one of the best the Kingdom has, and I'm going to give it all to you. My skills, my time, my life is dedicated to you now. I'll get you back to health."

"Ok. I'll do what I can. I can't do any more."

"You don't need to." He smiles, as he pulls away to retrieve the water. "Small sips."

"Jed, how can you be sure they'll let you keep me here?"

"They will. I'm in charge of them. Only the council have more authority than I do, and they won't care."

"Oh right." I narrow my eyes on him. It's amazing how far he's got himself in such a short period of time. I'm surprised he's willing to risk it all for a fantasy.

"I'm in a good position, don't worry. I've heard word of making it to the council next year, and to have that power would be perfect."

"It would."

Taking the small needle I spied earlier, Jedidiah approaches me again, holding it to my arm.

"What's that?" My body locks up.

"It's a nutrition boost. You need it," he asserts, jabbing me before I can protest. Tingles spread through my entire body, just below the skin but too deep to itch. I'm not so much concerned about that, however, than I am about Jedidiah's demeanor. His eyes have clouded over. He's not even smiling at my amusingly pathetic attempts to relieve my discomfort.

"What's wrong?"

"I'm just thinking about Dad." His response is swift. He gazes into me deeply, like he's trying to find something. "Allie, is he still alive?"

I'm in conflict, both deliriously happy from hearing his pet name for me, from his own mouth, but fully aware I can't answer his question. To put an end to something Jedidiah has hoped for all this time – to see his father again, and embrace him like I long to mine – I can't bear that weight. Pleading ignorance I shrug, knowing it will only make him more persistent, but no response comes to me. I don't even know how to *suggest* the truth, and I'm scared of saying it outright.

"You can tell me." He comes back with it, mounting on the pressure like bricks on my shoulders, and with every plea another brick is added. Straining my lungs.

"It's just…"

I don't know where I'm going with it, but I have to speak. The pain of it all is crushing me, and I'm welling up again. I can't let him see that. I turn my head away.

"It's ok."

He guides my head back to his, and in his sad yet calming countenance I see honesty, like he's become the embodiment of it. He knows I'm struggling, and he wants me to know it really is ok. He doesn't lie to me.

"I knew Dad wouldn't be able to survive so many hits," he continues, stroking my hair again. "I saw it all, before they took me out the house…and I see it every time I sleep. Play it over and over like I'm watching it on a screen, and I can't progress any further. It just keeps pausing and rewinding back."

I want to cry for him, but I'm already cried out.

"So you don't sleep. You stay awake for as long as possible."

"As long as possible," he agrees, smiling like it's only a minor concern. "And with you here, that's just become a lot easier."

"Jed."

He takes my hand again and holds it in both of his, still looking at me, not breaking eye contact. He's not weeping, but there's definitely something melancholic about his once uplifting smile, and I find seeing him is having the opposite effect. It's bringing me down.

"We can't change the past; I know that. But now we've got a grip on the future, and this day starts a new chapter, okay? We're going to work, and we'll reap the rewards. I promise."

Ever the optimist, I smile. Comforted by his presence, I drift into a deep slumber, and for all that night, I dream of only one thing: his voice, and what it tells me.

I promise.

CHAPTER XVII

LETHAL SECRET

I SIT DOWN on a plush sofa, brimming with anticipation. Jedidiah searches his cabinets for something; it's hard to stay still. He brings forward another needle and sits beside me, only it's different from the last one. The serum is a radiant red, which appears as though it's florescent, and the needle neck is longer.

"So there's only one way to one-up the other trialists, ok?"

"Ok."

He puts the syringe in my hand.

"It's with this. This has been specifically developed for Hane's soldiers so that they constantly grow, and constantly get stronger."

"What, a steroid? Like the kind which shrinks your...?"

"No." He eyes me curiously. "This is a fairly young serum. It prevents overtraining by recovering broken muscle fibers immediately, no drawbacks. Every officer takes it, as it allows them to train all day, giving them all the benefits at no cost."

"And you want me to take this?"

"If you take this, you'll be able to participate in your regular sessions with your advisor, and then, while the others are resting you can train with me."

"That doesn't sound right. How can I train during my recovery periods too, and what if…?" Worried I'm coming across pessimistic, I bite my tongue, literally. He takes my response lightly, however, and smiles in that glorious way I could never forget.

"Don't worry, it *is* right," he chuckles. "You won't need your recovery periods because the serum does it for you, all in the second you inject it. I was skeptical about it too, but it really does work."

"Won't I be tired, though?" I smile back. I can't help it when he smiles at me.

"Yes, but I'll make sure you get enough sleep."

He straightens out slightly.

"The other girls won't have the advantage you do. They'll have to make do with sticking to a strict dietary program to get the most from their workouts-"

"Which I won't have to do, right?" I wink at him, girlishly, with fudge cakes on the mind. It's clear that I'm not taking this seriously anymore. He scolds me.

"Of course you will! This serum isn't a free pass to do what you want, Aletheia! You need to work, and do everything you can to ensure you survive, understand?"

I know he's only looking out for me, but I don't like seeing him this stern. I nod, ashamed, at which he mellows.

"Look, I'm sorry. You're funny, and you haven't changed, and I love that, I do. We need to focus though, and you've got to do everything I say."

"Ok." I give one last faint smile to show I'm not offended, and sit forward.

"You'll have the edge over your adversaries if you put your max into training, and your diet, and if you attend these additional sessions. Yes, you will feel really rough, but it's psychological. Your body will be able to take it thanks to this, but emotionally it's going to be a battle. I'll ensure you get all the rest you need, but whenever you aren't resting, you're training, understand?"

He steers off into reflection.

"I've done it, Allie. I know how it feels, so I'm going to direct you the best I can – better than what anyone did for me. In a moment, I'm going to call a friend, and he'll take you back to your quarters. Don't tell anyone what's happened. Your advisor will know but they won't know about me. Don't tell them. This all stays between us. I'll send for my friend to collect you whenever you finish your sessions, and no one will ask why, so it's safe. You'll take the recovery serum here and here only. It's illegal for anyone but the officials to have this in their possession, and if anyone finds out we're history for sure. I know this is a lot to take in right now, but are you still with me on this?"

"I'm with you." I move in closer to Jedidiah until our noses are almost touching. I think I'm going in for a kiss, that's what I fool myself into believing anyway, but I panic. I quickly point my head up and give him a gentle peck on the forehead as he'd done for me, and back away again. He pauses, but shakes his head.

"Ok. I'm going to call Ladarius. He'll send you back for your morning session. You should be able to make it before it starts if you leave now."

"What about you?"

Suddenly I'm concerned for Jedidiah's sake, he was bold before Celadus and the other guards with him. He put his neck on the line for me, but this is the Kingdom, and those events don't go unnoticed.

No.

A picture of Celadus informing Hane detonates in my mind, the vision so lifelike it surges through me like electricity, causing my heart to race. Jedidiah sees it immediately.

"What's wrong?" He pulls closer to me again, but I move further away. I'm seeing it: the Kingdom sentencing him to death. The moment I lose him.

"Aletheia? What is it?"

"Nothing," I snap. Not aggressively, but in a guilty way like children do when they know they've done something wrong. "I'm just scared, Jed. About everything."

"I know. Don't worry." He looks at me assuredly, like he already knows what the future has in store for us, gets up and reports to his colleague via a communication device. It's similar to the hologram technology in the Gymnasium, except it projects a lifelike image of the recipient out of a blank white table. It's as if his colleague is in the room with us, accurate to even his height, who happens to be the same man that helped me out of the cells. When the call ends, the projection vanishes in the way I imagine a ghost to, and the white table folds into itself until it's the width of a thread.

"That's clever."

"I thought so too," he laughs, as he returns to me. "It's essentially a TV. Every household in the Kingdom has one, and you can also use it to make calls. They used a supersized version to project The Purge into the arena."

"You saw it?"

"No, the Trials are sick."

There's an uncomfortable pause, so I dig for a new topic.

"You look better with a beard."

⤚⟡⤙

The serum is injected once in my forearm, and once in my back. Jedidiah reminds me even though I'm tired, I don't have to worry about damaging my body and I can go all out in his session. His quarters are very large, and there's a basement at the far end which I'm led down carefully. It's dark, but as we reach the bottom, the light appears. Although I wasn't sure what to expect, it wasn't a lone punching bag hanging in the middle of the room. There's a standalone frame with a bar attached to it at the far left, but aside from that there's no equipment at all. I'm asked to stay where I am so he can demonstrate, at which he walks to the center of the room facing the bag. The floor below him pulses blue, and a voice identical to the Chance Globe's speaks to him.

"Good evening, Jedidiah. How may I help you?"

"Lois, prepare level three, one set, three-minute duration."

"Preparing."

Jedidiah reaches for a pair of boxing gloves and waits. A bright blue flash promptly floods the room, and with that, Jedidiah hits the bag. His punches are so rapid it's hard to tell, but there's a moment where a spot on the bag glows blue, and that's where he directs his punch. This goes on. Jedidiah ducks and swerves around the bag forcing his fists into the blue at the speed a fly changes direction. Not once missing a target, or hitting any other part of the bag. By the time he's finished, he's glistening all over, dripping from head to toe. But he's not even out of breath.

"And *that* is the level you'll be at by the time this three-month period is over," he smiles, chucking the gloves to the side as he walks toward me. "We'll work on body conditioning and target practice, making sure all your strikes land where you want them to, exactly where you want them to. But first…" He takes my arm and leads me to the middle. "We'll start you off on level one."

"What's level one?" I squeeze on the gloves he hands me, which fit perfectly, and suppress a giggle. They're still the same size as his.

"Focus. Ensuring you get the hang of aiming for a small area and that you always hit it. Speed comes later, just take it slow and steady."

He commands Lois to start me on the level one setting, with only two-minute rounds and eight sets in total. As I anticipate the flash, Jedidiah shouts over to me from the back of the room, reminding me to hit the blue areas only. He also informs me the gloves I'm wearing are linked to it, and they know if I hit the non-blue areas. If I do, small pads inside the gloves will zap me with a swift jolt of electricity. Apparently, it's bearable, but harsh enough to deter you from making a mistake.

I take a deep breath and ready myself. The first few strikes are fine; I hit the blue and then about a couple of seconds afterwards another area illuminates. I overshoot the next strike however, and the electricity grapples me immediately. I suppose it's 'bearable' for someone like Jedidiah, but the sudden voltage nearly drops me to the ground. I cry out holding my knees for support.

"It's okay, Allie, compose yourself and take it easy! No pressure!"

I stand up straight and hit the bag, which lands fine, but a few punches later, I miss again, and the ruthless stab of the electrical current leaves my mouth gaping.

"I can't do this!" I grunt, looking to Jedidiah who resists coming to my aid. He wants me to get through it on my own. Fueled by his repeated encouragement. I continue with the exercise until the round is done, gulp down heaps of water and then return for my second attempt. Every time I get the shock, I want to punch the bag in frustration, but knowing that will only worsen the experience, I'm forced to take on Jedidiah's advice. Compose myself.

After the eight sets have passed and I'm wobbling from the brutality of enduring twenty-seven electric jolts, Jedidiah shows me to the pull-up bar. This is his body conditioning. He doesn't simply do pull-ups. I watch in nervous awe as he raises himself slowly on the bar for three reps, then keeping himself at the peak of the pull performs three reps of leg raises. He repeats the whole process again and again, practically with no effort until five minutes are up.

How does he do that?

I pull off the first three pull-ups and leg raises fine, keeping the movement slow and controlled as Jedidiah instructed. As I lower my body back down however it's like all my energy has been drained, and it takes enormous effort to even do the next three pull-ups. My arms are shot from hitting the bag, and even with the continuous push of Jedidiah willing me on, assuring me my form is perfect and I 'have it in me' I can barely do the leg raises. I shake violently as I try to keep myself at the pinnacle of the lift – my hands sweaty and slipping. I only have to work through one minute, not five like Jedidiah, but when the leg raises are done, I have nothing left to offer. Instead, I hold on lifelessly, strained at the hands, until Jedidiah tells me that my time is up, and I drop.

⁓

Days pass, as do weeks, and with every day that does, I try to improve, if only remotely, so I am constantly bettering myself, breaking the boundaries for what I thought possible. I can run faster and for longer in the Ludus – one session Happy only has me run, but I manage it, even though the session was six hours. And I don't stop there. Taking the serum at Jedidiah's quarters is all I need to keep going, and I progress to level two. Same rules as level one only the bag gives you a time limit to hit the blue areas before they vanish, and if they do then you get the shock. I'm adjusting to the shock though, I can fight through it, and my speed is increasing with every week.

Jedidiah also spends some time teaching me about vital areas of the body: the locations of the major arteries and where to strike so my opponent bleeds out. Sometimes this is the only way to overcome an enemy, he tells me, if you face someone of equal strength and skill. In those situations, I must rely on inflicting wounds that put a time limit on how long my opponent can fight.

"Apply this to your target practice, and you'll be lethal," he assures me, also pointing out where I shouldn't strike. "There are no vital organs in these places," he continues. "And even if you cut deep, adrenaline will usually keep your opponent going."

When I reach level three, I can undergo body conditioning for a full five minutes as Jedidiah can. He starts me off on eight sets of two minutes, warning me the jump to a third minute is brutal. I make level three in the middle of the last month however, and by the end of that month, I've moved up to three minutes, too. I truly doubted him, but Jedidiah has done it. *I've* done it. I am at Jedidiah's physical capabilities, and all within the three-month break from the Trials my group won when Olivia was made to replace me in the Parlay – something she was ecstatic to tell me when I made it back to our quarters. Not as much as I was though, when I discovered my friends had survived the arena.

"I did what you told me to, Jed. I kept my promise," I blurt, once he's finished his pep talk.

He looks at me confused, so I elaborate.

"You gave me the spear the day you were kidnapped, and I used it every day from that point. I became a fish merchant, and I provided fish for the whole town."

For a second, Jedidiah is expressionless, but then a huge grin develops. He laughs, and moves in to hug me tightly.

"I knew you could do it. You must've done your parents proud."

"I did, but it wasn't them I was trying to make proud."

I pause to let my words sink in.

"When I first came to the Kingdom, I was hopeless. I wasn't strong, I wasn't built like the rest. I could run, but running was going to get me nowhere."

I stop, trying to work out why I am saying this, but then assured I'm on the right track I carry on.

"I was useless with the weapons, my chances of survival were zero, but then my advisor saw something in me. She saw I could use a spear, and I always hit my mark. *You* gave me that. You gave me a spear you built yourself. You inscribed my name on it. You didn't just give me a spear that day – you gave me hope. Because of that, I learned to fish, and that's why I can fight. That's why I'm still here, just because you…gave me that spear in the first place. I wouldn't have tried that hard if it was from anyone else but it was from you, and now, thanks to you, I have a chance, a real chance at winning this. Thank you."

There's silence, during which I process everything I've blurted, but I decide I'm happy with the words I chose. His eyes are watery, but before I'm given the chance to ask why he speaks.

"Allie, that's all you. I gave you the spear because I already knew you had the ability, the *capability* to be someone. It wasn't me; I didn't do anything for you. You're an overcomer. You take a challenge head-on and work until you get the results. That's why you're going to do this. You're going to bring down the Kingdom, and I'm just happy I get to see it. It's always been you, Allie."

After our talk he takes me to the same small chamber beside the entry to the arena. It's time for my second fight. Rested and strong, I wait for our anthem, the Star-Spangled Banner playing victoriously over the raging cheers of the crowd. I'm not afraid.

I'm going to win.

My name is called over the mic, and I walk forward, my armor materializing on my chest, waist and arms, with an eagle-like helmet mounted to my head. It's pointed like a bird beak, and constructed of a wire which holds the structure of the helmet together. Essentially an exoskeleton, not a full helmet that covers the face. It offers little protection, presumably so the audience can still see me. It doesn't even conceal the top of my head, but wraps itself around like a tiara.

I enter the arena and take my stance, spear in hand, and ready. At this point, I couldn't care less if someone like Sophie were to walk through the opposite gate. I'm going to give it everything I have, the hatred of the crowd being my fuel. I'm not intimidated. I'm going to show them how big a mistake they've made putting me here. I'm angry with them, and that makes me dangerous.

The gong sounds, and I move in cautiously, keeping my guard as I eye the dark-haired, olive-skinned woman who appears to be in her mid-twenties. I glare at her, reading her moves, not about to compromise myself for the sake of a potential stab. She lunges at me fiercely with her sword, but not without exposing herself for my counter. She's a one-shot killer, but I'm not that easy anymore. I avoid the lethal strike swiftly and in the same breath jab forward. My spear plunges through her throat, until half of my blood-drenched weapon is wedged in her neck. I watch as the life falls from her eyes and with that her entire body, and as it does, I retract the spear in a brief, firm jolt.

The crowd are stone still.

I walk in the direction of my entry, looking up to Happy whose eyes are locked to me. She doesn't smile, or even frown, but simply stares. Stopping, I turn back to the crowd who still refuse to whisper, throw off my helmet and gaze at them. I'm furious, and I want them to see it. Turning my back to them the outrage commences.

I keep walking.

CHAPTER XVIII

HER NAME IS FORN

THAT NIGHT I have a nightmare, and one like I've never experienced. It had always been falling, never any pictures or sounds ever, but I hear voices. First, they're small and quiet, like a spring breeze. So quiet I can't work out what they're saying, or where they're coming from, until they're all around me, growing louder and more urgent with every passing second. Jenny's is the first I recognize, and she's in pain, crying. I can't see her though. Confused as to where the noise is coming from, I grow desperate myself, only to hear Lucy's voice cry out above her. She calls for me, just as she did in the arena, but I can't get to her. Darkness is everywhere, and whenever I try to answer, no words follow. I'm mute and helpless.

More voices scream for me, and I don't recognize them, but Jedidiah's outpowers the rest, and I fall to the ground. I awake to my violent heartbeat, which pulses faster than I've ever known. For a moment, it was real. It was like everything I heard was real. Jenny and the others are sleeping soundly a few beds up, so I collapse back into my pillow. I can't even bring myself to blink.

In the morning, I'm roused by Happy, who takes me away from breakfast early and leads me into an unoccupied room. There's a nervous energy to her, which is strange, because I've only done what she asked. I've stepped up my game.

"What's wrong?" I call it out immediately – I see it in her eyes, and twitching fingers.

"Well done for yesterday."

"Thank you."

"I've been watching Hane. He's furious. He has a new plan."

Normally I squirm, and shiver at the mention of Hane, but I'm confident. I have something which he is steadily losing. Support.

"Ok, what plan?"

"After yesterday, most of the public held accusations against him for giving you a special advantage. They believe you must be receiving some type of training that the others don't have, and that Hane's rigged the Trials in your favor, which would explain your disappearance and sudden improvement."

"Right, well we know that's not true so what's the deal?" I cross my arms.

"The 'deal' is Hane wants you dead, but only so he can kill me which means you have to die in the Trials, and the longer that takes the more his people will accuse him of the opposite. They think Hane's cheating to keep you alive, which will only drive them to greater extremes to have you killed!" explodes Happy. "Why aren't you taking this seriously? Why are you always-?"

"No, no! I *am* taking this seriously," I urge, trying to calm her. "I just...don't get what you want from me! I fail the first fight and I've got work to do, but when I improve you say that's making the public angrier? What do I do? How the hell can I just move on at a pace that everyone's happy with? That *might* give me a chance at actually surviving?"

As I continue, the emotion rises – emotion once dormant, now furious to have been reawakened.

"*Every time* there's something I haven't done or shouldn't do. *Every time* you just look at me like I'm the same stupid kid that arrived here four years ago, and you never give me any encouragement! You're always belittling everything I do; we have no connection-hell, I don't even know your name!"

The words spew from my tongue like vomit, and I regret them almost immediately. I believe I've made Happy so angry she's about to strike me. But she doesn't. She breathes in, and exhales. Her face loosens.

"No, you don't," she mutters, at which she sits, her face sullen. "I've never told anyone here. No one knows."

She pauses for a second.

"It reminds me of my past, and that's something I want to leave behind. Not to mention it's dangerous."

"Dangerous?"

I don't know where this is heading, but seeing her like this – vulnerable – that's enough to shut me up and bring me to her side.

"Why?"

"I can't tell you now. I can't." She looks up from the floor. "But I will tell you this. My name is Forn."

"Thorn? Like what grows on roses?"

"No, not that. *Forn.*" She smiles slightly.

"I'm still hearing thorn?"

She spells it out for me. "F-o-r-n. Forn."

"Sorry, I've never heard that name before."

"I've never met a girl named Aletheia. Why'd they name you that?"

"Haven't you heard?"

She gives me an unconvinced gaze.

"I thought maybe you might have. Olivia has."

"Heard what?"

"Oh, just some Ancient Greek myth about a girl who had the power of a god that saved her people from captivity. Both my parents used to have it read to them when they were little, so they named me after her."

"I see. Well, it makes sense. That name suits you."

"What about your name? What does that mean?" I try to bring the topic back to her. We've never had a conversation like this before and maybe, just maybe she'll open up to me.

"I...don't know." She stares out, a far away look in her eye. I try to bring her back.

"Didn't your parents ever tell you?"

"A kind couple adopted me when I was young, that's when I got my name. I guess they just liked it."

"You can't ask?"

"Dead now. Well, my mom went missing, but she's probably dead too."

"Don't say that." I try to stay positive for her – her expression is fierce. "I'm sure you can find her somehow?"

"No, I can't."

She takes another deep breath and looks to me again.

"And anyway, I'm happy with the memories. They were good to me."

"Did you ever know your real parents?"

"Let's get back to Hane. I need you to be prepared for what's in store," she sighs, avoiding the question altogether. I respect what she's already told me, so I yield. "Hane has instructed his professionals to rate the skill of each girl who does not originate from your nation."

"So all of my adversaries?"

"Yes, and determine a list of the strongest. The list will be ongoing and forever changing, but those who appear at the top are to be paired against you, and only you. You're now the target, the standard only the fiercest competitors will be measured against."

"Then I have to fight, Forn. I have to try my hardest."

"I'm worried for you," she chokes. Never have I seen so much emotion from my advisor, and all in the space of a few minutes.

"I'm sorry for what I said earlier." I clutch her armor tightly; it rubs against the calluses on my palms. Her arms return the gesture, and we hug each other, as a mother and daughter would. "You chose me. You did all you could for me. You have to let me do the same."

Still holding me and on the brink of tearing up she pulls back so she can face me. She knows I'm right, and nods to show she acknowledges it, but she doesn't say a word. Locked to my eyes and finally letting the tears fall she tells me she's proud of me, and readies herself to usher me to the Colosseum.

Jedidiah is waiting for me, but Forn leaves before she sees. At first, I don't even see him, but he emerges from the shadows while I wait for my call. It's dark in the waiting chamber.

"How are you feeling?" He walks up to me and puts his hands on my shoulders. "Are you ready?"

I smile and nod, but his carefree expression shifts to a deep concern.

"Are you ok?"

He must be able to see I've been crying too.

"I'm fine. I'm ready." I grasp his own shoulders, and he releases me. Star-Spangled Banner is playing outside.

As I walk through the manifestor I pause, run back to Jedidiah, and remove my newly-materialized helmet. I hand it to him.

"What are you doing?" He tries to give it back to me.

"I want them to see me."

"Ok," is his response, nothing else, but if there's any disapproval behind it, he's sure to keep it concealed. Our eyes stay connected for the last remaining steps back to the passage, which is electric – a cable linked to the outlet of the spectators' boundless energy.

"Aletheia!" he calls, as I'm about to exit the gate.

I look back.

"Go and catch some fish."

I offer a smile and walk away, into the depths of the Colosseum.

Even now, on my third entry into the arena, nothing can prepare me for the assault of the crowd's sheer volume – my senses are overthrown and every bone in my body vibrates. I look up to Hane's place in the crowd, who's sat with his deputy and other members of the council. He gazes back at me. I know he can see me, but I don't break eye contact. Again, I don't recognize the anthem of my opponent, but even in my newfound state of composure, I'm taken aback as they enter. Forn wasn't exaggerating; this new threat towers over the last adversary, practically twice the size in thick armor similar to what Sophie wears. In fact, this opponent resembles Sophie in all aspects other than her weapon – a weapon I've never seen before – a mace ball on chain. In her other arm is the same enormous shield that Sophie carries, so already I know this girl's strong. Fortunately for me however, as I'd experienced practicing with Sophie, heavyweights are slow. Hane must think I stand no chance, but what he doesn't know is this is the type of opponent I prefer. I'd much rather spend my time looking for an opening than clash with someone who works at my speed. An adversary like this gives me a chance to rest and defend.

Grinning, Hane rouses the crowd further by standing and speaking out.

"People of the Kingdom, I give you a Trials favorite: Anica Balosak. One who has passed her physical examinations with a rating of ninety-seven percent. Enjoy, and remember to bet heavy. It will be worth your while."

Knowing Hane is simply trying to intimidate me, I block out the applause and ready my spear. The sun is as hot as ever, and already I'm sweating, but this won't hinder my performance. Jedidiah recently incorporated the humidity feature into my workout which simulates the heat here, so I'd be used to fighting at the same intensity.

The iron ball hurtles at me simultaneously with the sounding of the gong, so sudden I throw myself and fall flat on my front. I assume with such a heavy heap of metal I'll have enough time to recover while she retracts it, but I'm gravely mistaken. I roll hurriedly from harm's way as the opponent smashes her shield to the sand, inches from where I lie. As I try to scramble up, I'm forced to throw myself again to evade the ball, which I narrowly avoid. Fortunately, I land better and manage to thrust into a break fall which puts me at a distance from her. I'm not out of the ball's range however – she makes a third attempt at me as I jerk myself upright. I manage to stay on my feet though, and decide I'm going to stay far from her until I figure out how to proceed. No wonder she's been rated so high – the forearm strength to keep chucking the ball and hold up a shield, and all while being weighed down by thick armor. That's a brutal combination. The only chance I have is when she pulls the ball back to her, but as she's so quick, I'll have to move in swift, and out swifter. This will take everything.

Confident I have a strategy, I wait for her next throw carefully, but it appears she's predicted my counter. She's not launching the ball anymore, rather eyeing me out as I eye her. I decide to edge closer, tempting her with an easy shot, but she remains still behind her shield. Up close I'll have a chance – the ball is useless in comparison to my rapid strikes, especially combined with my accuracy. The danger is getting there though. It only takes a single lapse in judgment and the ball is going into me.

As I get closer her hands tense. She's going to throw it, but she's not revealing anything. I come within a foot of her, but she remains immobile, staring me down. Forced to make a blind prediction I watch, count in my head, and leap to the left. I'm lucky. The ball hurtles in the wrong direction, giving me the chance I need. There's a gap at her bicep which will do nicely – I jab it before she can pivot with her shield, and then move out again. That will trouble her. That's strike one.

She grits her teeth as she returns her focus to me. I knew the wound wouldn't make much impact, but all it seems to have done is angered her. I duck as the ball makes a beeline for my head, but as the iron propels past me the chain catches my spear, prying it from my grasp. Before I can retaliate the adversary seizes the moment and rushes me with her shield, leaving me no choice but to hurl myself further from my weapon.

The ball comes at me, faster than it did previously, and I find myself sprinting to the edge of the Colosseum, retreating. The crowd applaud and laugh, but instead of focusing on them, I look up to Forn. She stares back at me, intently.

Another throw is made, just as I turn from the stands. I shouldn't have taken my eyes off. Scrambling along the sand from chucking myself yet again, I claw for a rock which is lying close to me. The adversary comes in on me, hard, ready to ram her shield through my spine. Careful not to look behind me, I listen as the crashing of her footsteps get nearer and louder...

And I fling myself around.

Rolling rapidly to the left, I propel the rock at her face with all the force I can muster. It lands just shy of her eye; she's wearing a helmet but her nose and the skin around her eyes is exposed. She backs off and screams – I watch as a stream of blood rushes from the cut. Here's my opportunity.

I charge at her, head down as the shield falls to her side, bracing myself for the tackle. Her armor is hard and winds me upon impact, but I sweep her from her feet slamming her vigorously into the sand. She tries to fend me off, but I punch her nose before she can push me away.

Her head flings back, and with that I'm free to grab her chain which is lying by her side. I grapple her down as she attempts to raise herself and slip the chain around her neck, falling behind her as I do. It coils around her throat, and I manage to struggle into a position where I can tighten it from behind.

I keep the tension as firm as possible – she chokes and her body grows increasingly taut as I continue. I tug with all the strength I have, fighting her rigid movements with my legs – at one point her head slams into mine and nearly knocks me out cold. The thump in my skull grows harsher as the thrashing continues, but I hold on for my life. This is my life, and I only have one shot. This one.

My body trembles and my consciousness drains from me, as if it's leaking through my sweat, but the opponent soon slows, and ceases. The crowd is furious. They roar at me, but I can't concentrate on them. I use what last energy I have left to heave the body off my own to the side.

Wobbling, I rise to my feet, knees weak as I do, and stumble in the direction of my entry. An official comes to my aid, taking my arm over his shoulder as he assists me with the walk. *Never again,* I repeat to myself, but I know this is far from over. This will be the first of many.

"How are you?" Jedidiah urges, as I stagger back into the waiting chamber. He first grabs my waist, then my cheeks. Before I can steady myself enough to return the gesture however, he withdraws his hands, forcing a water bottle onto me. I sip from it.

"I'm ok. Just a little shaken."

"You're more than that," he rebukes, ordering the guard to fetch a doctor. "We'll skip today."

"No!" I burst. "I still want to do it."

"You're in no shape-"

"Just fix me up, and I'll be fine," I interrupt.

"Allie-"

"Jed!"

"Ok," he sighs. "Let the doctor check you over, and if you don't need any attention, I'll send Ladarius for you later."

"Thank you."

"Get some rest, ok?" He looks at me with sternness. Although I know I'll spend the next few hours lying on my bed with my eyes pried to the ceiling, I lie to him and agree. I don't want to worry him.

More footsteps emerge from behind me, but it isn't the doctor, or even the guard Jedidiah sent. It is a guard though, and he's with someone.

"Jenny!" I cry, reeling into her arms. The guard pushes me back.

"Stay away from her, slave!" he orders.

"Don't talk to her that way." Jedidiah walks over to me and opposes the guard. He backs down.

"Yes sir." The guard looks at the ground, not daring to look him in the eye. Jedidiah wasn't exaggerating. Over these years, he's worked his way up.

"What's your post?" Jedidiah inquires, as his attention slips to Jenny.

"I'm under orders to take this girl-"

"Jenny!" He embraces her before the guard can finish his sentence.

"Jedidiah! I knew it was you!" Jenny bursts, tightening her clutch on him. She overflows with tears, still locked to his hands even once they pull away from each other. "Jedidiah you're...so grown up. Handsome. A man!"

"So are you..."

The guard doesn't know what to do with himself. He takes a few steps back.

"Well, you know, not 'handsome,'" Jedidiah adds, scratching the back of his head. "But you're really pretty, Jen. Just beautiful. You've hardly changed at all."

Jenny turns to me, attempting to dry her eyes. "Aletheia, it's Jedidiah! He's here!"

"I know," I beam. It's beautiful to see the two of them reunite. "He's one of the top officials now."

"Did you just meet him, too?" Jenny asks, still holding him firmly. It's clear he's as dear to her as he is to me.

"No, actually I-"

"Yes, she did." Jedidiah speaks over me. I'm confused, until everything he warned me about hits me at once.

Of course!

"Yes! Just now, like you did."

I'm really not good at lying, though.

"Aletheia?" Her eyes narrow on me. "What do you mean?"

She's suspicious! screams my conscience. I try to keep cool, but I'm rubbing my fingers nervously. I'm really no good at lying.

"I mean we met just before you arrived, right here."

Realizing my gaze is drifting everywhere but toward Jenny, I focus on the floor. I'm afraid if she sees my eyes, she'll find the answer.

"Aletheia, what's wrong?" She pulls from Jedidiah. I look up to him, but he just stares. I'm on the brink of exposing our secret, and what will come next? I tell her about the serum? The official reports me? What will happen then? Jedidiah doesn't try to bring Jenny back to him, he must know that would only look more suspicious. It's up to me.

"Nothing's wrong." I force myself to look at her, but I can only manage it for a few seconds.

"Aletheia, I can tell you're hiding something."

I crack.

"I've been seeing Jedidiah for three months and he's been helping me but that's all, honest."

I say it fast as if there's a chance no one will hear it, but Jedidiah still palms his face.

"What?" Her sweet joy drains to disgust. "You're telling me you've known my cousin was here for three months, and you didn't think to tell me?"

"I couldn't Jenny. I-"

"She couldn't." Jedidiah rushes to my aid, trying to calm her down. But the damage has been done.

"Oh my God! He's been *helping* you? What, do you *favor* her, Jedidiah? Do you want your precious girlfriend to live and not me?"

"I didn't know you were here," he urges.

"No, of course you didn't, because I suppose she didn't tell you?" She jabs her finger at me ruthlessly. "*Did* you?"

"No, I-I didn't think about it Jenny. I'm sorry, I've been so-"

"Oh! You didn't 'think about it,' right? I'm Jedidiah's own family who hasn't seen him in years. I speak to you every day about how much I miss him, and the thought didn't even cross your mind? Is that what you're telling me?" She cries again, violently, shaking with fury. I've never seen her in so much despair, not since the desert.

"Jenny I'm sorry."

"No. No, *I'm* sorry, Aletheia. I'm sorry I ever met you, and I wish I'd died in that desert before I had."

With that, Jenny storms over to the guard, who's been watching all this time.

"I'm ready," she states, without bothering to look back as he escorts her to the arena.

Jedidiah and I stand there, speechless. For many years, I'd never known what it was like to have a friend, someone other than Jedidiah. Now, though, I know how it feels to lose one.

CHAPTER XIX

BIRTH OF CHANGE

"So, who will it be tomorrow?" I pant, as I conclude the day's session. I lean on my spear to keep myself upright.

"You won't be fighting a conventional match tomorrow," Forn frowns, throwing me a towel. "Tomorrow marks the Trial's one-year anniversary. To commemorate it, Hane has added a sixth phase: a multi-duel. You and a select group of allies will compete against another group of adversaries."

I'm both shocked I've lasted and it's been that long, but I'm given no time to process it.

"And another thing. Hane has decided to take me back. I'm still your advisor, but he's returning me to my previous position."

"W-What? Why?"

My stomach tightens. Of all the things I know about Hane, this conflicts his very nature.

"I don't know, believe me, I'm working on finding out, but at least now I can watch him closely."

"Are you still at risk if I die?"

"Not according to his rules, I'm not an official advisor. But don't talk like that!" she snaps. "You're not going to die."

Her comfort doesn't help. My head's a daze. There's no logic behind bringing her back, in fact there's no sense to any of this hellhole Hane calls the Trials.

"This doesn't make any sense, Forn! Why is Hane doing all this, anyway? You said he needed girls, so why not you? What the hell is Hane planning? Why? Why can't you just-"

"He needs real women," Forn blurts, but then her face flashes dread. It's only brief, but impossible to miss. "Forget I said that. The point is he needs you, ok? I don't know what he's thinking right now, but I'm on your side, understand? You're an adult now. You've got to stop acting like this."

I don't press her any further. Her look is unnerving. I force myself to breathe, and with that Forn walks me back to my quarters, but such a strain in my chest keeps me from walking inside. I turn back to her, afraid to ask the question.

"Wait. Do you know who my allies will be?"

Her response makes me numb.

"Jenny, Tobi, and Olivia."

I don't get to sleep that night. I'm too busy playing over all the possible scenarios of the day ahead of us: what horrors await us in the arena, and who my adversaries could be. Will I have fought them before? It's possible to draw in the arena, that is if you don't have to kill your fallen opponent because the public grant their plea. Sometimes the time limit would be the cause, but rarely. In the arena, people die, and if they don't, they hold grudges.

I can't block it out. First, I'm worrying about who my adversaries could be, then I'm thinking about all the ones I've slain. Murdered. None of that compares to the moment my mind drifts to my friends however, who haven't spoken to me since they took sides with Jenny nine months ago. Knowing I'll be fighting alongside them, that my life will be in their hands, that's something that makes my other worries look trivial. A torture that gnaws at my sanity to such an extent that by the time morning comes and Forn fetches me for breakfast, I break. In front of everyone.

"Please don't make me go out there! Please! Please!"

Naturally Forn can't accept what is happening to me, having not seen me this way for years. Taking me to one side but still within earshot of everybody she tries to hush me. She doesn't understand me, not in a literal sense, but she still understands me. In her eyes, I see a compassion that tells me she's been where I am before, and she's here to stay with me every step of the way. She reminds me of my capabilities, the fact I'm a contender, and that I wouldn't have made it this far if I wasn't, even as I argue against her. As we're talking, I notice Jenny – who's never gone near me since our fall out – stop and watch us. I try to listen to Forn, but her presence is distracting and abnormal, and my eyes constantly flicker to her. She sees me, but regardless of this, she stays where she is. Watching. Forn hands me a cloth to wipe my eyes, and gives me one last embrace before taking me to breakfast. Jenny has left when Forn's finished.

Because the four of us are to fight in only a couple of hours, we are excluded from the morning session and allowed to rest within our quarters. Everything in me wants to get up off my bed, walk over to Jenny and find out why she watched me. None of them are talking however, not even between themselves, so I sit in silence.

The atmosphere is chilly and awkward. Not chilly in the sense of cold, there are no windows in the quarters. No, not cold, there's an eeriness about the silence so unnerving I almost shatter it by crying out, screaming at my former friends out of rebuke for their abandonment. I don't though; I keep it together, just until our advisors return for us. There's Forn, Jenny's, then two others whom I barely recognize. I don't know their names, and although they understand the severity of our situation, they do not speak to me. Not even an attempt to ask how I am or offer some form of encouragement before I walk to my death. The only comfort I can draw from is how assuredly Forn grips my hand as we're escorted. None of the other girls' advisors are doing the same for them, but she is for me, and I cherish that.

When we reach the waiting chamber Forn holds my shoulder, but doesn't say a word. The rest of the advisors do, they tell their students they are strong, that they're going to be fine, but Forn doesn't need to say that. She's said all she needs to. In a way, as I watch her disappear into the darkness, it's like she's letting me go, like a bird encouraging its young to fly for the first time. This is my push, and it's time to leave the nest.

As I turn toward the gateway a familiar face emerges. I'm always relieved to see Jedidiah. No matter what storm of emotions I'm experiencing, there's always room to let him in. The other girls are still preoccupied with their advisors, so he knows there's no risk to appear. Taking my hand, he cups it, and after a pause, runs his fingers through my hair like he always does. He recognizes my fear, he sees it straight away, but he doesn't dwell on it. Instead, he repeats everything Forn reminded me, and every sweet word soothes my tension like warm honey for a sore throat. But he never lies to me. He warns that although I have this, I need to be careful, and I need to stick with my allies. I try to explain that's an option I no longer have, but he quiets me. I don't know why, and I try to speak again, much more urgently, but he points me toward Jenny whose advisor has left. Before leaving me he walks up to her, kisses her on the forehead and embraces her. I'm left alone, with Jenny opposed to me, and the other two allies still in conversation.

"Hi," I mutter, looking at the ground.

"I'm here to establish something with you," Jenny snaps. "I hate you; you hate me."

"Well-" I stumble, not sure how to continue.

"We're not friends," Jenny interrupts abruptly. "But you did save my life once. For that I owe you, and I'm going to protect you."

She pauses for a moment, and then continues, reaching her hand to me.

"Today, I'm your ally, and I've told the others to be the same. You're safe."

I take her hand, holding in the tears, and whisper my thanks. It's the only thing I'll allow myself to say without letting all my emotion flow out, which I know will only make me look weak. I consider this is a taunt of some kind, a horrible lie, but I dismiss it the moment I look up. Just as she could see through me, I know when she's lying, and upon realizing I'm not going to fight alone the stockpile of fear just leaves me, leaving in the same way Jenny is as she returns to the girls. It walks away.

I drop my helmet to the ground as I always do, and the other girls eye me. Ignoring them, I turn my attention to the crowd waiting for us, and Hane's announcer who is about to introduce us over the mic. I know the girls despise me, but they've agreed to help me. That's all I need, nothing else.

As our anthem comes to its end, we're ushered forward by an official. Neither of the girls look at me, but keep their gazes straight and true, probably taking in the enormity of what lies ahead. I find my eyes stray to the stands, however, and as I do, I notice something peculiar. I see Tobi, Jenny, and Olivia's advisors, but not my own.

I'm confused why she's not in her rightful place, but then it clicks, and I see Forn beside Hane and the other deputy. She's watching me as usual, but seeing her in the new place reminds me…nothing is the same anymore.

Everything's changed.

I keep my head locked in her direction, ignoring the adversary anthem and the all-too-familiar taunts from the crowd. She nods at me, serious but with strong intent. It's as if she's communicating with me, and I to her. I'm asking her for advice and she's responding with something else. Not what I'm hoping for, but simply 'you can do it.' *But how?* I don't receive anything else, she turns her head from me, which angers me initially but then I remind myself that I have this. I don't need a smile or nod from her to know it'll be ok. I believe her, and Jedidiah. It will be ok.

The opposing gate gives way to four of the most daunting opponents I've ever seen. Two of them I recognize, having drawn with them both. One of them I drew with on two occasions: a woman slightly older than me who carries a shield and sword. Closest to one of the traditional gladiators I've seen, she wears a helmet that covers her face, though twice I managed to knock it off. Currently, she's holding it to her side so everyone can see her, and she's waving to the spectators too, rousing them against us already. The shield in her other hand is small, not like the giant ones popular with the heavyweights, so there's still a chance to land a strike. The problem I've faced fighting this adversary is her phenomenal speed. I've been training hard, but on both occasions, I couldn't match her. We equalized by my accuracy alone, because though I couldn't keep with her pace, whatever prospect I saw to injure her always landed.

Next to her is the other adversary, one who wields a double-edged trident and famously the only one to do so. The audience is in love with her too, chanting her name as we speak. She wasn't as quick as the other opponent, so I wasn't straining myself to keep up with her strikes, but she's identical in fitness. Whenever I'd attempt to jab her, she'd counter me, I'd counter her, and the process wouldn't end. She is the closest I've come to fighting myself, always knowing what I'm about to do, but I'm confident with three allies, I'll find a way around her defense. The other two adversaries though, I'm not so confident. One of them is holding a pair of nunchucks, which I've seen before but are very rare. These, though, are unlike any I've known. There are blades on them – one hit would finish me and nunchucks are fast. Blinding.

Trying to stay optimistic, I turn my attention to my allies' weapons: Jenny uses axes and daggers for throwing at range, and Olivia is holding a bow. She never used to speak of her skill, and I'd always been too busy to watch her, but looking at her I'm pleasantly surprised. Olivia's bow is bladed across the upper and lower limbs, so she's proficient in close combat as well as providing utility. It seems we have a special weapon of our own.

The final adversary is a large built woman holding two enormous maces, one in each hand. She's not carrying a shield like most heavy opponents, but that worries me – her defense is offense. I look to Tobi. She's considerably smaller than her but strong, holding a large shield and with a thick scythe fastened to her other arm. I'm not suited to taking on heavyweights, but Tobi is. She's standing next to me, so I whisper to her I'm going for the sword and trident girls, and that she should cover me. She doesn't respond but nods, without returning a glance. I question if I'm really safe at all, if my allies will try to keep me alive, but I don't let myself sink into panic. If Jenny says they'll help me that's enough. Wiping the sweat from my forehead, I look up to Hane and wait.

Before the gong sounds, silence floods the Colosseum. I've been fighting here for a year, and never have I experienced such a sensation as this. One where you know every eye is peeled but this time because they're certain you're going to die.

Slam!

As the fight commences, Mace makes a beeline for me, and she's quick, I have no time to respond. I watch in horror as Tobi leaps forward to take the impact into her shield. The clash rings loud as the two collide.

I'm stunned in shock, then realize Nunchucks and Sword are also headed toward me. Jenny pushes me from Nunchucks, swiping at her with axes, leaving me face-to-face with Sword. I inhale sharply.

Sword doesn't pause – she drives her sword at my stomach

before I've even taken in the pace this duel is moving. My reflexes enable me to deflect her first attempt, but her strikes keep coming fast. Even faster than I remember, and I find myself stumbling backward trying desperately to keep on top. Fortunately, the sessions with Jedidiah have prepared me for this level of assault, and I find a rhythm in which to guard myself while I scan for an opening.

We push to the edge of the arena in fierce combat, so much so I can't keep track of where anyone else is. I'm locked in a heated showdown with my rival, and she's just as keen to bring me down as the spectators are. I catch a brief chance to thrust my spear in her helmet as her arms drop, and she falls a few steps backward, allowing me to go in for another strike. She's quick to recover however, and my spearhead crashes into the thick steel of her shield.

An arrow impales her arm from nowhere, forcing her to drop the shield. She's still got a firm grasp on the sword, but I seize the opportunity and barrage her with a flurry of strikes. Many of them she manages to fend off even while grasping her arm, but I knock her helmet clean from her head, and the force of my jabs shove her to the ground.

"Aletheia!"

Olivia shrieks before I can conclude the kill; I turn immediately, raising my spear to prevent a near fatal strike by Trident. I think I have it in control, forwarding my attacks and pushing her back, but I'm dropped hard to the ground.

I wail as I return my attention to the fallen opponent, who has scrambled to her knees and plunged her sword in my thigh. It's in deep. I try to pull it out, but Sword leaps and grapples me ruthlessly. Trident hovers over me, ready to heave her blades in my chest.

I scrunch my eyes shut.

But she doesn't. She leaps away, weaving between arrows hurtling in her direction. Olivia is still covering me. Knowing this is my only chance, I writhe frantically, desperate to escape Sword's hold. I manage to flip myself and straddle her.

Aggressively we wrestle, the sharp clangs of bow against trident filling the air around us. Spurred on by my determination to help, I bind down my rival with my limbs enough to remove the sword from my thigh and plunge it into her stomach. All this time, all the hours spent trying to better myself so I could defeat her are finally over.

In pain but still with enough strength to get up, I look out to take in my surroundings. Tobi is still struggling with Mace, Jenny is in a violent engagement with Nunchucks, and Olivia is fending off Trident. Gasping I move to Olivia, who is closest to me, and hurriedly limp to her aid. She slashes at Trident relentlessly, but Trident is faster.

"Olivia!" I cry.

Trident finds a way around Olivia's defense and forces the five points of her weapon into Olivia's shoulder, who screams and falls. I'm not close enough to stop her – her hand raises to finish the job. I stop. I don't think.

I just throw.

CHAPTER XX

RE:UNITED

TIME FREEZES. I watch as my only weapon cuts through the thick, humid air, narrowed down on Trident who is moments from murdering my friend. She sees it, but not in enough time – it hits her, impaling her through the head. Her body drops into her own pool of blood.

The sight is gruesome, but I ignore it and stumble to Olivia, who is sprawled on the sand holding her shoulder. It's worse than I thought it would be. Close up, I see the trident has marked deep into the muscle and in five places too. She grabs my arm and begs me to leave. I don't want to, but I have no choice. Tobi is ok, but Jenny is in danger. I yank my weapon from Trident's head and run as best I can toward the four remaining women. Adrenaline circulates my veins thick and fast; I grow oblivious to the gushing wound in my leg.

My spearhead rushes Nunchucks before Jenny is even aware of my presence. She retaliates by swinging her nunchucks in a frenzy which forces me to leap back, knocking my spear away as it catches on one of the blades. I land beside Jenny, who is cut all over her arms and face but nowhere serious.

"What happened? Get back!" she yells, staring at my leg. "Aletheia, get back!"

"No!" I urge, as I brace myself for the onslaught.

As Nunchucks comes in, Jenny attempts to jump in the way, but is flung back by a powerful thrust to her breastplate. The opponent doesn't move in on her however – disinterested in Jenny, she advances on me, having me rapidly maneuver my spear to avoid her flying razors. I catch Jenny from the corner of my eye. She's sitting up but clutching her chest, and she's lost an axe.

Furiously I launch forward and manage to hit Nunchuck's hip, but as I try to follow-through she gets a clean swipe of my neck. It doesn't go in deep, but it stops me in my tracks. She's about to strike me again – which I'm too close to avoid – only she's stopped by a dagger that scarcely misses her head. Her attention returns to Jenny, who has primed herself with another dagger. She tries to rush her, but Jenny somersaults away from harm.

My wound bleeds relentlessly; it drips down my arm and onto my armor, but I block it out. Jenny is toiling hard with her one axe, but the other has been knocked away too far for me to reach. I try to run to her but find myself leaping further away – Mace charges me again, hurling her sturdy weapon to the sand as I jump. Even against the sand it sounds like a thundering crash, reverberating within my chest. As Mace heaves the hunk of spiked iron again, I scan frantically for Tobi, and locate her at the far left. She's lying motionless.

A second swing is made, which is powerful but slow, and I take several steps backward so I can pick her off at a distance. With shaking bloody hands, I hold tight on my spear pole, jabbing at Mace to force her back. One jab hits her vambrace, then a second her groin, but nothing breaks through to her flesh. I'm tiring with every jolt, and my shoulders are seizing.

Clang! Clang!

The gong forces me to stop. Mace stops. We look to Hane who has stood up, leaning over the stands. Is it finished? Have they had enough? No. The rattle of the surrounding gates echoes the Colosseum, and the crowd cry in joyful uproar. Officials rush to the gates to release them, and as they open come the stomps of something terrible-*many* terrible things.

Out of the gates emerge large beasts – elephants – with long jagged horns, but also with additional horns beside their natural ones and spreading out at the sides. I've seen them in pictures but never like this. Even the eyes are different. It's like I can see their bloodlust. The three of them trudge into the arena, guided by the slaps from the officials' whips. For a second I even forget about Mace. I'm too horrified yet mesmerized by the sheer bulk of the impending predators. It's as if they're living tanks. Biological weapons. I watch as one of them retaliates on a guard, throwing him higher than its own body as its gargantuan horn runs him through like he was sponge.

Lost so wholly in awe, I don't even notice the macehead my opponent drives toward my face – I only see it in my peripheral in time to fall to the ground. I flounder at her feet, rolling and diving as the continued frenzy of strikes keeps me from recovering my stance. Clinging to my spear, I attempt to thrust it upward just as she's about to hit again. Catching on her swift swipe, my spear is pried from my grasp and thrown high.

I tauten as she lifts her mace to deliver the final impact, but it doesn't come. I ask myself why it hasn't, glaring at the horrific spikes as they fall to her side, but the roar behind me confirms Mace's motives promptly. The ground beneath me quakes. As Mace leaps a strong rush in my chest urges me to do the same, despite being wounded and scraping the borderline of consciousness.

My body lands in a bloody heap. At this point, I wonder if it's possible I'll bleed out, and staring at the drenched sand doesn't convince me otherwise. Despite this, there's no time to be paranoid. My concerns shift to the elephant which is turning back to me.

I bring myself to my feet, directly opposed to the beast. I can't see Mace, she's somewhere behind it, but I quickly decide I'd rather be facing her. The elephant stomps over to me, so close I can smell its breath. The moisture of its exhalations dampens my face, but my eyes keep trained to its horns, wavering from one to another as I try to decide which horn I'd least wish to be impaled by.

"Aletheia! Stay there!" cries Jenny, who has rushed closer to me but is still a distance from the elephant. I don't know where the other two are or even where Nunchucks is, but at this point I don't care. I'm not watching the elephant anymore; I'm fixed to her. Stunned in panic.

"Jenny," I utter, trying to keep my voice down, but also making it apparent to her I'm scared out of my wits. I don't want to die. Not like this.

I jump as a second elephant emerges behind me – I know it's there; I can hear it, but I refuse to turn from Jenny. If I must die, I want my dying glimpse to be of her, my friend, who has always been there for me. Even if I'm no longer hers.

"Aletheia, don't move." She creeps closer to me. A thousand thoughts attack me at once, and I try to decide if there's one possible scenario in which I could escape this. Nothing comes to mind, but then I'm distracted. Jenny hollers at the elephants so loud I jump again, and as she does her only axe leaves her hand. I gaze as it flies toward the elephant's side, landing a perfect dent in the beast's skin. It groans and leaves me immediately, charging full force at her. The other elephant follows, raging furiously at Jenny with its head bowed.

She dives from the first rampant beast and sprints hurriedly from the second, leaping onto one of the gates and climbing it with haste. It smashes into the gate without hesitation, sheering the entire steel frame clean from its brackets. Jenny hops to the second gate in just enough time, and the elephant wails as it struggles to remove the gate from its head.

Leaping down from the gate, she signals me to join her. I pick up my spear and run, then duck, as Mace ambushes me from nowhere. Seeing I'm in trouble Jenny races toward me, but I see Nunchucks again as I avoid another sharp blow from a macehead.

"Jenny, behind you!"

She stops and leaps as Nunchucks flanks her with successive swings, forcing her further from me. I wonder where the elephants are, desperately searching for them as I continue to fend off Mace, but then my attention returns to Jenny. She's fallen – Nunchucks is above her.

"Jenny!"

Disregarding Mace entirely, I hurl myself toward Nunchucks, who upon seeing me ignores Jenny and moves in to strike with increased violence. Mace pursues me, but she's heavy and slow, and I know I have time. Our weapons clash with resounding power. I've never known such eagerness to kill, but this adversary reeks of it. Tirelessly we rage on, steel on steel, and as we do my anxiety falls away – with every blow, with every clash. I'm determined to save Jenny.

Mace reaches me but is held off by one of the elephants. She runs for her life, screaming, but not even that can drown the roars of the elephant afar, still trapped in the iron. Nunchucks is limping; I see it clearly, and although I'm in no better shape, I know I have the advantage. Because my reason is stronger.

The jeering of the crowd keeps my strikes evermore violent – every clash of metal is a failed attempt of ending it, and with every failed attempt, my anger only climbs. I overpower her, and she stumbles, but Mace manages to return, making it two on one.

I duck and sway as spiked handles and maces tear at me from

all angles, all while Jenny squirms on the floor. The spectators cheer; they think it's over for me.

It's not.

Screaming I plunge my spear into the heart of Nunchucks – I don't watch her fall, rather withdraw the weapon immediately. Proceeding to stagger Mace with a sequence of accurate jabs, I pierce her hand, disarming a mace, and then follow-through to do the same with the other, dropping her to her knees from the sharp stab I land in her kneecap. Hesitating at nothing, I pry her head from her shoulders.

First, there's silence, then an almighty uproar which doesn't even rattle me. Without looking to the crowd, I march to the dying Nunchucks who is still alive and reaching for me. My spear promptly thrusts into and retracts from her neck, putting an end to her writhing for good. My stomach twists, but I remind myself she's no longer suffering.

Still heedless to the audience I stumble over to Jenny. She's in a bad state. There's a deep wound in her side, and gashes all over her body. She's able to stand as I help her up, though. She moans.

"It's okay. I've got you," I assure, and as we stagger to Olivia, I whisper to her. "I love you."

She looks back at me, red in the eyes, but with no words.

We pick up Olivia who holds onto me by my arm, and as I support two of my dearest friends, we arrive at Tobi's body. She's unconscious still but alive.

"She's breathing!" I yell, toward the officials at the edge. They come running. "She's breathing! Help her!"

It takes three of them to transfer Tobi to a medical tray, which they offer to carry Olivia and Jenny on too.

"No, I'll take them myself," I insist. "They're staying with me."

CHAPTER XXI

RISE OF A HERO

I'm cried out because no one has returned. I've been discharged from the medics, but the rest of my friends are yet to be released. I'm sitting here alone. Not even the girls who were taken to the Ludus are back, and it's well into the afternoon. The sun is balancing on the horizon.

I look down at my bloodied leg. The ointment they used has caused it to scab over, but it stings and it's unpleasant to look at. I don't know how long I've been here, but I've never sat in the quarters by myself. I may have felt alone in the past, but to be alone is torture.

Jed!

I leap from my bed and throw myself into his arms as he enters. He returns the embrace tightly, and he doesn't let go. He's been crying.

"What's wrong?"

"I just-don't worry. I thought I'd lost you," is his quick response, still holding me close to his chest.

"I won't leave you, Jed. You know I won't do that."

"Not by choice," he mutters, pulling away. "But they can try…the Kingdom. They'll keep trying to take you from me, no matter what. No matter what!"

I gasp as Jedidiah flips one of the beds, shattering it. They're especially large, and he launches it like it's a sack of flour.

"Jed, stop! That was one of the girl's beds!" I urge, pulling at his arm. He does. His breathing is frantic, but he tries to relax himself. "It's okay. It's okay," I hush, as I move in to hug him again. He sobs over my shoulder, vulnerable and shaking as if he were a deer, desperate to escape its poachers.

"Why are you like this? Tell me what's wrong."

"Hane just wants this over with, Allie. He'll try anything…" He looks worn, and can't seem to muster the words, but then the door to my quarters opens again.

Over his shoulder, I notice the figure immediately, and fear grapples me. Forn walks over to us, her face stern and racked with confusion. I pull from Jedidiah.

"Aletheia?" she probes, approaching us cautiously. "What's this?"

"This is Jedidiah-"

"Yes, I know," she interrupts. "What is he doing here with you?" She turns to him. "What are you doing here?"

Drying his eyes, he takes a deep breath, and explains everything. Forn doesn't bleat a sound during his explanation, which only worries me more. She frowns.

"This was a mistake."

"No. Don't be that way," I beg.

I choke. Despair is clogging my throat, and it's dense.

"She's right, don't blame this on her, it was my idea. It was the only way-"

"It was *not* the only way!" she snaps. "I chose to raise Aletheia because *I* knew she had it in her to pass the Trials legally! She's already in the thick of it as it is, do you really think your support has helped, given her any measurable chance of surviving even if she *does* win?"

Jedidiah remains silent, his face set to the ground. I want to defend him, but there is truth to Forn's argument. Trying to compose herself, she rubs her face and returns her attention to me.

"Aletheia, it's almost time. Your allies aren't coming back."

"What?"

The words lodge in my heart like a blade.

"It's what I was trying to tell you, Aletheia," Jedidiah adds. "After your fight, Hane ordered everyone to enter the arena. All surviving girls, from all nations."

"No, that's not right," I contest, against my better judgment. "We were given a warning before we went in? We were prepared the day before. We didn't go to training but the others did-"

"That's because you were originally intended to be the only ones. Hane really thought he had you this time, but you proved him wrong. He's decided to kill off the weak so you have to fight the best."

Jedidiah grows more defeated as he explains it, and each word is like another blade jabbing me, until I'm overwhelmed with pain.

"What about my friends? What about *them?*" I'm losing it. Forn grabs and shakes me.

"Calm down, *calm* Aletheia! They're still being treated by the doctors. Their wounds were worse than yours, but they're ok, stop worrying. They're ok." She hands me a handkerchief. Tears and snot are flowing down my face. I'm a wreck.

Slowly, she sits me back on my bed, and Jedidiah sits beside me, keeping his arm around my waist.

"This is all the plan, Aletheia, to mess with your head so that when you walk into that arena you're a pushover. You can't let Hane do this to you."

"No, you can't," Forn agrees.

I give each of them a nod to show them I'm still listening, and Forn goes over her strategy for tomorrow. It's straightforward, but involves revisiting The Purge zone and using it as preparation for what will surely be the toughest fights of my life.

"It only gets harder from here," Forn warns. "You'll spend the day with me. You shouldn't interfere from here on out, Cadman."

"That's not going to happen." He rises from me, with bladed eyes.

"*Excuse* me?" Her eyebrows raise high, accentuating every crease across her forehead.

"Look, I respect you for everything you've done for Aletheia." He walks right up to her, without flinching. Her eyes bear down on him, but even their height difference doesn't deter him. "And I owe you my life for choosing her in the first place. But I am her friend, and I have always been her friend, and as her friend I have a duty to give her everything I possibly can to ensure she stays alive. If that means risking my life for the sake of seeing her pull through then I take that in my stride, and I accept the consequences. With or without me, she either lives or dies, but with me, you and I both know she has a better chance, and I will not let you take that from her. Aletheia trains with you in the morning, and in the evening she trains with me."

My eyes have opened. I always knew Jedidiah was never one to back down, but even in the face of Forn who has all the authority…he is still willing to stand in my name, and give a statement so profound it renders the recipient incapable of speech. Gazing at him, I think back to the time he also stood up to Celadus in the presence of the other officials. The significance eluded me then, but here I understand. I *get it* now.

Silent but heart racing, I watch as Forn withdraws, at which she calls back to me she'll come for me in the morning, but without turning around. I don't mind. I don't mind if she's angry. I'm here with Jedidiah again, and as I stare into his miraculously transparent eyes, I'm finally aware of something that I've always known but never believed. He has to leave before I can say anything; the girls have returned, patched up and washed of blood. I half-cry as I hold them.

Olivia had a broken ankle and torn calf, as well as other deep wounds, but she was the worst of it. Tobi had a concussion, which was caused by the steel handle of the adversary's mace. It should have been serious, but in the Kingdom such injuries are no issue thanks to their technology. If only our doctors had it at home. Aunt Olivia could've beat her illness.

Like many nights recently, I find it almost impossible to sleep – I catch around two hours, but most of the night, I talk with Jenny. She's moved into the bed next to me, but the other two are finding it hard. They're lying in their usual place, squirming in their sleep alone. Jenny notices I keep eyeing them through the night, and how I'm constantly staring at the vast emptiness. The silent beds and lonely bathroom.

We talk for ages, just in general. I don't think either of us can handle accepting what the days ahead hold, even though we're both dying to talk about it. Instead, we fill each other in on the gaps, gaps that haven't been filled for almost a year. Me explaining my sessions with Jedidiah, and her talking about how she took walks with her advisor out in the corridors.

"Why?"

"Just so we could chat," she explains. "I mostly used to talk about you."

"Me?"

"I missed you."

I pull on my boots and journey to breakfast smiling – I even talk to my friends during the meal, a luxury I thought had long passed. I notice Forn is still in a bad way, but I smile at her and invite her into the conversation. She doesn't, but at least she realizes where I stand with her. She does give me something though, a little something, as we walk back to the Ludus. She smiles back.

She's right, I don't have any difficulty returning to The Purge. I'm apprehensive of the fire walls, but that's merely psychological. I twist and dive through the obstacles, reaching the swinging bags and axes just as Jenny described. In my imagination, it seemed worse, but I find I'm more suited to the challenge than I ever could have hoped. With only my sweat to tell of the experience, I reach the finish…a survivor.

A winner.

Taking care to ensure no one notices, Ladarius collects me from the Ludus as normal. This time however, Jedidiah invites Ladarius to join us, pulling him into the basement where I demonstrate my abilities. I've reached the stage where I can endure four minutes on the bags for eight rounds, and I can also keep up the body conditioning for seven minutes. I've exceeded Jedidiah, but it hasn't made him bitter. He's singing my praises to Ladarius. He's never been happier.

By the time the session is over Ladarius doesn't have much else to say other than 'good luck,' and he walks out of the quarters, leaving Jedidiah to cover the details of my upcoming fight. Only one adversary is left, the rest were killed in the bloodbath. It's just her and my closest friends, and they won't have to fight because I'm not going to lose. Utter delight hits me as firm as a punch to my gut, only painless. Knowing this could soon all be over, that I only have one more fight to go and then we're free to live our lives again keeps me going. Free. It ignites my heart, immerses me in hope again. That's how I feel, at least, until Jedidiah brings me back. This is the Kingdom. From the high place I was I fall and crash with broken wings.

"Aletheia, only one person survives this."

He pauses so I can take it in.

"You mean the fight? There's not going to be a time limit?"

"No, I mean the Trials." He takes my hand, but I pull it back.

"What? But the rules state we only fight adversaries? Surely-"

Over the last five years I'd forgotten what Forn warned me: to not get attached, and that there could only be one. I'd forgotten. How could I let myself forget? My anger simmers.

"Those rules were only put in place for the beginning. I'm sorry."

Something happens to me inside. I lose it.

"No! You're lying!" I cry, as if denying it could change the truth. This is worse. This is worse than learning we were the last ones left, that my group wouldn't come back. These are my friends. My dear friends. "You're lying!" I repeat, eyes flowing as I scream at the top of my voice. I leap up from the sofa and run. Jedidiah doesn't follow. "*No!*" I shriek, reaching his door and pounding it until the sensors detect me, and it opens. I fall out. Ladarius is waiting and catches me in his arms where I cry, slumped in desolation.

I cry constantly, coughing and losing my breath from screaming for so long. In the end, I'm left sniffling, heart pounding, lying on the floor with Ladarius gripping me. Jedidiah doesn't return for me, and Ladarius says nothing either. We just sit there, until I muster the strength to turn to him and whisper.

"I'm ready to go."

As we walk down the corridor, footsteps emerge behind us. I'm still wiping my eyes with one hand, but something clamps my other wrist, jolting me from Ladarius. I turn in horror – it's someone I recognize. Hane's deputy.

"You're coming with me," he states.

Ladarius pauses in disbelief, but speaks out before I've been fully dragged away. The guard stops.

"Sir, with respect, I am to escort this girl back to her quarters."

The guard stares back at him, aggressively.

"By orders of?"

Ladarius is hesitant. He opens his mouth, but no words follow. This is Hane's deputy, and if he learns of Jedidiah…

"By orders of?" He presses closer to him.

"Nobody, sir."

The man doesn't question him further, but tugs me into a room and has me sit down. It's a small room, plain and dull. He sits opposite me. There's a table to separate us.

"You appear upset," he proclaims, stroking his beard. He extends his palm for me, but I keep my hands far away, tucked to my side. I say nothing. The room echoes with my snuffling as I try to contain my emotions.

"The name's Jurgen. Do you know who I am?"

His harmless façade is almost convincing, but again I don't respond, which breaks his front immediately.

"I'm going to make this straightforward. Either you lose tomorrow, or your life won't be worth living."

"My life's never been worth living." I bite back my resentment. I don't want to be angry like he is, I want to prove I'm strong. That my words run deeper than personal feelings. "But I'm not living for me – I'm living for the people, and I'm going to make their life worth living. You watch me."

"The people don't like you, Aletheia," he smirks.

"They will."

He lets out a condescending laugh.

"What makes you think you can save *anyone?*"

"Faith," I counter, discounting his ridicule. I'm not frightened by him, rather stimulated. His dark, deathly stare is the source of my passion. In his presence, I'm assured of myself. If his plans were to dislodge my confidence, he's made a grave mistake.

"Then I hope for your sake Hane puts an end to your fantasies quickly," he grunts.

I focus on his rough, cracked lips, his beaten hands and greying hair. His skin looks much younger, but it's clear stress has taken its toll. We stare at each other for a moment, fiercely, then he proceeds to get up and stroke my cheek as he passes. I keep my sights fixed dead ahead, and I don't flinch. I want him to know I'm not afraid. I want him to regret we ever met.

"Such a pretty girl. What a waste," he mutters, at which he leaves me in isolation.

꩜

When I wake up, I'm fully rested, which Forn questions as she knows I've been having rough nights lately thinking too much, never stopping. I don't tell her the real reason though – how Jurgen put my mind at ease. Assured me of my purpose.

"I had a hard session yesterday," I smile, excusing myself from breakfast. "I was tired."

I've figured there are things Forn doesn't have a right to know, not after how she treated Jedidiah, and I want him to know I'm on his side. Oddly, I don't see him this morning or even receive a message from him, which is unusual because he mentioned he would drop by my quarters before the fight.

While I sit on the bed alone, I reflect on what he briefed me regarding my adversary: my build, similar armor type, and quick. Her weapon of choice – a sword. That's it. No shield or any other weapon. All the weird shapes and sizes of the Kingdom weapons, all the many imaginative ways to kill a person, and the girl who is left carries nothing but a sword.

That fact plays over and over in my mind as I wait, and I find myself fidgeting as it does. *She must be good,* I tell myself, watching the sweat in my hands drip to the floor. The more I think the worse I feel, and as I grow increasingly nervous it's as if the flow of time runs dry altogether. Good is an understatement. This adversary has managed to survive where all else failed, and all with a basic weapon, not even a shield. Is it because she doesn't like the other weapons? Is she more suited to a sword? How skilled must she be to survive with just one sword?

The sun lowers to midway – it's late afternoon and still no one's returned for me. Maybe the sword isn't her preferred skill? Maybe she doesn't need anything else because she knows she'll always win? When Forn comes for me, she asks why I'm sweating so much; there's a puddle by my feet, and my sheets are ruined. I want to see my friends one last time. I want to hug them and remind them how I feel just once more. Knowing I can't, and that the next few minutes are critical I get up, Forn takes me out, and as I look back a horrid feeling grapples me.

It tells me this will be the last time I see these quarters.

CHAPTER XXII

DEFIANCE

GREETED BY THE usual boos and hisses, I press forward into the sun-soaked court. Jedidiah has failed to find me like he promised, but I'm not concerned. No, as I look up to Hane and Jurgen in the stands, I know there's a job to be done, and that's all I'm thinking about. That's all I-I don't believe it. Listening to the adversary anthem I recognize the opponent is Spanish. I gasp at the horror of what confronts me.

The adversary enters through the gates. She's dark and slender, the embodiment of exotic beauty, and I've seen her before. I've never fought her, she's not a rival. She's the girl I saw at my fitness assessment five years ago. The first adversary I'd ever seen.

She saw me too that night, and I remember how I felt. I remember how I went to bed afterward, praying on my knees that I would never have to fight her, that our paths would never cross again. She seemed too delicate, too innocent to kill, too young. I thought that prayer had been answered. Now I've learned God is as ruthless as the Kingdom.

We get closer to each other. I'm certain she recognizes me too. I have never been this close to an adversary before the fight: we're only two or three paces from each other as I gaze up at Forn one last time. She is sat to Hane's left while Jurgen is to his right, and Hane himself is also staring at me, just as before. I quickly pry my gaze from him. Even in my certainty, his eyes are still jarring.

The sun rains down like fire from hell. The heat is worse than before, but I don't let it distract me. We're both panting already, but we're focused, raring to strike. Jedidiah didn't describe what type of sword she wields, but it's half the length I expected. It's longer than a dagger, but compared to a traditional sword it's small, and it makes her seem less threatening. Which is even more worrying.

The gong clangs louder than the jeers of the thousands upon thousands of spectators. There are so many in the arena that many are without seats, crammed into the stands like a flock of sheep. Sheep are calm in confined spaces though, and here the people are moving vigorously, pushing and shouting and pumping their fists. An angry mob.

I lunge upon hearing the gong, bracing myself for the inevitable counter. The adversary, however, backs off and twists her body around so the sword comes flying across my waist. A move I did not predict.

The blade slams into my armor, tearing into it and partially cutting my flesh. She withdraws it immediately which brings on a sting. I step back gasping, expecting her to proceed, but she stays where she is, eyeing me. I pause, digging for all scraps of sense. I'm tired already – the heat is not aiding my cause – and now I have an idea of how fast this opponent moves. It's faster than anyone I've ever encountered. It's faster than Jedidiah.

Swallowing and noticing my throat is dry, I decide to wait no longer. I go in again, hard, this time aware of the pace I must work. I know it will be rough, I know it will take everything, but I can do it. Her second strike fails – it only takes once to learn from my mistakes. I throttle her with flurries of jabs, twirling my pole from one hand to the other to deflect her vicious counters.

Our metals clash faster and more forcefully than I've ever known – there's no time to pause, we're barely into two minutes and my lungs are screaming for air. We grunt and moan but still move at the same pace. This is harder than my brawl with Nunchucks. This is more demanding than my body-to-body struggle with Ball on Chain. There's a reason this girl is still alive, and it's because she's the strongest I've ever seen.

Roars from the crowd vibrate my bones, as do the repeated conflicts between her blade and my pole. Every blow rattles it so violently it's hard to keep hold. The adversary tries to sweep my legs, but I predict it and leap forward – I think for a second my spear will find her chest, but she knocks it away. Her blade narrowly misses my neck as she does.

We're back to square one, diving and twining round the other's strikes. None of us can land another injury; we're caught in stalemate. Our defenses won't give way. Stopping at once the two of us gaze on at each other as if we're trying to say something, but without knowing what. Her eyes are sweet yet darkened. I'm so tired I can barely hold my weapon…but from her red face and quivering fingers, I notice neither can she.

Again I charge for the first strike, which smashes against her fast deflection and immediately we're pounding at each other again. We're fast, agile, keeping our breaths steady and moving in for blinding, seemingly unavoidable thrusts. Her grit is all too evident. Neither of us are going to give in. We throw kicks, launching our feet for the other's head but always missing. I scream as more swings are dealt; the impact throws us back, but we only come in for more. I'm on the edge but neither of us are slowing. The sword slashes my lips leaving a rusty tang in my mouth, but that creates an opening to scrape her wrist: it pours.

We fight on, bathed in sweat and exhaustion but rapt to each other's eyes. Spitting phlegm but pushing. Not slowing down. Not ceasing to end the other's life. Her sword rams so intensely into my spear, I lose my balance and my feet slip from beneath me, but she attacks with such power she overthrows herself too.

As we fall our weapons clash, and as we sit up in the same motion, in the same breath as our fall...I see it. An opportunity to put an end to adversaries. To be the last girl standing and put the adversaries behind me. To end it. Her neck is wide open – I go in for the swipe. I pause.

She's seen the same opportunity.

My heart pounds as we kneel there, our blades a fraction from the other's neck. Neither of us have followed through. I can't understand why, we could kill the other by the flick of our wrist, but neither of us have taken it. My eyes lock to the adversary. She sets hers on my own. Our chests heave with heavy breaths, and our hands shudder. I look up to the crowd around me. No one is speaking, not even a murmur. The roaring lion has been tamed, and it's waiting to see what we do next.

Trailing my attention back to the opponent, I notice her nod at me. I think for a moment I'm hallucinating and maybe even dead. Perhaps this is what the afterlife is? Maybe this is why ghosts never leave the spot they died, because they're unable to escape their final moments? She nods again however, and this time I know what I feel.

My other hand rises, and as it does the hand holding my spear to the adversary's neck lowers. She does the same, and slowly yet firmly our hands meet and join, while our weapons lower to our sides. It's a simultaneous reaction, neither of us have prompted it...but something great, a large and powerful sensation directs me, one which tells me to rise with the adversary – still linked by the hands – lifting my spear high to the sky as I gaze at the shell-shocked crowd. We both do, standing proud and confident on our feet, driven to the audience who wish me dead. If I was myself, I'd have crumbled, but I'm not. This isn't me. I don't know who it is. But I don't care either. As I look to Hane's stand, I see him holding his face, Forn too, speechless but not taking her eyes off us. Jurgen looks down at me, shaking his head. His eyes are cold, but my heart burns. The grip of my opponent tightens, and I squeeze harder in response, raising my spear to the people. My adversary too, keeps her sword high for all to see.

As if someone has triggered the anger in every heart of the thousands watching the crowd uproar in a commanding, instant response which hits my core like iron. Their wrath powers through me like I'm not material, like I'm merely an observer of something inexplicable. I keep standing, however, absorbing the abuse that pours down like verbal daggers. I keep my spear raised, my head pointed high, and listen. I listen as the pleas of death grow louder and louder. But I still stand.

"Kill them!" they cry, and a scattering of shrieks follow.

"Hang them!" order some.

"Crucify them!" demand others, and the voices hit me. They keep hitting me. I grit my teeth, still refusing to cry.

"Throw em to the lions!"

"Set their heads on a poll!"

Both our hands quake, but I look to her, and she looks at me. This is how it should be. I can't hear myself think, I can't feel my fear, only the hatred that thickens the air. Then my eyes well up, but not with tears. The atmosphere waters out, and I know I've felt this way before. I can't move. I can't speak. Everything fades.

I'm in a cell. I think I dreamed about waking in the medical facility, but I know it's all in my mind – I'm hot and alone in darkness again, and Rose is nowhere in sight. Immediate thoughts follow on what could possibly happen next, where I'm headed after this, but I shrug them off. I don't regret what I did. For now, at least, everyone is unharmed and safe. I can still taste the tiniest trace of blood from my lips, but the wound has closed. The brickwork of the cell is flickering in the torchlight, but I can't see it well enough, so I stroke along its rough surface. There's no tally chart on the wall, so I'm not in the same cell from all those years back, but there's still a tatted rag and old pillow at the back that's positioned exactly how I remember leaving it. I crawl to it and rest down, clutching the rag tightly.

As the world starts to fade, a pair of feet rushes down the staircase, but as the rumbling grows louder it becomes clear there's two people. One of them stops against my cell, an official, and in the light, I can just make out his features. Ladarius again, I'm sure of it. I breathe a sigh of relief.

"I've been ordered to take you to the Ludus." Reaching for his waist, he pulls out something made of steel. I can't see it, but I recognize the clanging as the metal clatters against itself. I know what it is. "And I have to put these on," he continues, in a defeated tone.

Gently he reaches for my hands, which I give to him, and secures the cuffs in front of me. I don't say anything.

"I'm so sorry this happened to you." A tear flees down his cheek despite his effort to contain it.

"It's fine. It needed to be done. Thank you."

He leads me by the arm to the stairway. My adversary and her guard are behind us, but I refuse to look back.

As my boots brace the paving of the Ludus, I'm overthrown by the atmosphere immediately. The seats surrounding our court, although there's hundreds, were never filled in all the years I've been here, only in part by those who paid to watch us train so they knew who to cast bets on. Now though, many spectators flood the court, there's not a spare seat anywhere, and all of them are chanting the same abuse they had previously. To kill us. Ladarius and the other guard walk us into the center, where four different guards take their place. Isolated and surrounded by ongoing abuse, we stand in wait with the guards positioned around us, weapons drawn.

People do strange things when they're desperate; I'm looking to the sky, hoping for a miracle, but knowing full well it will never come. Hane comes forward from the front, Jurgen and Forn follow beside him, and upon seeing them, the crowd instantly cease with their insults. I see no mic by Hane's lips, but his voice thunders louder than the audience combined.

"Aletheia. Erin. By refusing to fight each other you have openly defiled the principles of the Kingdom, and the code of The Kingdom Trials. *This* is a severe offense punishable by death without question. By order of the public, I should take your lives right here in this court."

I keep my sight fixed to his daunting figure. The suit he wears is still clean and crisp even in the heat, and he appears brawnier than before. Slowly I scan his body, heeding every word he says but more concerned for the man himself. How he stands, how he looks at us. How he bears the very resemblance of death.

"But," he continues. "I am a gracious man, and though you have brought shame upon yourselves and therefore *all* trialists…"

A signal of his hand has some guards open a gate, and for a second, I expect lions or more elephants. What I see however, is worse than all of that. Guards appear, holding my friends. They lead them to where we stand.

"I am going to give you the chance to prove your loyalties… by allowing each of you to fight one last time."

Jenny is dragged close to me, and her eyes alone break my heart: endlessly streaming, half-drooped from fatigue. I want to reach for her, but my cuffs prevent me. This is worse than the death I was expecting. Whatever is happening, I've brought my friends into it. Olivia, Tobi, and Jenny. They're all involved.

"For the finale of The Kingdom Trials, each of you will fight one of my elites – not each other – in determining who lives as champion. The fights shall be to the death, there will be no mercy pleas, and the winner will be rewarded for their valor by securing citizenship to the Kingdom."

No one says a word, not us or even the crowd who are glued to their seats. No one moves a muscle. Hane smiles, then shouts to the guards below him who are standing beside the gateway opposed to us.

"Bring forth the opponents!"

In response the officials grab the chains and tug, raising the bars for Hane's strongest warriors to emerge. Celadus is at the front of the pack, but following him are many other officials I've never seen before. They appear even stronger than the advisors. All of them are armed.

One of them is beaten severely.

I gasp, close my eyes and open them again to ensure I'm not imagining it. I'm not. It's Jedidiah. His face is cut and his body is bruised, and there he stands amongst the rest, silent. This is all happening too fast. I can't take it in.

The men position themselves in a horizontal line, but they're twelve strong, and there's only five of us.

"These are my fiercest warriors, a worthy challenge to you, the last surviving trialists," Hane states, speaking over my thoughts. "Who you fight will be determined by the Chance Globe which, in a moment, will scan your identities and state your name. It will then return to one of these men, scan them and announce their identity, and hence they will be your opponent for tomorrow."

I can't concentrate. I'm still focusing on my friends who are all shaking and breathing rapidly. Agitated my hands squirm within their cuffs, rubbing my wrists sore. They shouldn't be here. My friends shouldn't be here. *What have I done?* I beg myself for an answer, but I'm quickly drawn from my nervous writhing. The

Globe has come beside me, over to Jenny who stares at it, panicked. It scans her and calls out her name, still in the assuring voice.

I watch as it hovers to the long line of threats, but looking back to Jenny, I see her head's planted to the ground. I keep my eyes fixed to her as the name of her opponent is announced.

"Celadus Mardas."

A gentle tear drops from her eyes as the name is called. I follow it to the stone below us, and watch it splash against the surface where it evaporates instantly.

I'm the last to be called. My friends and Erin are paired with officials I've never known, and there are eight left. I stare deeply into Jedidiah's eyes. He catches my gaze. I've never seen him so wounded, so miserable. The glint in his pupils has gone, it's dead, and as he watches me from the line, I see fear. All of his emotion as clear and as bright as if it were being displayed on screen, both for me and all of the audience to see. It's a cry for help but to deaf ears. It's a presentation of pain but to blind hearts.

"Aletheia Mirabel."

The Globe has scanned my face and is flying to the line, giving no indication as to where it might land. When I think it might stop it shifts to another person and another. I look down as Jenny did, not capable of watching any longer. I squeeze my throbbing hands into fists and tighten my jaw, refusing to look up. The atmosphere is dark despite the brightness of the sun, and I only wish for this moment to pass. To end.

"Jedidiah Cadman," states the Globe.

I collapse to my knees, head bowed.

CHAPTER XXIII

WORTH IT

HERE I AM one final time, sitting silent in the cells waiting for evening to pass. I refuse to sleep. I know sleep will get me nowhere anyway – I don't need rest. I'm not going to fight him. I keep telling myself over and over, until I'm convinced of it.

This is what Hane's wanted all along: to have me killed. Well now he gets it. He's won, but I will not let Jedidiah suffer my fate. I will not give Hane the pleasure of trying to kill my friend. That's where he's underestimated me. I'm not afraid of death; as long as Jedidiah stays alive, I care nothing for my life. I was never going to stand a chance against the Kingdom regardless of whether I lived. Jedidiah though, he has a chance. That's being realistic, and my duty is to ensure he sees it through. I sigh, distraught but assured of my purpose. I've done my part. Jedidiah will do the rest.

It's hotter than it's ever been inside the dungeon, despite the fact it's well into the evening. I don't know what month it is, but it's never been this hot even in the middle of summer. Caring for my dignity no longer, I strip to my underclothes and toss the soggy uniform behind me. My skin is wet from head to toe, and the air is thin. Knowing full well I'll never get comfortable, I lie on my side. The floor's too hard to sit on.

I flip positions whenever my ribs start to ache. There's no pillow in this cell, or even a rag, but it's closer to the torchlight so I have a better view of what I'm doing. For the first time in these cells, I can see my hands in front of me. My head spins with thoughts: thoughts of my old life, my mother and father. But also my fights. Each and every one of them, and how much I resent the Kingdom and what it stands for. I think about Jedidiah – the moment I realized how he felt. I also remind myself of the JJs, my brother and sister whom I haven't seen for years, even two years before I was taken. I ponder how their lives must be, if they still look the same. If they're happy or in a relationship maybe. Everything. I think of everything all in one confusing, horrible blend of scattered memories. My dehydration isn't helping, but no water has been provided to ease it. I was so hysterical after the Globe's announcement I don't even remember what happened after, or how I'm here again. I think one of the guards offered me water, I have a faint recollection of it, but if he did, I didn't take it. I don't know what I was thinking, but whatever trance I sank into offered no reprieve. It wasn't like drifting into a daydream or blacking out, it was far worse. It was agony. A prison of pain. And I'm not sure I've even escaped.

For a long while, I gaze at the torchlight, watching as its flames flicker and dance as I remind myself of the fires I used to light by the river. I remember my first catch, and how I built a fire to cook it myself because Jedidiah showed me what to do. All of it feels so long ago, so distant, as if I've lived a separate lifetime, but at the same time it's as though time's flashed. Weary and growing delirious, I question if it had all been a long dream, and if I'll wake up as a happy twelve-year-old, lying by the fire. I've endured this delusion before though, I know it, so I rebuke the thought and try to muster some sense. I still need something though, something to pull me through the night, so I consider the alternative that I could be dreaming after all. Not as far back as home, but possibly that I'm still in the cells after the fight with Erin, in aching sleep. That the scenario with the Chance Globe was all in my imagination, and that in reality my friends are safe. Feeling better about myself I decide not to discount it as a possibility, and growing giddy but a little more relaxed, I lay my head down. I can't keep it down for long, but at least I've found a brief sense of security to do so. Even if it is false.

I'm aware I'm alone. I don't know where they are keeping the others, but they're not here. The silence only adds to my torment, and I deliberate if this is what hell might be like. Not the burning torture of your soul like many believe, but an eternal, inescapable silence where there's no one to hold me. Where I still have full consciousness and I keep thinking back to my loved ones, but I know full well they're not coming for me. I study the bars of my cell, pondering for a second if I may fit through. I devise a rash and impractical escape which I could try as a last resort, when someone comes to take me. *I could leave it all.* I think about what opportunities could possibly aid the plan. *I could leave it all behind,* I repeat, picturing a scenario where I steal the weapon of the guard, kill him and then try to leave the Colosseum unnoticed. If I reach society, the city itself, maybe someone will take me to the desert discretely? I could explain I'm a friend of Jedidiah's, someone who's well-known within the Kingdom. I could bribe them, saying that when Jedidiah overthrows Hane, I'll have him reward them. Until that day, I'd stay within the desert – people can survive in the desert. I'd eat lizard meat and scorpions, and there are limitless cacti so water wouldn't be an issue. I'd take refuge there, where no one will find me, and stay out of sight until the right time to return.

I slump back against the wall not able to lie on my sides any longer. I hit my head hard as I do, and weep, knowing everything I've imagined is a lie. There's no chance anyone in the Kingdom would help me, and even less chance of fleeing from here in the first place. These jagged stone walls are as real as my tears, and I'm not dreaming. I have to face Jedidiah tomorrow. I have to take his blade into my body and say my last goodbye. My last vision will be of him, broken as he plunges his weapon inside me, knowing it's the only way we can move forward. He has to live, but not me. Have I failed though? Was there something I could have done, someway this might have ended differently? I picture my friends' faces and cry harder. If I hadn't been so foolish, so reckless, they would be safe. They wouldn't be in this with me. *What have I done?*

I slam my head again – this time deliberately – and absorbing all the sharp pain that follows, I scream, concentrating on the throb as it travels my spine. What did they do anyway? They've always played by the rules, the public has nothing against them. How can Hane throw them in this too, and make the excuse my shame reflects on them? Can the crowd really allow that, considering they already hate Hane for letting me live unfairly? Can't they see he's stepped out of line again, and that he's about to murder three innocent girls? Surely. Surely if the Kingdom is as angry as what Forn describes, they will protest it? I don't know if I fight first tomorrow, or if I'll see Forn, but if I do, I'll beg her. I'll drop to my knees and beg her to rouse the public against punishing my friends.

At that moment someone approaches, walking slowly, until they reach my cell with a set of keys. I listen to the clangs of metal and harsh thud as the lock on my door releases, but I don't look up. I'm too defeated to, too ashamed of myself. I decide that until I see Forn, if I ever see her, I'm going to stay silent. The official closes the gate behind him, which is unusual, but locked in a spell of pessimism, I decide he's here to beat me.

"Allie?" calls the voice, which obliterates my despondency immediately and I rocket from the floor, straight into Jedidiah's arms. I clutch him tighter than ever before, certain this is the last opportunity to do so. We stand there for a few seconds, both of us saying nothing, but then I pull back to examine his face.

"What did they do to you? Who did this-?"

"*Shhh*," he hushes. "I'm ok. They didn't do much."

"I'm not going to fight you, Jed. I'm not," I assert. I'm in no mood to be preached to. I've made up my mind.

"If you don't, we both die."

"No."

"They know about us, Allie. They must." There's sadness in his eyes, but he's trying to stay strong.

"How?" My tears are forcing through. "We were careful. We-" He interrupts me again.

"I don't know, but if you don't fight, they'll kill us both," he reiterates, which only makes me more frantic.

"I'm not losing you, Jed! Kill me! I'll die!"

"Allie, you know I won't do that. The people need you, you're going to give them a hope they've never known. You can stop the Kingdom."

"Can you hear yourself?" I rebuke. "*No one* can stop the Kingdom! It's all hopeless! There's nothing we can do! But you, you must live. I won't let them take you."

"Allie…"

Aware my explosion has disheartened him, I pause and try to breathe, but it's impossible to compose my thoughts. Blood pulses through my head.

"Maybe one day, there'll be a chance, I don't know. Maybe you'll find an opportunity to do something about the poverty and…" I think hard, eyeing Jedidiah whose face appears as distraught as what I'd picture mine to look. It breaks my very soul. "Jed, you could still bring Hane down. You could. But not me. I was never going to make it, but that doesn't matter because it was never my goal. It was always you, Jed, from the day you left me. It was always to find you."

I reach for him again, but he takes a step back.

"Allie, you've come a long way since you were brought here, but is this really how you want to be remembered? The girl who sacrificed herself for a boy when she could've done so much more?"

"And do you want to be remembered as the boy who gave his life for a girl who could do nowhere near as much as he could?" I counter, stepping in again.

"No," he states, which stuns me. "I'd die for you in a heartbeat, but then I won't be around to protect you, and I didn't come all this way for you to face the Kingdom alone so here's what we're going to do. There's a chance we can both live, but if it fails, we both die."

"What? What chance?"

"We draw. Hane is expecting one of us to die, and if we both refuse to fight, we die anyway. But he's not expecting a draw, and a draw could ensure our survival."

I stop to process this. If we draw, surely we would evade prosecution. Hane wouldn't be able to justify it. To draw however, means to fight. Hane's not going to stop the fight, he made it clear it's to the death, so how do we draw?

My heart sinks.

"You mean…we both lose."

"Yes," he agrees. "Make it appear as if we're both going to die, when really we have a chance of surviving."

"How?"

"We both know where the vital areas of the body are, right? Well, when we fight we just need to avoid them."

"It won't work," I sigh, having already given up on hope. "What if we hit one of those areas by mistake?"

"I won't hit them at all. And you know what you're doing,

you're more than skilled enough to keep your strikes precise. It doesn't matter if we get scrapes, we just need to ensure the audience believe our fight."

"So, what if we do, and we just get minor injuries? The audience would still know it's not enough to kill us so if we fall and pretend we can't keep going we'd just be caught."

"No." He takes my hands. "We use those injuries to keep the public convinced, then we strike each other at the same time in a place that should keep us alive but end the fight."

I stare at him. His stubble is sharp and his skin is worn with cuts and slight imperfections, but his features haven't changed at all. His eyes, though saddened, embody honesty in its truest form, and I believe suddenly. I believe what he's saying could be our way out.

"There's still a chance it could fail," he continues. "If we don't make it to the medics fast enough, we'll lose too much blood. It's risky. But it's all we have."

He breathes softly into my ear; he's close. Refusing to look away, I nod, readying myself for the plan. Our only opportunity but an opportunity nonetheless.

"Ok. How will we know when to strike?"

"I'll leave myself open, and when you go in to take it, you'll also do the same." He swallows hard. He's clearly thought about it, but there's a side to him that's nervous. That doesn't want to go through with it.

"What if I don't see it?" A horrible vision of me screwing up the entire plan follows, and I shudder. "What if I miss the chance completely and the crowd realizes it's a ruse? What if they catch us?"

"Trust me, you'll see it," he assures, nodding slowly. "You're better than you think you are. Just relax and the rest will follow."

"I'm scared. I see it going wrong." I'm panicking the more I think of it. "Just kill me! Forget the idea and just kill me, then at least you live!"

He pulls away from me and sits in a corner, holding his face, and I fall back against the wall, allowing my body to slip down until I'm on the floor again, opposite him. After some silence, his eyes narrow on my cheek, which is directly in the torchlight.

"How did you get that scar?"

"Commodus." I keep my voice low. "His baton."

"You know what that looks like, don't you?" He studies my face intently, his pupils blazing in the torchlight. "It's very close to the symbol of Aletheia."

"How do you know about that?"

"I know the myth," he smiles. "I asked your parents why they named you Aletheia, and they taught me the story. Your scar is identical to her symbol."

"I don't know why," I mutter.

"I do." The smile on his face grows larger. "In the story, Aletheia frees her people from captivity, and she does it by fighting. The first female to ever lead a war."

He looks out the cell toward the torchlight, which seems to be intensifying as he talks. I can see his face clearly – it's soft in that lighting, like I'm seeing him as a child again.

"Aletheia means truth, and with her truth, she gave the people hope. The truth of a better tomorrow and a nearing salvation."

"What are you saying?"

None of this is making sense. I know the story, so why is he repeating it to me?

"I'm saying I think you have that scar for a reason. It's a reminder of who you are, who you really are, and your purpose is to free the people through fighting, not by giving way for another to fight in your place."

I pause, thinking about all the times I've watched the townsfolk suffer, knowing I've always wanted to do something but never being in the position to.

"Allie, you love the people," he continues. "The people are going to love you back, but you can't let these circumstances change you. You can't let this determine who you're going to be."

I keep watching him, but my lips are held tight. I have nothing, no words to respond.

"You know, I never told you what happened when I was brought here, did I?" His eyes are resolute. I'm silent but partially shake my head.

"When they took me to the Kingdom, first they beat me. A lot worse than how they have now." He half snickers. "They wanted to get through to me that they owned me, and if I didn't cooperate there would be consequences. Course, I was the one who agreed to their training, but if I hadn't, they would've killed me, so joining them was my only option."

A profound sadness comes over me as he speaks on. If I had been there, I would've tried something, anything to stop them hurting him. But I was away, far away. All I can do is listen.

"Afterward I was left in prison, similar to here, with no food or water. I was in such bad shape when they took me out, I needed a hydration capsule, which led to the worst night of my life." He becomes reflective, gazing out of the cell bars. "I thought about you though, all through the withdrawal phase. Picturing you was the only strength I could find to get through it, and I did get through it." He smiles again, as if he's remembering the happiness he felt from thinking of me, and not just the brutality of his torture. "Once I'd recovered, I was put in training immediately. At first, they offered nothing – no serum, no medicine – because they didn't want me to improve, they just wanted me to suffer. I would run every day, out in the sun for hours, eat and then proceed to combat. The more it went on, the worse it got. Soon they had me sparring against their elites, and I'd always leave bleeding.

"I trained all day, with four hours sleep and only one rest day each fortnight. There were times I considered taking my life, seeing no point going on, but whenever I had those feelings, I always pictured you smiling at me. Willing me on. See, the Kingdom can do what they want to your body, but they can't touch your mind. Not if you don't let them.

"They made me run until it felt like my blood was being drained from me, and all my body would go heavy and pull me back. But you pulled me forward. If I was too tired to lift a weight, I'd remind myself the suffering's only temporary, that one day I'd be beside you again, and then I'd lift it.

"I grew for you, just as I knew you would for me, and I was convinced without a hint of doubt in my mind that one day we'd not only meet again, we'd be strong enough to change things. Not me, or just you, but both of us together. Allie, looking back at it all, my convictions of where I'd be, and how far I pushed myself to see it through. All of that pain, while hoping – dreaming – I might find you…it was worth it. I'm here now, with you. It was worth it."

His attention shifts to my back, which he notices in the half light as I pull closer to him. I tingle as his hands catch me, stroking lightly across the scarring where I'd been flogged. I'm still sweating, but his hands are cold. They were always cold as a child, and sometimes he used to tease me by sticking them down my neck – he knew I hated that. As his fingers feel the marks of the whip, I hear my heart again. It's beating faster, and as the seconds pass the pulsing grows louder, until I can't hear my thoughts. My heart is speaking to me.

"Allie," he whispers, arching his head over my body to see the scars clearer. "I'm so sorry-"

I don't let him continue but promptly hush him with a smile. "*Shhh*. It's okay."

"He would've killed you if I hadn't-" He ignores me, trying to speak again, but I press my finger to his lips.

"Don't speak," I smile, moving my finger away again. He doesn't, but pulls me in closer until our noses are barely apart. Our lips meet, and the pain falls away.

I shudder as his hands work further up my back until they rest on my cheeks, and wrapping my arms around his shoulders, I let my body melt into his. Tensions fading and muscles relaxed, holding Jedidiah as if he's my own, and I am his.

I can't get enough. The more he takes me in closer and intimate, the more I want the moment to never end. I've never felt this before, this yearning for touch, but he separates from me again. Our eyes are locked; our breathing heavy. With a regretful voice, he ends the silence.

"I can't stay here."

"I know," I groan, remembering where we are. I refuse to back away from him. I stay as close as he'll allow.

"The guards are going to come for you soon, it's morning. I have to leave before they find us." He peers out of the cell through the bars again, eyeing the torchlight that floods his face. He's beautiful. I nod, eyes fallen in sorrow.

He pushes his forehead against mine, bringing my gaze back to him.

"Allie, I know this seems lost. Just trust me." With that, he gets up, causing my head to droop, and opens the door, locking it behind him as he moves away.

I stare at the ground as his footsteps fade to the distance, considering everything that's happened as the silence returns. *'Trust me.'* He's not going to kill me in the arena, and if I refuse then that's the end for both of us.

CHAPTER XXIV

FAITH

ONLY ANOTHER HOUR or so passes before someone else arrives to take me, but during that time I'm left wrestling with my mind. Even as I walk my last ever journey to the arena, wrists bound in steel and with two guards holding my arms, I still don't know what I'll do. I gaze down, picturing the spear that may kill Jedidiah. His blood on my hands. I almost vomit, but swallow hard.

Forn is nowhere inside the waiting chamber, but there are other guards waiting for me. My cuffs are broken free as one of them pulls toward me, getting uncomfortably close and forcing me to step back. I notice he's one of the elites I could've potentially paired up against, had fate not despised me.

"Where is my advisor?" I'm intimidated but not scared to question him. All I'm thinking about is reaching Forn, one last time, and pleading for my friends' exclusion from the fights. He laughs, calling over to the others so they can add to the mocking.

"Guys, this one wants to know where her advisor is!"

They all erupt with evil, patronizing cheer.

"And where *is* she?"

My response throws the official off, and he steps closer to me, aggressively. I push away, but he continues to move in.

"Advisors are for good slaves, sweetheart. You don't have an advisor," he scorns. There's a baton in his sheath he reaches for, but I don't flinch. He raises it to head height as the other guards close in on me. "You know, I asked Lord Hane if we could have a little fun with you before the fight." He traces the weapon along the length of my scar. I ignore the surrounding guards and concentrate only on him. "But he insisted you come out fresh so we can see every wound you'll suffer. I suppose he's right," he grunts. "But isn't it a shame we can't at least prepare you for what's to come. You know, out of sympathy."

Finally the baton is removed from my skin and pushed back into his sheath, then chuckling to himself he walks away from me. Other guards move from me too, but some remain where they are and continue to jeer at me. No one touches me, but their insults cut deep. Some of them taunt how my parents would be proud of me for getting so far, while other's try to convince me Jedidiah is ruthless, listing off all the people he's killed. All in graphic detail.

When it's time to step forward I'm confused – my anthem hasn't been played, nor has my name been announced either. As my armor materializes, I throw my helmet to the ground, and taking one last breath, I pause, gathering my thoughts from the cell in a desperate bid for conviction of what I must do. A guard pushes me from behind before I've found the answer, and I find myself stumbling into the viewpoint of the seemingly limitless crowd. The orchestra of hate, whose symphonies quake the spear I hold and tear at my spirit with psychological blades. It breaks me down, as if to the mentality of a child all of a sudden.

Simultaneously the urge to run back grapples me like a tiger, roaring at me to retreat. *I can't do this!* I wheeze, halting in my path. But then I see Jedidiah, his composure as he enters the arena opposite me. I draw toward him like a magnet, pulling deeper into the abuse of the audience but setting my sights on him and him only. A magnet, but which am I – positive or negative? I haven't decided, but I don't care. My fear minimizes with every step, until the tiger is a tiny cat whose cries I no longer hear. I'm not thinking about anything except him.

In his usual place in the stands, Hane rises to give an announcement, but not for the crowd. It's directed at me.

"Aletheia." His voice ceases the crowd as before, and every head turns to him. "This is your opportunity to prove your worth to myself and the people. Win, and your fortune will be restored. Die, and know that your nation's honor, your family's name, and your opportunity to build a greater future dies with you." Hane then turns to Jedidiah, still with the same sinister glare he'd given me. "Jedidiah. As punishment for her actions Aletheia is to fight you, and you are to fight her. Hold nothing back. Do not hesitate, and do not forget who is watching. God, and his covenant, rests on your shoulders to restore order. Do not fail him, and do not fail me."

Jedidiah stares up at him for the entire speech, his eyes relentlessly focused. The sun's rays envelop him like a divinity, and as he turns to me, I find myself in awe of his presence. It's as if he's not here to fight me at all, but fight *for* me, as my protector. My angel.

I study his armor in anticipation of the gong – it's unique, I've never seen anything like it. Like me, he's not wearing a helmet, but whether it's because he prefers to fight without them or wants me to see him I'm not sure. The armor itself is a similar construction to my eagle helmet, mounted to his body like an exoskeleton and formed of thick wire. It flows around the contours of his physique, with wire around his chest and abdominals at the front, down his obliques at the sides, and over his shoulders, biceps and forearms. He has no lower protection but sturdy boots like mine, and in each of his hands are swords. I'd never seen what his weapon skill was, but it's hardly surprising. At best it's logical, because although he was a keen spear fisher uncle Hamza was always teaching him how to use swords. He already had that skill before he arrived in the Kingdom, so I can only imagine how talented he is.

Looking to the stands, I eye Forn, who is watching me closely as she always does. As our gazes meet, I wonder if there was truth to the official's ridicule, and that she hadn't been separated from me by Hane but through choice. I haven't seen her since the situation with Erin, and I know she could never forgive it. Maybe I'm on my-my thoughts are overcome by the crowd, who are chanting Jedidiah's name in aggressive cohesion. He doesn't respond to them like I'd expect him to, not even with a wave, but instead gazes head-on, readying his blades in stance. Responding to his stance with my own, I tremble. It may be an act, but I'm starting to believe it. We have a plan, but this is all too real.

The most least-welcome sound – more so than all the voices of the crowd – strikes me in the form of the gong. Jedidiah wastes no time in throwing the first jab, and his force is unlike anything I've experienced. Fearful I can't match him, I counter his attack and blitz him with a flurry of my own, which he deflects effortlessly. I try again, more urgently, with the knowledge I can't afford to waver searing at my thoughts. My mind's processing so much it's already brought on pain, and I can barely think straight.

Jedidiah nearly knocks my spear away altogether as I'm hurled to the ground, but I manage to recover and fend him backward. My arm has been slashed already, and there's blood on the sand from where I fell. He drives forward again but I side roll to safety, clashing with his blade in the same motion. Another assault follows, and I swipe at his arm. It breaks through but bounces off his armor with a loud clang, and Jedidiah continues to besiege me with his fast-flying swings. His attacks only just skim my face, at one point avoiding my chin by a fraction. I panic, and lose my footing again. I hope he will acknowledge my struggle, at least give me a chance to get up, but he launches on top of me and tears a gash on my shoulder, proceeding to throttle me with a sequence of slashes.

Hurriedly I spin my spear to deflect a majority of his attacks, but some get through and force me to jolt my body. His weight bears down on me, making it difficult to guard. With an almighty cry, I snap my legs upright, pounding him in the back of his head. It doesn't get him off me, but it dazes him and allows me the chance to swivel my torso and throw him to the side. We both leap to our feet and the engagement continues – the crowd bellow their frustrations, but I disregard it. Jedidiah's glare has softened, reminding me I'm on the right track, and very quickly I push a strike through which does cause injury. A deep cut along his forearm.

I'm overwhelmed by his combination of speed and power, but I notice patterns in his movements, which I predict, landing more wounds as I do. There's a gouge in my calf which is hindering my balance, and I'm bruised and bloodied all over, but this is what we wanted. The crowd is captivated, cheering and applauding on the edge of their seats. We're fooling them. It's almost time.

I'm knocked back by a sword handle being too crippled to evade his arm, and as he moves in, he punctures my left glute. I gasp, lifting my spear to avoid his follow-up but his strength pushes me further. People scream with excitement, and I grow disorientated. I want to cry for him to stop, but then I remember his plea: 'trust me.' I think back to the moment I was holding him, and he was holding me. I envision his lips stroking my own, and his cold but delicate touch…reaching out to calm me, not cause harm. I picture his smile when he explained what he lived for, what he believed when he was faced with adversity. A sword comes barreling for my ribs but my spear reaches it before impact. Everything is spinning; everything is spinning but Jedidiah's eyes. They tell me to focus, to concentrate on him. He attacks ruthlessly, but his eyes remain loving, like a father's gaze who watches me from a distance while I learn to ride my bike. I fall and injure myself, but I keep going, and he keeps willing me on, telling me to follow him. To get back on the bike and follow him. He knows I'll make it, and then the cuts and grazes are worth it because I can finally ride my bike. And then I reach him, cycling into his embrace.

It's almost through. It's almost finished. My limbs weaken and my body rocks from pain, but still I manage to counter his blows. Still I push on, urging myself further and harder and desperate to reach the end. I'm at breaking point; Jedidiah can see it. And then it happens. Like the earth has slowed and halted, I see an opening – the first opening of the fight's long, excruciating duration – I see it as if it's calling me, begging me to take it. To let all my deepest fears fall away and just take it, not considering what could go wrong. Not willing me to play the possible scenarios over and over in my head until I vomit, but to trust and dive in. A commitment to Jedidiah that says yes, I don't think it will work, but if it means I could still be with you-if there's still a chance we can be together, I'll do it. *I trust you,* I tell myself, one final time. And I step in. I let go of my fear, neglect my own safety and target his spleen – spearhead honed in, firm and without hesitation. As my arm reaches forward, I twist into it, moving with the strike and offering a clear gap for his sword. My other arm drops, preventing the urge to defend, and as the point of my weapon penetrates his skin and drives deep a horrid pain tears at my nerves. It's ruthless, and my body convulses. Jedidiah's sword has hit me, pushing all the way through and tearing out behind. We both gasp with desperate, agitated gulps. The audience have stopped their chanting. I look up from my wound to Jedidiah, whose eyes tear up and lips tremble. I well up in response, overcome by pain I cannot describe.

Reaching one hand to steady me while keeping the other pressed to his sword, Jedidiah's head meets my own. Neither of us can say a word...only shudder as our mouths gape for oxygen, eager to numb the pain. My strength is draining from me. Tears are flowing rapidly. As we fall to our knees, I reach back for him, my other hand grasped tight to the spear, and hold his shoulder to support myself. Our watery eyes stare into each other's, refusing to look away, and I realize his hand is working up to my cheek. It's just me now. Me and Jedidiah.

Shots of pain torment me as I try to lift my arm higher to his face, but I grit through it, squeezing my spear with a hand already buried in his blood. I heave, fighting the spasms. His mouth opens again, his hand shaking violently on my face.

"Allie…I love you," he splutters.

I swallow and realize my mouth is dry, but coughing I manage to find the words.

"I love you, too."

Linked by our blades, we kneel, knees burning on the heated sand. My eyelids are heavy, but I won't let them close. I keep my unsteady hand glued to his cheek and accept this is our moment. This is what had to be done, and it's over.

END OF BOOK 1.

ACKNOWLEDGMENTS

First and foremost, I'd like to honor God for giving me this story. This is your story, I've written it, and now it's out there. I only hope it encourages others as much as it's encouraged me. Man or woman, rich or poor, no matter their race or background, let them believe anyone can become a hero. Please show them what a true hero is.

Now I know it's cliché to thank your friends and family, and at this point it's even becoming cliché to say it's cliché! But my heart overflows when I think of the amazing people in my life, I'm truly undeserving. Mom and Dad, you have supported me in every conceivable way, and I only wish to make you proud. Nan and Grandad, you're the most loving grandparents I could ask for and I'm so lucky to have you. I have way too many friends to list but you all know who you are, and you have all shaped me into the person I am today. Words on a page can't express my love for all of you.

Of course, I have to give massive shoutouts to the people who even made this book possible: Joel Newton for taking me under your wing; Kathleen Gillett for obediently sharing God's word for me to publish; the team at Damonza for their beautiful formatting and cover design, and my wonderful editor Stephanie Taylor. From the bottom of my heart, thank you. I had no idea what it would entail actually publishing a book myself, and you have all been a blessing and made the road smooth. This couldn't have turned out better because of you.

And finally, to the one most precious to me, Ma-chan. Thank you for believing in me. I love you as much as Jedidiah loves Aletheia.

ABOUT THE AUTHOR

Daniel JP Harris is the author of 'The Kingdom's Daughter,' a project that was eight years in the making. Around the time of writing, he left his home in the UK to pursue his dreams as an actor and writer in Hollywood, striving to achieve what he was told was impossible so others would do it too. Before you go, he'd like to leave you with one final message:

Have any questions, concerns, philosophies of life? (I stole that from my drama teacher) I'd love to hear from you! I can be reached on Instagram, Twitter, and TikTok @danieljpharris, and I make a point of posting encouragements daily so hopefully you'll get more than you came for! Even if you just want to discuss what you think the best food in the world is and why it's pizza, you're welcome on my page.

Shine on, hero.

Printed in Great Britain
by Amazon